Audrey Whiting is recognised as one of Fleet Street's
most distinguished commentators on British royalty. Her
knowledge of the Royal Family spans three decades: she was
present at the Queen's coronation in Westminster Abbey in
1953 and attended the wedding of The Prince and Princess of
Wales in Saint Paul's Cathedral in 1981. Over the years
she has written extensively on the structure of monarchy for
publication both in Britain and Europe and her articles for
the Mirror group have been widely quoted all over the world.
She is a well known broadcaster on royal affairs and works for
television in Britain, the United States and France.

Audrey Whiting

THE KENTS

Futura

A Futura BOOK

Copyright © Audrey Whiting 1985

First published in Great Britain in 1985
by Hutchinson & Co (Publishers) Ltd

This Futura Edition published 1986

ISBN 0 7088 3061 7

Printed in Great Britain by
The Guernsey Press Co. Ltd
Guernsey, Channel Islands '

Futura Publications
A Division of
Macdonald & Co (Publishers) Ltd
Greater London House
Hampstead Road
London NW1 7QX

A BPCC plc Company

FOR

NANCY SWIFT

Photographic Acknowledgements

For permission to reproduce copyright photographs the publishers would like to thank Aspect Picture Library, BBC Hulton Picture Library, Camera Press, *Daily Mirror*, Tim Graham, The Photo Source, Syndication International, and Topham Picture Library.

Contents

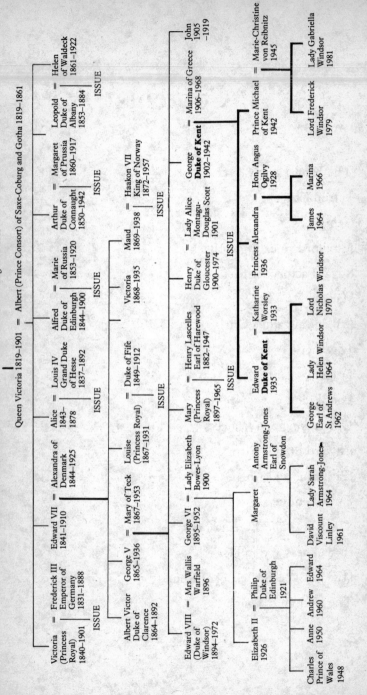

Introduction

The Duke of Kent, Princess Alexandra of Kent and Prince Michael of Kent are an integral part of the Royal Family. They are each married to highly complementary partners, the lovely Duchess of Kent, business-man the Honourable Angus Ogilvy and the extrovert Princess Michael. Few families are as close to one another as the Kents who have seven children between them, the youngest, Lady Gabriella Windsor, five, in her first term at school, and the eldest, twenty-two year old Cambridge undergraduate, George, Earl of St Andrews. Over the years the Duke and Princess Alexandra have carried out thousands of public engage-ments, and since his marriage in 1978 Prince Michael has joined them on the royal rota.

The often dramatic story of their parents, George, Duke of Kent and Princess Marina and their impact on the royal scene is fascinating. Accounts of some individuals are available and informed. Yet despite their consistent achievements and popularity over the years, the unfold-ing saga of this whole family has not been presented until now.

When senior members of the Royal Family are alone together they are among the best raconteurs in the world, telling stories at the expense of one another which are mostly taken in good part. Only occasionally do some of the men and women of the House of Windsor feel sufficiently relaxed in the presence of an outsider to express some frank opinions about themselves and the family to which they belong. It is, therefore, a rare occurrence when a royal agrees to a wide-ranging interview without restricting the discussion to the respective merits of a particular favourite cause or charity. It was in the spring of 1972 in the course of such a series of frank and open meetings with the late Prince William of Gloucester that my serious interest in 'The Kents' was aroused. Reminiscing over the years, the Prince told me that the two people whom he most admired in the Royal Family were his cousins, the Queen and Princess Alexandra of Kent.

When I asked him to explain more about Princess Alexandra he said,

She is the most marvellous person. I do not think I can honestly fault her in anything. To me, she epitomizes all that is best in the family – she is so sure, so stable. She really enjoys her work, unlike someone like myself who would prefer a quite different career. There are always difficulties in bringing up royal children in these modern days, keeping them with two feet firmly on the ground and so on, but somehow she is managing to surmount these sort of problems and has established a really happy family life of her own. She has experienced a time of deep personal sadness but even this she managed to keep very much to herself.

Prince William, a bachelor, said that he not only admired Princess Alexandra but also envied her. He was talking to me at a time in his life when he had had to give up a career in the Diplomatic Service in order to take on the responsibilities of his seriously ill father, the late Duke of Gloucester, whose heir he then was, and also the running of the family estate, Barnwell, in Northamptonshire. After talking at length about Princess Alexandra and her brother, the present Duke of Kent, Prince William said, 'The Kents really are a wonderful team.'

Prince William's views about the Duke of Kent and Princess Alexandra were more than supported by the late Lord Mountbatten, whom I first met in 1960 when he invited me to lunch at his home, Broadlands in Hampshire. Only a few weeks before he was murdered in Ireland in August 1979, I spent my last happy day with him there, when he described the senior Kents as 'two of the most remarkable people' in the Royal Family. In the last interview he ever gave he talked freely to me about his royal relatives and of his hopes for the future which would, one day, rest in the hands of his beloved great-nephew, Prince Charles. 'It may prove far more difficult for him in the years ahead,' said Lord Mountbatten, and continued:

Hopefully that will be a long time from now since the Queen is tremendously fit and will never abdicate. Nevertheless no matter how monarchy changes – and change it must – Charles will need the support of people like Alexandra and Eddie. They don't grow on trees, you know. To be a monarch and have cousins like the Kents is of untold value – they are both relatives, friends and, at the same time, bloody hard-working people.

Lord Mountbatten paused, as he always did when he was intent upon making a serious comment with a humorous twist,

I like to think that I helped to make the Kents the people they are today. I taught them how to shake hands faster than anyone else – at least, when pushed, twenty people a minute!

Their parents, the late Duke and Duchess of Kent, were a magnetic couple. I am always taken aback when I see Princess Alexandra since she bears an incredible resemblance to her mother, who was quite one of the most brilliant and beautiful women I ever met.

Over the years I began to understand part of the reason why Prince William, a shrewd man capable of sound critical assessment, and Lord Mountbatten, never one to lavish unnecessary praise, admired the Kent branch of the Royal Family so much. Unlike other monarchs both in this century and the not so recent past, Queen Elizabeth II has been remarkably fortunate in her relatives. Her own children, Charles, Anne, Andrew and Edward, all grew up knowing that, unless some disaster befell them, they were destined to carry out royal duties for the rest of their lives. For her Kent cousins, however, the future was quite a different matter: they could have opted out of the royal scene if they had so wished. The Queen would never have brought regal pressure to bear upon them had they chosen this course, one which would have left them free to pursue careers or lifestyles which they may have felt better suited their individual inclinations and temperaments. While such a decision would have proved a bitter disappointment to the Queen, especially as their maturity coincided with a period in her reign when she needed the support of young and experienced relatives, she would have accepted it without question.

It has never been part of the Queen's nature to urge members of her family to take an active part in the 'royal business' if it has no appeal. Prince William, for instance, who had lived abroad for many years, never received a command to return home and take over the mantle of his sick father. He came back to England of his own free will because, as he told me, 'of an innate sense of duty to the Queen'.

The Queen did not protest when Prince Michael, the younger brother of Princess Alexandra and the Duke of Kent, decided upon a full-time career in the Army. On rare occasions he carried out some public duties, but only when illness or over-taxed schedules meant that no other senior member of the Royal Family was available at the time. His attitude did not change for many years until he married at the age of thirty-five in 1978, and later decided to give up his service life. A new career in the City provided him with an opportunity to perform some public duties, albeit of a far less important nature than those carried out by his brother and sister.

The Queen is devoted to her three cousins, children of the late Duke and Duchess of Kent, who were even more glamorous in the 1930s than the Prince and Princess of Wales are in the 1980s. Yet the mists of time have strangely tended to obscure the fascinating and highly gifted personalities of these earlier members of the Kent family. Even the present generation of Kents, with all their combined talents, became overshadowed by the intense interest in Prince Charles, the Princess of Wales and their children. Although inevitable, so shortly after the marriage of the future King and the birth of his heir, Prince William, this is regrettable, since without the years of support from the Kents the business of running the modern monarchy would have been that much harder for the Queen. She calls them her 'second eleven', an apt description for a superbly professional royal team.

In private, Princess Alexandra is very close to her cousin, the Queen. Despite their ten-year age difference the two women are compatible. Both have great mutual empathy and both have had ample opportunity to demonstrate a need of one another in times of difficulty or stress. The Princess's brother, the Duke of Kent, a precise man with a military bearing, often appears a somewhat austere personality, yet his make-up contains much of the infectious humour that was so pronounced when he was young. Prince Michael, a more outgoing person, has gradually been drawn into public life by his Czechoslovak-born wife, Princess Michael, who, with her exuberant personality and natural love of the arts, has added yet another dimension to the Kents.

This book aspires to recount the story of a family which, over the course of the years, has produced powerful personalities surrounding and supporting the monarchy. The Kents have been involved in royal dramas in the twentieth century, but they were also playing for high stakes way back in the eleventh century.

The Kent Peerage

From 1066 to 1465 there were five creations of the earldom of Kent – the first and third were royal or semi-royal. In 1710 Queen Anne made the last of the non-royal earls of Kent Duke of Kent. When he died in 1740 the title became extinct until George III created his fourth son, Edward, Duke of Kent in 1799. He was to become the father of Queen Victoria. On his death the title was again extinct until 1934 when the present dukedom was bestowed by George V on his fourth son, Prince George, just before his marriage to Princess Marina of Greece.

The history of the Kent peerage is a dramatic story and began with Odo, Bishop of Bayeux, who was made the first Earl of Kent by his half-brother, William the Conqueror, as an expression of gratitude for help at the battle of Hastings in 1066. Odo had gathered together men and arms for the 1066 expedition and supplied ships to transport troops across the English Channel. The famous Bayeux Tapestry may have been made for him.

The next Earl of Kent was Hubert de Burgh, who received the title in 1227. He was gaoler to Prince Arthur, who was murdered by his uncle, King John. According to Shakespeare, Hubert refused an order to blind the young Prince.

Among the many succeeding descendants of this line there were several of particular interest. In March 1330 Edmund of Woodstock, Earl of Kent, youngest son of Edward I, was arrested and executed for treason outside the gates of Winchester Castle. His death was delayed for five hours because his executioner fled from the scene. Ultimately a criminal from Marshalsea in Kent agreed to do the deed. His condition, that he should receive a free pardon, was granted.

After the death of Edmund's two sons, the title went to his daughter, known as Joan, the 'Fair Maid of Kent', and regarded as one of the most ambitious and beautiful women of her time. She is said to have inspired Edward III to create the Order of the Garter by deliberately dropping her garter at court in his presence.

Her grandson, Thomas Holland, who succeeded in 1397, was involved in a plot to seize the interloper Henry IV, who had taken the throne of Richard II. It failed, and Holland was captured by a mob and beheaded in January 1400. His head was placed on a spike on London Bridge for two months – then sent to his widow for disposal. He was thus the second Earl of Kent to lose his head.

William Neville, a member of the great Neville family and a distinguished Yorkist noble, was a later famous Earl of Kent. This peerage was granted in 1461 by Edward IV after the battle of Towton. William died a year later. He was once Admiral of England and is referred to in Shakespeare's *Henry VI*: 'Stern Falconbridge commands the narrow seas. . . .'

Two years afterwards, Edward IV made the Yorkist Edmund Grey, Lord Grey of Ruthin, Earl of Kent. The Greys were originally Lancastrians, but Edmund changed sides during the battle of Northampton in the Wars of the Roses. Edmund was a sword-bearer at

Richard III's coronation and died in 1490 at the ripe old age of seventy-three.

Richard Grey, his grandson, who eventually inherited the title in 1503, was regarded as a waster, became a notorious gambler and fell deeply into debt. Nevertheless, he managed to live in magnificent style and took part with Henry VIII in the diplomatic mission known as the Field of the Cloth of Gold. He died in his house 'at the sign of the George' in Lombard Street, London, in 1523 and, having no children of his own, left a vast trail of debts for his half-brother.

A century later, in 1639, the earldom passed to a clergyman of extraordinary longevity for the times, the eighty-two-year-old Anthony Grey. When he died in 1643 he had been rector of Aston Flamville in Leicestershire for no less than fifty-three years.

His pastoral life was in striking contrast to that of his grandson, Henry Grey, who was Lord Chamberlain for six years. He was a courtier held in great esteem by Queen Anne, who made him Marquess of Kent in 1706 and Duke of Kent in 1710. After the Queen's death, George I made him Lord of the Bedchamber and Constable of Windsor Castle. His son and heir choked to death on an ear of barley, and when Henry died the Kent title again became extinct.

It was not until 1799 that George III gave the dukedom of Kent to his fourth son, Prince Edward. When Edward, Duke of Kent, reached middle age an event took place in his life which ensured that his name and his place in British history would never be forgotten.

The Pregnancy Race

In a cobbled courtyard outside the dilapidated old castle of Amorbach in the wooded uplands of Bavaria ladies in waiting, valets, cooks, seamstresses, maids, extra coachmen and two doctors clambered into the waiting coaches that were to carry them over 400 miles of rough roads to the Channel port of Calais. It was late March 1819, and the skies were ominous. As Edward, Duke of Kent eyed the vast mountain of luggage, which included song birds, musical clocks, a pair of Russian lap dogs and a huge bed with vast quantities of fine linen, he made a sudden, bold decision: so much was at stake on the journey that he pulled himself on to the box of the leading coach and took the reins himself.

Only too well aware of the hazards ahead, he knew it would take the royal party at least three weeks to reach their destination – provided the weather was good and provided his wife was not taken ill en route. At fifty-one, even with his great fitness and stamina, he felt that cool nerves would be needed if the party was to reach Calais safely. Inside the carriage was his wife, the former Princess Victoria of Leiningen, a widow with two children, whom he had married the previous year.

At thirty-three she was small, plump, with deep brown eyes and a rosy complexion, cheerful and exuberant: when she caught the Duke's anxious eye she registered no sign of personal fear at the punishing days that lay ahead of them all. Despite a relatively hastily-arranged marriage brought about by circumstances, they cared deeply for one another.

The journey, with the coaches swaying, jolting and pitching, would have been bad enough under ordinary circumstances – but the Duchess of Kent was more than seven months pregnant. Any great jolt on the road or significant delay caused by bad weather could have serious or even fatal results for both the Duchess and her unborn child. Husband and wife had earlier discussed all the possible risks, and both were in total agreement that the baby must be born in London.

The Duke and Duchess of Kent were participants in the great royal pregnancy race which followed the death in 1817 of Princess Charlotte, only child and heir of the Prince Regent (later George IV), in giving birth to a stillborn son. This catastrophe destroyed at a stroke two generations of heirs to the throne, the Princess and her son. If the crown was not to pass to the Duke of Brunswick, a young cousin of George III living in Hanover, the Royal Family had to produce another heir as soon as possible.

The Prince Regent was out of the running. At fifty-five he was tied to Queen Caroline. The royal couple disliked each other intensely and had lived apart for many years. They had had no children other than the unfortunate Charlotte – and there was no prospect of any more.

Only two of his brothers, the Dukes of York and Cumberland, were married and they had no legitimate heirs. So the direct line of succession depended upon at least one of his three unmarried brothers – the Duke of Cambridge, the Duke of Kent and the Duke of Clarence – marrying and presenting the country with a desperately needed heir. All found suitable brides and in 1818 the air was heavy with belated nuptials: Cambridge married Augusta of Hesse-Cassel on 7 May, Kent married Victoria of Leiningen on 29 May, and Clarence married Adelaide of Saxe-Meiningen on 11 July. The question was: which couple would prove fertile? In the event only Edward, Duke of Kent, fathered a viable child.

As the Kents proceeded over potholed roads across Belgium and northern France, the party was described by an Englishwoman who watched them as 'an unbelievably odd caravan'. The Duke had taken the precaution of enlisting the services of Charlotte Heiland, a remarkable German midwife who had been given the title of Doctor of Midwifery by a German medical college, to take care of the cheerful Duchess. To help her supervise his wife's health was the Duke's personal physician, a Dr Wilson, a former naval surgeon.

The party reached Calais with the Duchess tired but well. The Channel winds were strong and the seas running so high that the royal couple were advised to wait for calmer weather before risking the voyage to Dover, since the Duchess was only eight weeks from her confinement. Seven days passed and, although the storms had abated only slightly, the Duke and Duchess decided that their journey could not be delayed any longer and boarded the ship; it was to take more than three hours to cross the choppy seas to Dover.

The Duchess was seasick but, to the relief of Charlotte Heiland, once on land she soon recovered her spirits. It was with great relief and joy that the royal couple finally reached London and settled down in the quiet of Kensington Palace to await the birth of their baby. As he watched over his wife, the Duke of Kent wrote to a friend, 'I trust my countrymen will duly appreciate the great sacrifice and exertion made by the Duchess at travelling at a period drawing so near her confinement . . . .' At 4.15 a.m. on Monday 24 May 1819, after a relatively easy six-hour labour, a baby girl was born – Victoria, the future Queen of England and Empress of India.

In the autumn of 1820 the Duke and Duchess left London with their daughter to stay at Woolbrook, Glent, a small two-storeyed white house less than a quarter of a mile from the sea at Sidmouth in Devon. On 22 January 1821, after a series of severe colds which developed into pneumonia, the Duke of Kent lapsed into unconsciousness and died the following morning. Within a century his descendants were to sit on the thrones of England, Germany, Russia, Norway, Romania and Spain. His royal dukedom died with him and it was not to be revived until 1934 when Prince George, fourth son of George V and Queen Mary, fell in love with Princess Marina of Greece. Shortly before his wedding in Westminster Abbey, Prince George was created Duke of Kent.

Key

David	Edward, Prince of Wales, later Edward VIII, Duke of Windsor (1894–1972)
Bertie	Prince Albert, later Duke of York, George VI (1895–1952)
Mary	Later Princess Royal, Countess of Harewood (1897–1965)
Harry	Prince Henry, later Duke of Gloucester (1900–1974)
Georgie	Prince George, later Duke of Kent (1902–42)
John	Prince John (1905–19)

1

Georgie

The weather was crisp and cold and, as the Christmas of 1902 drew nearer, four boisterous royal children eagerly awaited the first sign of hard frost. They were longing to skate on the lake, half hidden by laurels and thick clumps of evergreen rhododendrons which reached down almost to the edge of their garden. Even the youngest boy, the delicate, two-year-old Harry with his not very strong legs, had been promised that he could join in the fun provided he took great care not to tumble. The prospect, however, of cutting a dash on the ice faded into oblivion when, to their immense joy, they were told they were going to spend the festive season in the nearby 'Big House' with their grandparents, Edward VII and Queen Alexandra.

For David, eight, Bertie aged seven, Mary, five, and little Harry, it was like being given an open sesame to a glorious and glittering Dickensian world. There, from peepholes known only to themselves, the children could gaze upon vast drawing rooms heated by huge log fires burning in great hearths and adorned by elegant men in court dress and bejewelled women gliding in tight-waisted, stately Edwardian gowns to the lilting music of Gottlieb's Vienna Orchestra.

Little wonder that they ran breathlessly the quarter of a mile up the hill, as fast as their young legs could carry them. They were going to be utterly and outrageously spoiled by grandparents whose practical jokes always sent them into paroxysms of helpless laughter. That Christmas was destined to stay in all their minds for the rest of their lives.

In their exuberance and haste, the manner in which they said goodbye to their parents, the Prince and Princess of Wales, later to become George V and Queen Mary, was almost perfunctory. The little boys, though already well versed in royal protocol, paid small heed to the bows they made before their father, and Mary's curtsey left much to be desired. For their preoccupied parents, it came as a great relief to be temporarily free of their excitable and often explosive children whose multifarious activities, always accompanied by shouts and guffaws, had become for the moment unbearable. What their mother wanted most of all, as she rested on the sofa in her first-floor boudoir with its large bay window looking over the great lawns of the Sandringham Estate, was peace and quiet and time in which to relax. For the fifth time since she had married in great splendour nine years earlier in the Chapel Royal in St James's Palace, the Princess was enduring the anxious hours before the onset of labour. Two doctors of the Royal Household were already in residence in an overcrowded home and, while the Princess prepared to face her imminent confinement with fortitude and stoicism, she was, nevertheless, desperately hoping that her fifth delivery would be as straightforward as those she had experienced earlier in her marriage. She also hoped it would be her last.

She had already produced a future heir to the throne in David, now second in direct line of succession, followed by a daughter and two more sons, and this Christmas the Princess felt that she had done her duty not only by the nation, but also by her husband and family as well. She ardently hoped that she would never again find herself waiting for physicians, in their black frock coats and starched white collars, supported by three midwives ready to usher her into the adjoining bedroom and confirm that the time had arrived for the *accouchement*.

Like Queen Victoria, who had died the year before, the Princess wholeheartedly disliked pregnancy and all the physical aspects of childbirth, an attitude common to most of her royal relatives and aristocratic friends, and not without reason. In 1902 even royal mothers-to-be faced a hazardous ordeal that was very much a hit-and-miss affair when infection of one kind or another, notably puerperal fever, was a killer. There were no blood transfusions, no antibiotics and no ante-natal care whatsoever. The Princess's bedroom had been cleared of large pieces of furniture, but tables bearing jardinieres and framed family photographs still remained in place. The carpets were covered with sheets. Both doctors were extremely deferential towards their patient and did not take off their coats until the last possible moment. Even then, they only cautiously rolled up their shirtsleeves.

Waiting for the birth, Princess May – a familial shortening of Mary – was as composed as she possibly could be under the circumstances, comforted in the knowledge that her husband was nearby, quietly reading downstairs in his cluttered study, the walls covered with dark red cloth. Neither parent nor, for that matter, any of their relations was unduly concerned about the sex of the new baby. If it were a girl it would be a companion for Mary, who was already under the strong influence of her mischievous older brothers and showing every sign of becoming a tomboy; if it were a boy, he would soon be initiated into the secret world of fun and games that David and Bertie were already introducing to little Harry. As she passed the time, sometimes reading, sometimes endeavouring to concentrate on her crochet, Princess May could have had little sense of privacy. Not only was her home filled with members of the entourage but, in addition, Queen Alexandra had used it as an annexe for the 'Big House' to accommodate some of her overspill of parcel-laden guests, who were already arriving from all parts of Britain and the Continent well before the festive celebrations got underway on Christmas Eve. There were barely enough rooms to go round at the best of times, and this Christmas her home was seriously overcrowded and not an ideal atmosphere for a mother-to-be almost at the end of her term.

Princess May was resigned to the imposition, accustomed as she had become to the thoughtless and sometimes antagonistic attitude her mother-in-law adopted towards her. Queen Alexandra could at least have tried to make better arrangements not only for the comfort of her guests but also for the peace of her daughter-in-law.

It is unlikely that Queen Alexandra, with her possessive love for her son, George, would ever have come to terms with any daughter-in-law. She was not the most considerate or understanding of mothers-in-law. She would address letters not to 'Her Royal Highness the Princess of Wales' but to 'Her Royal Highness Victory Mary, Princess of Wales': a subtly incorrect designation that implied the existence of a whole host of variously named Princesses of Wales. Sometimes the Queen's disparagement of Princess May was more overt. Suffering from a cold the day before a court, she asked King Edward (VII) to cancel it. This he refused to do at such short notice. Instead he invited the Princess of Wales to take his wife's place. The Queen was furious, and, as Kenneth Rose recounts in *King George V*, allowed neither her Mistress of the Robes nor her other ladies to be present in attendance on the usurper . . . she failed to conceal her jealousy of the woman who had won her son's love.

The house in which Princess May was being confined was York Cottage on the Sandringham Estate – given to her husband as a wedding present by his father and, although over the years nearly every visitor disparagingly criticized it as 'poky', with her commonsense and practical mind, combined with natural good taste, she had made the best of what was undoubtedly the smallest and most unprepossessing of all the royal residences. With its narrow corridors, imitation Tudor beams and stained glass fanlights, York Cottage was a mockery of a royal home. Even on the brightest summer day most of the rooms were gloomy because of surrounding high trees which kept out the sunlight. By modern standards the cottage would be regarded as a more than adequate country home for a very affluent couple with a growing family, but in 1902 and for two very senior members of the Royal Family, constantly surrounded by lords and ladies in waiting, nannies, tutors and domestic staff, space was at such a premium that as each child was born some sort of extension had to be added.

In her boudoir Princess May could hear muffled voices coming from people circulating downstairs in the small entrance hall, the library, two drawing rooms and dining room. Only the massive billiard room, *de rigueur* for any gentleman's establishment built in the nineteenth century, was totally silent. Nevertheless, despite comparison with their other principal homes of York House in St James's Palace, Frogmore in the grounds of Windsor Castle and Abergeldie on the Balmoral Estate, York Cottage, with all its limitations and drawbacks, had come to represent 'home' for both Princess May and her husband.

They loved it dearly and it was here on the morning of Monday 20 December that their fourth son and fifth child, a lusty, normal boy, came into the world. While everyone was delighted that both mother and child were doing well, there were no great national celebrations since the new Prince, christened George Edward Alexander Edmund in the small Sandringham church, was well down the line of succession, distanced from the throne by three elder brothers. His future role was expected to be no more than supportive to the monarchy. Yet Georgie – as the baby became known – was to have an extraordinarily powerful and lasting impact, not only on members of his family, but also upon ordinary men and women, some of whom were far more inclined towards republicanism than to the establishment. Possibly more than any other man or woman born so close to the throne this century, Georgie, in spite of being the fourth son of the monarch, possessed all the qualities most needed in a king.

A boy with ideas and imagination, he could not have chosen a better time to be born. It was a period when the late Victorian era with all the rigidity and gloom that had surrounded the court for so long was rapidly disappearing and being replaced with new attitudes. However, there was no wind of change in the nursery routine at York Cottage, which adhered strictly to traditional lines. Georgie's parents were relieved to discover that their latest addition to the family was in every way a fine specimen of a boy. He was a contented child with a mass of dark hair and deep blue eyes who cried very little, and Princess May recovered rapidly from her confinement, which had been relatively easy and had presented no complications. They might have had reason to hover anxiously over Georgie in his early days, since two of their sons, Bertie and Harry, were delicate: in 1901 all the children had gone down with a severe bout of German measles, and at one stage in his illness, when Harry had had a very high temperature, there had been real fears that he might succomb to the disease, which then accounted for so many infant deaths.

As the Princess rested in her bedroom her husband went to great lengths to ensure that she was made as comfortable as possible. Ever a meticulous and obsessively punctual man, he prepared her breakfast himself every morning, and promptly on the dot of nine o'clock placed an elegantly laid-out tray before her in bed. At regular intervals during the day he would sit in an armchair reading aloud to her, once making the wry comment that they should feel proud of themselves as parents since they had now produced 'a regiment of princes'. If anything he was glad that he had yet another son, since it would have been almost impossible for a second daughter to have encroached upon the deep affection he felt for Mary, who was always to remain the apple of his eye.

Far from being insensitive parents, as has often been alleged, George V and Queen Mary were both caring and loving when their children were young. George V was certainly not always a fault-finding martinet. While in later years he had cause to speak harshly to the difficult and wayward David and Bertie, to the often truculent Harry, and on very rare occasions to Georgie, as children they had no reason to reproach their father. Indeed, the present Queen Elizabeth II, who is in a better position than almost anyone to know the truth about her grandfather, will have no ill word spoken about him. She remembers the grandfather who played with her and pushed her in her pram, and whom she adored because he was kind and loving to children not only in her own generation but also in her father's.

As Georgie grew up, George V presented the picture of a happy, domesticated man who would joke and chaff with his children as they splashed and played in an old tin hip bath that every evening was filled and emptied by a fleet of servants carrying water upstairs to the nursery. Despite his outwardly stern appearance with his naval beard and moustache, penetrating eyes and a voice that was deep to the point of gruffness, he had an inner jollity that Georgie often recalled when he was older. For his fourth son, George V would build wonderful towers and forts of bricks on the nursery floor and set out armies of tin soldiers marching across a drawbridge and posted on the towers and battlements of a toy castle.

An equally unsympathetic image of Princess May as a mother has been built up over the years. People outside the Royal Family were so accustomed to seeing her stiff and unsmiling, straight-backed in an elegant, close-fitting coat with a fur collar, the inevitable toque on her head and umbrella clenched in one hand, that they failed to accept that, while she was terribly shy in public, she was a different person at home. They forgot, too, that she had often been considered a handful as a child, and her husband's cousin, Princess Marie Louise, often liked to recall these times. In *My Memories of Six Reigns* she wrote: 'I remember her as a tomboy up to any pranks and games, even after her first years of marriage.'

Georgie came into his parents' lives at a happy time, nine years before they became immersed in, and oppressed by, the duties of state which followed their coronation in 1911. He took his first steps in the grounds of Sandringham, idyllic for children. Active days would contrast with the early evening when, with four sons and a daughter gathered around her feet, Princess May, with her prodigious knowledge of royal history, would hold them all spellbound with stories of her youth. Sometimes they would play card games like beggar my neighbour, old maid, happy families and the like. It was in these very early years that Georgie developed his mother's love of languages. She would turn to him and use words and phrases in German and French which, unlike his siblings, he learned to pronounce correctly, almost without an accent. He rapidly built up vocabularies in both languages.

Georgie's early years marked the period when his parents, in spite of an arranged marriage, had already grown very close to one another and had established a devoted relationship which was to last for the rest of their lives. Although the Prince of Wales was essentially the dominant partner in the marriage, his wife asserted herself in quiet but effective ways, especially as far as the young children were concerned.

It did not take the parents long to realize that Georgie had a completely different temperament from his brothers. He did not share David's mercurial moods, never displayed sudden bursts of temper and rage like Bertie, and was clearly quite unlike the slow and plodding Harry who seemed almost backward at times. Georgie had a far more loving and generous disposition than Mary, and while he got into his fair share of scrapes it was apparent that he was already intellectually, artistically and musically more gifted than any of the other children. To all those who came in contact with him, especially his mother with her highly cultured background, it became clear that he represented the élite in the Royal Family.

David, Bertie and Harry were each in their various ways difficult to teach, and reports from their tutors revealed only poor progress made in the restricted confines of their small schoolroom, with its desks and blackboard, in York Cottage. Admittedly they were taught by the tall, gaunt bachelor, Henry Hansell, who had taken second class honours in history, an unimaginative man who did little to inspire his pupils and was in constant despair over their lack of achievement.

He found his stimulus in the striking contrast presented by Georgie, who sailed through his lessons with ease and, although nearly three years younger than Harry, rapidly rivalled his brother's performance in every subject. He responded well to discipline and nearly always managed to outmanoeuvre any attempts at domination by David and Bertie. Yet his brightness never produced bad feelings between them: left to their own devices, and almost entirely cut off from boys and girls of their own age, the children developed private games, usually spurred on by the inventive Georgie. All of them learned to ride ponies and jump fences at an early age, and one of their greatest delights was cycling down a steep hill to watch the steam trains drawing in and pulling out of Wolferton, the local station for Sandringham. In those days no one so much as gave the royal children a second glance as they got up to daredevil acrobatic feats on their bicycles, riding with no hands or pedalling hell for leather in the direction of one of the sweetshops in the neighbourhood, to watch toffees and boiled sweets being carefully scooped out from huge jars and weighed on gleaming brass scales on the polished wooden counter. Once their parents left

York Cottage to attend Royal Ascot and, much to their disappointment, the children were left behind; it was Georgie who arranged what he called the Ascot Cycle Stakes. Because he was the youngest Georgie was given a start of a yard, but it was Mary, with her flowing fair hair and billowing long skirts, who, much to her younger brother's chagrin, came in first. The children never had lavish toys and they had as much fun playing with a set of old golf clubs as with anything else.

Loath though they were to leave York Cottage, there were times in the year when for official engagements or seasonal family gatherings the royal parents and their children were obliged to spend weeks in far more magnificent homes. When Georgie was only a few months old Edward VII and Queen Alexandra had reluctantly moved into Buckingham Palace and handed over their old residence, Marlborough House, to his parents, the Prince and Princess of Wales, as their new London home. Georgie would sleep outside in the garden in his pram as his mother and her ladies in waiting arranged furniture and hung pictures, sometimes working as long as eight hours a day. All seemed well with the family until the winter of 1904, when Princess May's hopes that she had experienced her last pregnancy were dashed: on 12 July 1905 she gave birth to her sixth and last child, John, who was not only subject to epileptic fits but also seriously retarded. The way in which the family closed ranks and, as far as official duties permitted, kept the subnormal child lovingly in their midst, had a powerful and lasting effect upon Georgie. With his older brothers away at school he saw far more of the handicapped child, and in a gentle way played with and amused John for hours on end. When the time came for Georgie to follow his father and elder brother to the Royal Naval College at Osborne in September 1916, he always made sure that the little boy received a regular supply of picture postcards.

The latter part of John's short life was mostly spent in the seclusion of Wood Farm, on the Sandringham Estate, which is sometimes used today by Queen Elizabeth and Prince Philip. He was cared for by nurses and doted upon by his family until he died quite suddenly after an epileptic attack in 1919 when he was only thirteen. After the death of 'dear little Johnnie' Princess May, then Queen, wrote to a friend, 'For him it is a great release. . . . I cannot say how grateful we feel to God for having taken him in such a peaceful way . . . he just slept quietly into his heavenly home, no pain, no struggle, just peace for the poor little troubled spirit.' He is buried in the tiny churchyard at Sandringham.

It was in Georgie, cheerful, alert, well-balanced, and then doing so well at Dartmouth, that his mother found her greatest solace. He greatly helped to ease the deep sadness of the bereaved Queen by accompanying her, as he had always done since he was a little boy, on her private visits to antique shops where she indulged her great passion for collecting objets d'art. She was diligently beginning to build up collections for which she was later to become famous. Georgie had inherited his mother's love of the arts, and for her it was a joy to share her love of beautiful things with her engaging youngest son.

With skill and patience she imparted to Georgie her own historical sense, and before long he began to understand and share her liking for order and for cataloguing treasures in the many royal residences. The boy proved an apt pupil and came to rival his mother's remarkable memory, fired by her avid and catholic interests which embraced furniture, silver, porcelain, paintings and objets d'art, among them Chinese jades, enamels and miniature tea sets. Over the years Queen Mary enthused Georgie with her vast knowledge of royal history, and they were often together when she acquired pictures and objects of family interest to add to royal collections, some of which she paid for out of her private purse. She was a pioneer amongst the modern Royal Family in this field and it was a passion she once described, as quoted in James Pope-Hennessy's *Queen Mary*, as 'my one great hobby'. Her instincts were in essence conservative; she would never, for instance, have dreamed of initiating a collection of contemporary pictures – as George did later in life. Her passion for family history led her to discover and retrieve objects dispersed from royal collections of the past which had been lost through historical upheavals, or by mere negligence in years gone by.

Georgie was infected by her enthusiasm. So well tutored was he that later in life it was difficult to know which of the pair had the greater expertise. Their absorption in the arts, music and literature was something quite beyond the understanding of other members of the family. In comparison, Georgie's brothers seemed disinterested: they read very little and their father only paid lip service to the royal treasures which had surrounded him all his life. Georgie was the only one of her children who had the historical and aesthetic curiosity to discuss with his mother all those works of art which other royal eyes scarcely seemed to see. He was already showing signs of becoming a fine pianist.

It is hardly surprising, therefore, that Georgie, the tallest, most handsome and most charming of her sons, became the undoubted favourite of his seldom openly demonstrative mother. While she and, to a lesser degree, his more hard-headed father recognized Georgie's outstanding and brilliant qualities, others became aware of his remarkable personality long before he left home and went away to school. This sometimes came about quite by chance and a classic example happened in 1912 when David, by then Prince of Wales, was a sophisticated eighteen-year-old already impatient to be allowed greater freedom in life.

David had ended his training at the Naval Colleges of Osborne and Dartmouth, and after serving a short time at sea had several months on his hands before going up to Magdalen College, Oxford. His parents were abroad for the Coronation Durbar at Delhi and he was irked because they had refused to allow him to accompany them to India, on the grounds that he needed to prepare himself for the new subjects that would face him at university. The prospect of being forced to spend the autumn and winter months at York Cottage under the eagle eye of his old tutor, Mr Hansell, did not please him at all and he expected to be profoundly bored. Yet it was during those months that David, with his increasingly dominant personality and need for stimulation, established the most powerful and intimate relationship that he was ever to make, with the exception, many years later, of that with his wife, the future Duchess of Windsor.

Looking back upon this remarkable period for both himself and Georgie, David wrote in *A King's Story*:

In spite of all my disappointments I spent a pleasant enough autumn and winter at Sandringham. Mary and my two younger brothers were with me at York Cottage and we enjoyed this period of freedom from parental restraint. Although we were in the charge of Mademoiselle Dussau and Mr Hansell, the four years I had been away had given me a certain independence of tutorial discipline. I no longer stood for being ordered about in quite the same way as before. For the first time in my life I felt more or less on my own.

During this interlude at home between the Navy and my new life of study abroad and at Oxford, my constant companion was my brother George, the youngest but one of the family. My older brothers, Bertie and Harry, were both away at school and came back only for the holidays. Although George was eight and a half years my junior, I found in his character qualities that were akin to my own: we laughed at the same things. That winter we became more than brothers – we became close friends.

Nothing confirms Georgie's unusual and gifted make-up more than this observation made by David. One has to remember that at the time the elder boy, with the charisma of his youth and heritage, was about to become the world's Prince Charming. His spell at sea, where his jobs included the dirty, back-breaking task of coaling ship, had been hard and when he returned to York Cottage, a cocky Mr Know-All, no one, least of all David himself, ever dreamed that he would establish a powerful bond with a little boy of nine. It was a relationship that was later to undergo a terrible testing, but this only served to strengthen the bonds between the brothers. In Georgie, David found a young boy who had rarely ventured out of the cosseted home atmosphere, except when, with Mary and his brothers, he was involved in a minor scuffle in a royal landau during the 1911 coronation procession. David, on the other hand, was already well aware of his unique status which gave him precedence over peers of the realm and, as he well realized, potential power.

Georgie was already showing signs of becoming a fine pianist. Unlike Bertie and Harry, his health was as robust as David's and his drive and energy were legendary. Also David discovered that he could 'talk himself out' to the mature-for-his-years Georgie in a way that he found impossible with anyone else, inside or outside the family. He was a good listener and, although he had no liking for the sea himself, he was always entranced by David's stories of his experiences away from home and listened with glee to accounts of secret smoking when coaling ship. During those months David opened his heart and fooled around with a companion who, despite their great age difference (a gap usually unbridgeable between teenagers and little boys), had all the qualities he had yearned for in a contemporary but never found.

One person who watched and delighted in the increasing closeness of David and Georgie during their months together at Sandringham, and to whom many years later Georgie was to feel nothing but gratitude, was their Aunt Toria (Princess Victoria) who was staying at the 'Big House' with her mother, the widowed Queen Alexandra. Toria, Alexandra's only unmarried daughter, gave up her life to her mother and yet, as David later acknowledged in *A King's Story*, 'always encouraged our fun'.

Georgie detested the idea of going to sea, and during his happy years with Harry at St Peter's Court, a prep. school at Broadstairs on the Kent coast, his future scholastic sights were already set on some sort of academic future ahead of him. The omens were good. The first-rate reports his parents were receiving from the headmaster, Mr A.J. Richardson, were so impressive that George V made what was for him a remarkable decision: he decided to pay a special visit to the school with his wife. When he complimented the headmaster on Georgie's results the reply he received was, 'But Sir, Prince George applies himself to every subject. It is a joy to teach such a child.' When Georgie returned home at the beginning of each holiday, his talents vividly showing up as each term passed, he found himself 'quite a little hero'.

It was with a sense of outrage that, just before his fourteenth birthday, Georgie discovered that his father had entered him for the Royal Naval College at Osborne, to be followed by Dartmouth. The boy was distraught. His mother pleaded Georgie's case with George V, but to no avail. His father was adamant and at no point could Queen Mary make her husband realize that for their youngest son, with his artistic and academic bent, the Navy could prove a disaster. At first Georgie did well, but his bitterness and total lack of interest in a career that had been forced upon him showed up in later reports when his position in classes began to slip. Unlike David and Bertie at the same age, Georgie was an easy mixer, but that did not ease his sense of anger and personal defeat at being compelled against his will to endure long weeks of what was, for him, monotonous naval training with no outlet for his creative interests. He was also a bad sailor and the prospect of the final training cruise in foreign waters, which delighted other cadets, only filled him with horror. Not only was he the victim of seasickness but he was also bedevilled with insomnia when these attacks came on. The two maladies were to dog him whenever he set sail. Despite repeated and urgent protestations to be allowed to take up another career ashore, in 1921 Georgie was made a midshipman and appointed to the *Iron Duke*, the flagship of the Mediterranean Fleet. For the sensitive and brilliant son of George V and Queen Mary, who spent much of his spare time learning Italian, Spanish and Dutch in addition to the German and French he already spoke fluently, his future outlook must have seemed bleak indeed.

Ultimately the strain was to prove too much for him and his life was to take a strange turn some years later when, almost unknown to the public, he was to set forth on a career which was to take him along new paths never before trodden by a royal prince.

2

A Sailor Prince Fights Back

On 20 December 1923, almost three weeks after his twenty-first birthday, Prince George was appointed a Knight of the Garter by his father. Home on leave from the Navy, the King's youngest son was proud and delighted to join the oldest order of chivalry in the world, and that Christmas there was every reason to believe that he would continue the family path as a sailor prince like his father and grandfather. However George was, and remains, the only prince ever to have broken the tradition of serving in one of the armed forces until such time as he took over as his sole occupation the various assignments and official duties of a member of the Royal Family. His inclinations were to work as an ordinary member of the public and, by stubborn determination, he realized this goal during the years between his discharge from the Navy in 1929 and his marriage to Princess Marina of Greece in 1934. The story of this unique achievement began when he passed out from Dartmouth in May 1920; after a training cruise on board HMS *Temeraire* he was appointed as a midshipman on HMS *Iron Duke*. In retrospect it can be seen as the outcome of the conflicting influences of his mother, his father and his eldest brother, David.

Probably because of their birthright, which inevitably distanced them from other people, members of the Royal Family have always established their closest and strongest friendships within their own ranks, most of them going back to nursery and childhood days. In the 1980s this pattern is at last gradually beginning to break down, but when George V was on the throne it was still staunchly upheld, and for very understandable reasons. As children his four sons were almost bereft of contact with other boys and girls of their own age. Then and in their early teens the children came to be regarded as little more than oddities, and they were totally unprepared for the outside world when they were suddenly thrust out of the cocoon-like atmosphere of the royal residences into the harsh, rugged dormitories of naval colleges where they were ragged and teased by fellow cadets. They were lost and bewildered. Whenever their periods at Dartmouth overlapped, as David's and Bertie's did, they relied on one another for support, and it was always a relief when the holidays came and they found themselves once again in familiar surroundings. Away from home during termtime in those crucial formative years they craved to be once again in the heart of a family in which they were loved, if seldom demonstratively, and understood to some degree.

At Dartmouth George, gregarious by nature, fared far better than either David or Bertie before him, but he too yearned for the days that would take him home to his mother. To her favourite son she would recount stories of her tours with her husband both at home and abroad, and proudly show George some of her most recently acquired objects and pictures of royal historical interest. In turn, he was the only son in whom she could easily confide and with whom she did not find communication either inhibiting or difficult. The relationship was a joy to both mother and son for the rest of their lives.

Unlike his brother, George always had a good relationship with his father whose rapport, particularly with David, became steadily more blunted until his death on 20 January 1936. According to Kenneth Rose in *King George V*:

During his convalescence in 1929, the King had more than once confided to trusted members of his family that his eldest son would never succeed to the throne. Six years later, he broadcast his fears more widely. A lady-in-waiting heard him say: 'I pray to God that my eldest son will never marry and have children, and that nothing will come between Bertie and Lilibet and the throne.' He told Baldwin: 'After I am dead, the boy will ruin himself in twelve months.'

Because of his self-confidence and unusual personal insight George was always careful and avoided the sort of confrontations that his brothers seemed at times almost wilfully to seek. By sheer strength of character he refused to allow himself to be intimidated. Even as a young boy he had a disarming way of answering 'Papa' back in a manner that was simultaneously firm and charming. George was able to laugh his way out of tricky situations, whereas David, Bertie and more especially Harry faltered and foundered in the monarch's presence. George V, with his bark and bite, could run verbal rings round each of them, even to the point of frightening them – if he chose to do so. George acquired the knack of being able to stand up to his father without giving offence. Certainly, if there was anyone who had a way with George V, it was young George.

However, the most powerful bond that George was to make before he married in 1934 at the age of thirty-two was with David. The eight-year difference in their ages was largely bridged by the very opposite nature of their individual personalities: they complemented one another. David, in contrast with George and despite his position in the family and his apparent assurance in the presence of some of the most distinguished world personalities of the day, was fundamentally weak and emotionally immature. In spite of being the most idolized public figure of his generation, David was an uncertain person in his private life, often to the point of great indecision. When George was away at sea, he enjoyed the company of his cousin, 'Dickie' Mountbatten, who became his equerry and accompanied him on several world tours. This was never a totally fulfilling relationship, and when Dickie married the wealthy heiress Edwina Ashley in 1922 his marriage and his dedication to his naval career allowed him far less time to devote to his bachelor cousin.

It was in the mature George, his urbane and sophisticated sibling, a man of wit and understanding, that David found his soul mate. George was able to ease David's lonely, indeed often solitary, private world, once the flags and bunting had been taken down and the cheers of the crowds had faded away.

From childhood George had always openly adored his elder brother, and as he grew into a young man this hero worship never waned. Nevertheless, George was objective enough to recognize some of the imperfections in David's character, notably his nervousness and the restlessness that made it impossible for him to enjoy his own company for long. Thus it was possible for George to feel empathy with David, whose public image contrasted so strongly with his private self.

In many ways David adopted a highly protective attitude towards his younger brother, whom he knew to be so desperately unhappy at sea. Whenever the opportunity presented itself David urged his father to allow George to be given special leave from naval duties in order to prepare himself for a more active role in public life, should that, for one reason or another, become necessary at a future date.

For very different reasons both George and David needed each other's support. A deep and often unspoken understanding emerged. One of the most important aspects of their relationship was a shared sense of humour that equally embraced a sense of the ridiculous, a precious and intangible gift that drew them ever closer together.

It was no small triumph when in 1927 David persuaded George V that it would be helpful if George could accompany him on a short official visit to Spain, where he had been invited to stay with King Alfonso at his courts in Madrid and Seville. For David, who by 1925 had already completed four gruelling major world tours involving long sea voyages to Australia and New Zealand, India, Japan and the United States, the prospect of providing his brother with a short break from the Navy was a delight. He recognized that, from a psychological point of view, George could only benefit from the change, and, at a personal level, he cherished the idea of his brother's lively and stimulating company.

It proved to be a relaxing and untaxing visit to the luxurious Spanish court, where David and George received an enthusiastic welcome and were able to renew old friendships with distant relatives, many of whom were also descendants of their own great-grandmother, Queen Victoria. Not surprisingly, when they returned to London there was widespread and favourable comment in the Royal Family about the great change in George: he looked fit, bronzed and happy. So often when he came home on leave from the Navy his colour was poor and it could take the best part of his leave before he began to recuperate. George seldom complained, except in private to David, but frequent bouts of severe seasickness combined with chronic insomnia always played havoc with his health during long months at sea.

Even his early years as a midshipman were blighted. He was often very hard up, and on his father's instructions had to live on his pay of about five shillings a day. It was David who regularly came to his brother's rescue by helping him out with extra pocket money. He had one narrow escape from death. When the battleship *Queen Elizabeth* on which he was serving had a drifter called *Blue Sky* attached to her, young midshipmen were sent aboard in order to improve their skills in seamanship. George asked to be allowed to board the drifter, but the captain refused permission. In the event, the drifter ran into terrible weather, foundered and sank with the loss of all hands. George was so distraught that he asked to be transferred to another ship.

Nevertheless, there were some important rewards to be gained from life in the Navy. When George served as a lieutenant with the Mediterranean and Atlantic Fleets and the China Squadron, and on the South African and West Indies Stations, he was able to see for himself some of the greatest ports in the world. Given shore leave, and in the company of fellow officers who, from the beginning, had accepted his firm dictum that he was always to be treated as a sailor and not as a royal prince, he was able to wander in places as varied and as far apart as Shanghai and Rio de Janeiro. Without the modern encumbrances of detectives and equerries and without the hindrance of any form of protocol, he was able to see for himself the notorious red light districts as well as the perimeters of shanty towns. Entry to both types of dangerous waterfront areas in ports all around the world was officially barred to British sailors, but there were few young men who did not attempt to venture into them in the safety of groups at some time in their careers. The temptation was too great.

In the 1920s, therefore, George was the only royal prince in modern times able to witness at first hand some of the greatest inequalities which divided the world at that time. It is more than likely that the first stirrings of his social conscience, which was to become so evident a few years later, began during those impressionable years away from home. Nor was it only in foreign ports that George was brought into direct personal contact with suffering and hardship. At times, when he had short spells as duty officer on ships docked in some of the hard-hit British ports like Liverpool and Portsmouth, he became well aware that men who had fought for their country in World War I were finding it desperately hard to get work. Many were already living on the breadline.

Because his visit to the Spanish court had been so successful for everyone concerned, George V raised no objection later in 1927 when David asked him to let George accompany him on another trip, this time an engagement of far greater significance. David had been invited by the Canadian government to take part in the Diamond Jubilee of confederation in August 1927, which was to last several weeks. By a strange twist of fate the politician who was to oppose David at the time of the abdication in 1936 accompanied the royal brothers to the other side of the Atlantic. He was Stanley Baldwin, then Britain's Prime Minister and a devious man who throughout his political life was often the centre of attack and intrigue. Many theories have been put forward as to why Baldwin accepted the invitation to visit Canada that summer, leaving behind a deeply divided cabinet to clear up the wreckage of the Geneva Conference. Some historians hold the view that as early as this Baldwin was preoccupied with David's attitudes and behaviour, which he felt would be a problem when he became King. A more likely answer is that Baldwin went to Canada at that time simply because he had been invited. In *Edward VIII* Frances Donaldson wrote: 'His son, Earl Baldwin of Bewdley, believes that he travelled to Canada at this time for the simple reason that he had been invited to the Diamond Jubilee celebrations and had accepted at a much earlier date.'

While Baldwin had had previous contact with David at an official level and knew a great deal about him through his many private sources, George was an unknown quantity at the outset of the voyage. It is thought more than likely that through the Admiralty grapevine he had heard rumours circulating about George which implied that he sometimes expressed slightly left political views. This must have aroused great curiosity in the Prime Minister and spurred him to find out the truth for himself. Like her husband, Mrs Baldwin was intrigued at the opportunity which presented itself of observing the two princes at close quarters and getting to know them.

The Baldwins found both David and George engaging and highly entertaining, but it was the younger brother who appeared to impress the Prime Minister more. Also, by the end of the tour, which had taken the party to Quebec, Alberta and to the inauguration of the International Peace Bridge across the Niagara River, both princes were deeply impressed by Baldwin as a fluent conversationalist, although David harboured a greater sense of reserve about the man than did George. Many years later, as Duke of Windsor and looking back on the tour, David recalled in *A King's Story*:

Listening to him [Baldwin] expounding on such varied topics as the apple husbandry of Worcestershire, cricket and the revision of the Prayer Book – then a subject of violent controversy in Parliament – I was impressed by his erudition even more than by his reputation for political sagacity.

However, as I studied Mr Baldwin, I thought I detected traces of the arrogance that some Englishmen display when travelling abroad. The deeper we penetrated the North American continent, the more he became the embodiment of Old John Bull himself.

Like many people who met them together for the first time, Mrs Baldwin was surprised to discover how much smaller David was than George, and in repose how strangely wistful. The brothers, however, shared much more than their striking good looks and charm; sometimes when they were together and became bored by routine, or when official pressures seemed almost unbearable, they would find their escape in rebellious escapades that usually involved no one but themselves. Once, for example, when attending a ball given in their honour at Government House in Ottawa, they left the function in order to join a private party elsewhere. Some mild criticism was expressed at the time by Lady Willingdon, wife of the Governor General of Canada, but if Baldwin or his wife were privy to this breach of good manners they kept their silence.

At the end of 1927, with the glowing memories of his visits to Spain and Canada still at the forefront of his mind, George made his first serious appeal to his father to be allowed to leave the Navy. It fell on deaf ears but George was given some slight encouragement when David, using all the skill that was possible for him to summon up in the dreaded presence of his father, pleaded his brother's cause. He stressed that Bertie and himself were each carrying out an ever-increasing number of official duties, including deputizing for the King when he was away, and urged that George should be allowed to ease some of their load. He suggested that his brother should be given occasional special leave in order to try his hand at carrying out some royal engagements on his own. David received a half-hearted response but the next year, on 13 April 1928, George was initiated into freemasonry and became a master mason the following June.

During his periods of convalescence and before returning to sea, George appeared in public on a number of occasions, speaking on behalf of various charities and philanthropic organizations. With his excellent memory he was able to brief himself very quickly on the subjects on which he had to speak, and thoroughly enjoyed his small sorties into public life. He possessed another skill that was quite foreign to other members of the Royal Family: he made his speeches without notes. It is not surprising that every time he had to report back for naval duty, by now with the rank of commander, it was with an ever greater sense of bitterness and resentment.

His private revolt against his father's rule that he must remain a full-time serving officer in the Navy had reached a critical stage when he was on leave during Ascot Week in June 1929. Once again he pressed to be allowed to find a job ashore, and once again his request was turned down. There was an overriding reason why George V had so little sympathy with his younger son. The King may have envied George: he had loved his own years at sea and regarded it as a tragedy when his own naval career, to which he was utterly dedicated, had been abruptly cut short in 1892 on the death of the Duke of Clarence. He had been created Duke of York when the ageing Queen Victoria was in her last decade and, as second in line of succession, he had to accept that royal duties must take precedence over a life at sea.

There were some members of the Royal Family who feared a head-on clash between George V and his youngest son, but each felt helpless to prevent the conflict. Intervention occurred, quite by chance, at a large and splendid dinner given by the King at Windsor Castle for his Ascot guests, when George found himself sitting next to one of his mother's oldest and closest friends. She was Mabell, Countess of Airlie, a shrewd and clever woman with great empathy who had been a confidante of the Royal Family all her life. She was also lady in waiting to Queen Mary. There were few secrets that the two women did not share and Lady Airlie realized only too well that once George V had made up his mind about a family matter, there was little his wife – or anyone else for that matter – could do to dissuade him from the course upon which he was bent. Instinctively she sensed that the handsome young man at her side, whom she had known since he was a little boy, was restless and ill-at-ease. She bided her time and it was not long before George found himself confessing to Lady Airlie how much he was dreading his next voyage. In her book, *Thatched with Gold*, she recounts how he told her that he was desperately unhappy in the Navy and wanted to go into the civil service or the Foreign Office, but the King would not hear of it. 'His only reason for refusing is that it has never been done before,' said George. 'I've tried to make him see that I'm not cut out for the Navy but it's no use. What can I do?'

Lady Airlie knew that, much as he detested service life, there was also a strong pleasure-seeking aspect to his character. While George was passionately absorbed in his spare time in collecting antique furniture and works of art, and enthralled by the Russian ballet and the emerging world of films and jazz, he also enjoyed a less aesthetic private life when he was in London. In the daytime he would play a hard game of squash at the Bath Club and lunch at the best places, often the Ritz Grill. After dinner he could often be found with his friends dancing in night clubs until the early hours of the morning.

With his easy, informal approach, his complete lack of arrogance and a long-established habit of hiding his real status, he had no difficulty in passing for what he truthfully said he was, a commander in the Royal Navy. It was during the late 1920s that George first began to reveal certain fundamental weaknesses in his make-up. He was not always a good judge of character, and in enjoying some of his heady evenings on the town he was sometimes far from selective in his choice of companions, both male and female. Like many young men and women he made some decidedly unwise friendships.

Probably bearing these facts in mind, and yet at the same time doubtless recalling the day when George V had told her that his youngest son 'had the brains of the family', Lady Airlie paused before replying to the Prince. It had never been her habit to mince her words, and at this Ascot dinner she made no exception. 'I advised him not to waste time in arguing with the King – which would only make him angry – but to work hard while he was at sea, get the Civil Service papers and do them, and then let his father see the results. He told me sometime later that he had acted on my advice and that it had been successful.'

Lady Airlie's forthright advice, which was destined to change the entire course of George's life, was incredibly bold, bearing in mind the King's known and total opposition to his son's leaving the Navy. Had news of her opinions ever reached the ears of the King, it would undoubtedly have been regarded as an act of outrageous conduct on her part. There is little doubt that the repercussions on Lady Airlie would have been disastrous and ended her royal friendships. Her advice, as she must have known when she gave it, was in direct opposition to George V's stubborn refusal to understand his youngest son's desire for a worthwhile job, which he dismissed as nonsense. For George V there were only two careers for a royal prince: either in one of the services, as in the case of George, or performing public duties with meticulous attention to detail and in the manner prescribed by himself.

Whether Queen Mary was ever secretly told about the advice given by Lady Airlie is not clear, but it seems almost impossible that she was not. George was, after all, not only her favourite son but his plight had been observed by her great friend. However, the outcome of the Ascot dinner was that it eased the tension between the King and George who, having easily passed naval navigation, gunnery and torpedo courses, saw no reason why he should not also succeed in the civil service examinations. He set off on his last voyage at sea armed with all the necessary books and papers in order to prepare himself for his great objective – to become the first member of the Royal Family to join the civil service. He devoted all his spare hours to swotting and studying in his cramped cabin, and worked so hard that his colour was often ashen grey.

Ironically it was not his studies that finally made the King decide that George could leave the Navy in 1929, but chronic ill health. Medical evidence revealed that further periods at sea would only exacerbate George's digestive troubles and add to the general deterioration of his already impaired constitution.

Faced with what was tantamount to a *fait accompli*, the King agreed that George, provided he went through the usual official procedures and was considered suitable material, should be attached to the Foreign Office, and at the same time begin to share some of his brothers' royal duties. Not without certain misgivings, he also accepted David's advice that George would adjust better to his new life if he went to live with him at his own establishment, York House in St James's Palace, instead of Buckingham Palace. At the latter even Harry, at the age of thirty-two, had to be down for breakfast at 8.55 a.m. to await the arrival of his parents on the dot of nine.

George's health improved rapidly under the personal wing of David, and he soon acquired an impressive manner. Shortly before nine o'clock every morning from Monday to Friday, the tall, slim figure in a bowler hat, black overcoat and pin-stripe suit marched smartly out of the ancient wooden doorway of St James's Palace, jauntily swinging a tightly rolled umbrella. He made his way via Horse Guards Parade to the Foreign Office in Whitehall. George went unrecognized by the public, but his striking appearance combined with a general air of *joie de vivre* always made heads turn. He had every reason to feel buoyant: entirely due to his own initiative, drive and determination, he was the first son of a reigning monarch to have become a civil servant.

His years of close contact with men in the Navy, who came from all social groups, enabled him to build up a very extraordinary background for a royal prince of his time. He was never, unlike his brothers, cushioned from life's harsher realities. In *A King's Story*, some twenty years later, David wrote that he was generally regarded, in a kindly way, as 'somewhat of a Bohemian' by both his parents, and by his brothers and their circle. Even David accepted that George was 'sharply different in outlook and temperament from the rest of us'. Later in life

David was to describe George in 1930 as 'possessed of unusual charm of manner and a quick sense of humour and, talented in many directions, he had an undoubted flair for the arts. He played the piano, knew a good deal about music, and had a knowledgeable eye for antiques.'

Far more sophisticated than Bertie or Harry, wiser and more intelligent than David, George found his natural home at York House where he became increasingly involved in David's social activities which gave him greater insight into more important fields. He came into personal contact with visiting statesmen, businessmen, foreign diplomats and other distinguished professional men and women for whom David gave formal dinners. Guests were impressed, often deeply so, by this cultured and erudite young man, a fact that became increasingly more widely known in political circles.

By 1931 the numbers of unemployed in Britain had soared to more than two million and George made no secret of his great concern about their plight and about increasing social unrest. He spoke of his frustration at being helpless to do more at a personal level. Later, in 1936, during a visit to the industrial areas in South Wales, David, now Edward VIII, made a comment that was political dynamite at the time and was to echo down the decades. Bare-headed and clutching a bowler hat as he entered the poverty-stricken homes of Welsh miners who could not find a job, let alone feed or clothe their families, David murmured, 'Something must be done. . . .'

At once the unemployed all over the country identified themselves with him. He had seen for himself all the despair – and had shown by his words that he cared. That message went over to the lost generation of the years after World War I. It had such strong political overtones that many members of the cabinet and ordinary Members of Parliament became alarmed. They began to question and look more deeply into the nature of David, the man who had succeeded George V, who would never have made such an emotive statement in public. He appeared to be breaking ranks. And politicians, who were already afraid of increasing unrest among the unemployed, became afraid of David. What was he about? What had he in mind?

What no one at the time ever closely questioned was the source of the gradual build-up of David's detailed knowledge of the industrial disaster which drove him to utter that moving and revealing remark. The source, in the opinion of such senior royal relatives as Lord Mountbatten, was his closest friend and brother, George, the chameleon who to some appeared far too debonair to be taken seriously. Only those who knew George very well indeed, and David was among them, ever realized the true depth of the man – and his tremendous influence over David. Baldwin had had the chance of assessing George on the Canadian tour, but few other British politicians had had a similar opportunity.

To some people, George appeared as a dilettante. They judged him by his spare-time pursuits, which included driving fast cars: at one time he owned a six-litre Bentley. In the course of his hectic social life he was frequently seen in the company of the Mountbattens and their cosmopolitan friends. After gaining his pilot's licence in 1930 he acquired the reputation of a daredevil flier. In fact he was a skilled aviator who never took chances. As Stella King wrote in *Princess Marina*, 'He always looked younger than his age and so full of life that someone commented at this period that he had "all the eagerness for enjoyment which stamps a naval officer ashore for a bit of leave".' Unlike all the other members of his family, notably his father and David, George disliked shooting and he invented a game to while away the time at the magnificent luncheon parties given by George V on shooting days. He imposed a fine on anyone who spoke the word 'shoot' during the course of the meal. It became progressively more difficult the nearer a guest was seated to the King, whose conversation was entirely occupied by the morning's foray. The King's attention was drawn to George's joke, but whereas he would have raised cain if David, Bertie or Harry had been the instigator, he chose to ignore George. It was a telling sign of his warmer, understanding attitude towards his youngest son.

There were many moments of light relief shared by George and David, but neither found much relaxation in the many private parties to which they were invited. Mrs Dudley Ward, for so many years David's closest companion, observed, as recorded in *Edward VIII* by Frances Donaldson, 'It was difficult for David and George to meet any nice people. I often noticed that at parties. All the nice people stood around the walls while the pushing people pushed up to them. Speaking of people in general and naval officers in particular, George said, "Either they slap you on the back, or they get under the table . . .!" ' Unfortunately this unhappy state of affairs for children of the sovereign still continued in the 1970s and 1980s when Prince Charles, with a rueful air, made similar observations. While he never complained of being slapped on the back, he expressed regret that it seemed to take an awfully long time for people to make themselves relax in his presence.

George, who, had he lived, would have been a great-uncle of Prince Charles, found his own way of escape from stilted social parties, work and royal duties. When the mood seized him and the right opportunity presented itself, he relaxed in the resorts of the South of France, for so long the happy holiday haven of his great-grandmother, Queen Victoria, who loved Nice. Always a man of nocturnal habits until his marriage in 1934, George would link up with the sort of men and women he enjoyed and gamble in the casinos of Nice. He once returned to London after a visit to Cannes and proudly claimed that he had won a tango competition. He was light on his feet and, with his dark, wavy hair, his aquiline features and his dark blue eyes, he cut a real dash on the dance floors of night clubs like the Embassy, the 'in' rendezvous of the rich in the 1920s and 1930s.

That George and David could dance their way into the early hours of the morning was a matter of bewilderment to George V. His inability either to understand or come to terms with the changing times and the way in which George and David enjoyed them was epitomized when he once remarked sadly to a friend, as related by John Gore in *King George V*, 'I am devoted to children and good with them but they grow up, and you can only watch them going their own way and can do nothing to stop them. Nowadays young people don't seem to care what they do or what people think.' His words give a hint of an almost fatalistic belief in a barrier between generations. He more than once spoke with the same fatalism about the attitude of British sovereigns to their eldest sons in recent centuries. George V was a victim of the generation gap. He was completely out of touch with youth and made no serious effort to try and bridge it. Yet, curiously, the seemingly straitlaced Queen Mary was privately far more tolerant than her husband. When Princess Marie Louise, a cousin of George V, was discussing with Queen Mary the way in which George and David spent some of their leisure hours, she remarked that she wondered what Queen Victoria would have said about the younger members of the royal family going to night clubs to dance. Queen Mary thought for a moment and then replied, 'There are no big houses nowadays as there were when we were young, in which they can be entertained, and therefore where should they and their contemporaries meet and enjoy themselves?'

In every way 1931 was the turning point in George's life. The Navy was behind him but he saw no real future in the Foreign Office. He realized that, as the King's son, he was never likely to be given an important diplomatic appointment abroad. The sort of job for which he yearned would inevitably have taken him into political situations at some time or other, and this was, in his position, impossible. It was during the Christmas of that year that he decided his next move. It was to be a dramatic one.

3

Royal Factory Inspector

Although he belonged to the most privileged family in Britain and by 1931 had come to be regarded as the most dashing and debonair of George V's four sons, George was privately far from satisfied. He lacked a real sense of purpose. To his family and friends, however, he seemed to be riding the crest of the wave: in popularity he almost outshone David. Edgar Wallace, the influential and widely read journalist who was famous for his crime novels, was able to write in the *Daily Mail*, 'There are hundreds of charming creatures throughout the country who have a portrait of Prince George on their bedroom walls and can hardly keep their eyes off it.' At twenty-nine George could captivate, almost at will, any woman he encountered, but his amorous adventures, mostly brief, were always with people well removed from royal or aristocratic circles. He never invited them home. Some were shadowy personalities on the fringes of the stage and show business world, others were encountered on his private and official trips abroad. His public image, however, was glittering. George had a national romantic appeal that has never since been paralleled by anyone in the Royal Family, not even Prince Andrew, Queen Elizabeth II's second son.

George's looks were those of an archetypal thirties' Hollywood film star, and this attribute, combined with his royal birth, made him irresistible to people who had never even met him. His open, smiling features became familiar to millions of picturegoers who watched him on the weekly Gaumont-British newsreels as he carried out his official duties, or with his parents and brothers attended great state occasions like Trooping the Colour and the State Opening of Parliament. The public saw him on newsreels made in South America in January 1931 when he accompanied David to the opening of the British Empire Trade Exposition in Buenos Aires. It was a semi-official visit, but the private government brief to the two brothers before their departure was for them to make every effort to recapture some of the great South American markets for British manufacturers, who were losing out in the face of fierce competition from the United States.

David, never a linguist, had taken a crash course in order to make a major speech in Spanish. He was tutored every day, including weekends at his country house, Fort Belvedere near Windsor, by a Spanish professor from the University of London, but it was George, fluent in German, French, Italian and Spanish, whose presence on the tour had the greatest impact on government and industrial hosts in Argentina, Peru and Brazil. His extremely adept sales talk in Spanish did much to persuade South American businessmen that they should turn their sights towards the other side of the Atlantic. Whereas David always had a translator at his elbow, George was able to get a far better picture of what was going on in South American markets. When David made his speech opening the Trade Exposition he could only deliver half of it in Spanish, whereas it would have been an effortless exercise for George to have made the entire speech in that language. He was also, as mentioned earlier, a natural speaker who never needed notes. Nevertheless David received an ego boost in a cable from Stanley Baldwin which read, 'WELL DONE SIR STOP MY WARMEST AND MOST RESPECTFUL CONGRATULATIONS ON YOUR SPEECH STOP SPANISH PUNDITS DELIGHTED WITH YOUR PRONUNCI-ATION.' Working closely together, the brothers made a great impact on hard-headed businessmen, but they found it less easy to put the lessons they had learned to practical use on their return. As David wrote in *A King's Story*: 'It was no easy task with all Britain bogged down in the gloom of the world slump. In Birmingham I dumped some of my foreign samples on the desks of jewellery manufacturers. But instead of being seized upon avidly, they were regarded with brooding suspicion and almost disdain.' The brothers had collected Czechoslovakian costume jewellery which had captured the South American market from Birmingham.

He and David made a powerful team when they went abroad together – flying the flag for Britain. On this occasion when they returned home they pointed out that important markets were being lost for two reasons: English manufacturers, unlike American, were failing to keep up with new trends, and were also totally ignoring the emergence of new advertising techniques.

Cinema audiences knew George as a pilot, too. In 1930, three years after Charles Lindbergh's epic solo flight across the Atlantic, tremendous advances had been made in aviation and three of the royal brothers entered into a family competition. David, George and Harry vied with one another in a race to see which one of them could gain his pilot's licence first. They took lessons at Northolt airport in David's small De Havilland Gypsy Moth and it was the elder brother who won the race. David had a lead over George and Harry, since he had received many hours of dual instruction before they began their tuition. While David never piloted himself again, George found freedom in the air, and later in 1930 made his first official flight when he flew from Sunningdale to Hull to open a Civic and Empire Week. It was this sort of dashing gesture, breaking new ground for royalty, that helped to build up his daredevil image. On other private occasions he would borrow a blue Tiger Moth which belonged to David. Wearing goggles and a leather flying helmet he would fly himself to parties, often landing on rough airstrips or bumpy fields. His expertise as a pilot was such that no accident occurred, until finally destiny overcame him.

However, despite his raffish lifestyle, George harboured a deep sense of frustration. He wanted a 'real job'. The Foreign Office episode had proved disappointing. At the age of twenty-nine he identified with the restless, ever-growing ranks of the unemployed, but even his eagerness to embark on fact-finding tours of the hard-hit areas of the industrial north drew no favourable or encouraging response from either his father or politicians. David fully sympathized with his brother's desire to establish closer contact with the working classes but felt that the obstacles were insurmountable. Yet entirely as a result of his own tenacity, determination and persistence, George finally made royal history: he became a Home Office factory inspector. On 12 April 1932, the day he first reported for work, he became the first son of a reigning monarch to work alongside ordinary members of the public.

On his personal insistence his royal status was successfully played down to the minimum, so that in the early days he appeared to be just an ordinary trainee factory inspector learning his job. Always accompanied by a senior inspector, he began his tours of factories in the London area at 10 a.m. and rarely finished his duties before five o'clock. He then had to go home and prepare a detailed report of the day's activities. George was always hatless, dressed inconspicuously in a sports jacket and grey flannel trousers. He went about his business in the front passenger seat of a small saloon car, usually a Ford, owned by his boss. Quaintly, because one cannot see how it could have served its purpose, to keep his identity concealed the senior inspector had been advised never to address him as 'Your Royal Highness' but as 'Prince George'. In the event, when they were not alone it was found better to call him 'Mr George'. His period as a factory inspector was a remarkable and dramatic achievement still unique in the annals of the Royal Family, even after an interlude of more than fifty years.

It required all his skill in the art of persuasion and diplomacy for George to realize the goal he had set himself. Not only did he manage to win over on to his side the extremely dubious Prime Minister, Stanley Baldwin, but also George V, who had never even remotely pretended to understand his son's desire to have first-hand experience of industry and encounter workers at shop-floor level.

George knew he had overcome his first major hurdle when in February 1932 Sir Herbert Samuel, the Home Secretary, asked Sir Malcolm Delevigne, Permanent Deputy Under-Secretary of State, to examine the possibility of George becoming a Home Office factory inspector. One of the major problems that faced the two men was that, although George wanted to become a full-time inspector, the King stipulated that his son must remain available for royal duties. How could this issue be resolved? George was optimistic and felt that, with the full support of his three brothers, he could combine essential royal duties with his new job and would be able to report for duty on a regular basis. Impressed as they were by his enthusiasm, both Sir Herbert Samuel and Sir Malcolm Delevigne harboured doubts and were of the opinion that the conflicting pressures might well prove too great for him.

Nevertheless by mid-March Sir Malcolm had thoroughly researched the royal project and sent a confidential letter to the Home Secretary, saying that Prince George 'should be . . . a supernumerary inspector, and undertake the ordinary duties of an inspector, although not necessarily for the full number of working days in the week'. Because of the King's insistence that George must also perform royal duties, Sir Malcolm felt that in his early days the Prince should work in the London area. His report continued:

As his work will lie in the Metropolitan area, we would propose to attach him to three London districts, Southwark, Woolwich and South Essex, in order to give him as interesting a range of work as possible and at the same time allow of some concentration of interest in the more important and live issues of factory administration. . . .

Among the more important and live issues to which his attention might be given are the work in the London docks (loading and unloading of ships, which are processes fruitful of accident and are governed by an elaborate code of regulations, and which happen to be, at the moment, the subject of international discussion); the asbestos industry with its newly discovered dangers to health; different branches of the engineering and woodworking industries; the building industry with its recently amended code of safety regulations etc. It would also be arranged to let him see interesting developments in health and welfare work. . . .

. . . the actual visiting of the factories should be alternated with visits to the Home Office Industrial Museum . . . where he would be given some intensive instruction in the principles and practice of the safeguarding of machinery and the prevention of various kinds of accidents; the nature and prevention of industrial diseases and the promotion of industrial health and welfare; the principles of factory ventilation and lights; and so on. This is now part of the ordinary training of recruits to the Factory inspectorate.

Unfortunately . . . some of the staple industries of the country are hardly represented at all in the Metropolitan area, but it could easily be arranged that the Prince should pay visits of inspection to these when he happened to be in or near any of the industrial districts.

It is an essential part of the training of an Inspector that he should make himself acquainted as quickly as possible with the main provisions of the Factory Acts and orders and regulations made under them. . . .

It is presumed that the Prince is to be treated exactly as an ordinary Inspector, will be expected to work regularly and punctually (it will be convenient if it can be arranged that he should keep to the same days in the week, though, of course, it will always be possible to alter these days, by arrangement) – the Inspector whom he accompanies during his period of training will be carrying on his own actual inspection work, and it is important, therefore, that he should not be delayed by the Prince arriving late in the morning! . . .

The Home Secretary ended his answering memo with a sincere comment, 'I need not add that the Department will be very happy to give all the assistance possible to make the plan a success.'

Samuel, however, was anxious that his memorandum should not lay him open to criticism from any quarter, either political or royal. Instead of sending it for the immediate approval of the King he decided first to put the communication before the Prime Minister.

Having read the proposals, Baldwin, as Samuel suspected he might, raised specific questions. On 22 March 1932 he wrote to the Home Secretary:

I confine myself to practical considerations. 1. He must have exceptional treatment as to training, hours, discipline, work. Will this work? 2. Can his other public duties give him regular time to do this work? 3. Can he be regarded by owners and work people as an Inspector and not as a Prince? 4. Will he find it possible to stick to the work period sufficiently long (at least two or three years) to justify beginning it?

I need not point out the very serious effect of a termination which would be criticised by sections of working class opinion.

The difficulty is the very simple one of showing the public that this is a genuine desire to perform a public service, and not a whim or excuse or something of that nature. If His Royal Highness is willing to take his coat off and put his back into the job it would be a very fine piece of work, but he will have to get round some very dangerous corners, and must have the most vigilant guidance to start with by the Home Office.

What Baldwin may have feared most was that George, through no fault of his own, might become involved in scenes of unrest. The Home Secretary dealt with the four points raised in the Prime Minister's letter:

1. No exceptional treatment will be given except that he will not work more than four days a week;
2. The Home Office cannot say – but has not been impressed with any particular hindrance; his work with the Home Office ought to be regarded as his *first* public duty;
3. While he will be called Prince George, he will be treated, as far as one can possibly manage, as an Inspector – and not a Prince;
4. It would not be fair either to the Department or the Prince to stipulate so long a period as two or three years but I think we ought to get His Majesty, if he approves the scheme, to lay it down quite definitely that if the Prince enters on it, he is to stick it for at least (say) six months and that he won't be allowed to leave the job before.

George privately told the Home Secretary that he was anxious to undertake the work exactly on the lines of Samuel's memorandum. He fully accepted the Prime Minister's view that it would be very undesirable for him to start the work and then discontinue it after a short time. George said that he had discussed the new job with Queen Mary, who, according to a Home Office memorandum, 'cordially approved' the project. Neither mother nor son saw any reason why royal duties should interfere with the clear-cut plans so carefully drawn up by the Home Office.

George V finally gave George his full blessing to go ahead when they dined together at Windsor Castle on 7 April. That same evening the King's Private Secretary, Colonel Sir Clive Wigram, wrote to the Home Secretary informing him that 'His Majesty is glad to approve of these proposals which should provide an active and interesting life for the Prince.'

Anxious that there should be no delay or that the King should have second thoughts about his new job, George paid an informal visit to the Home Office the following day. He received encouragement and praise for his initiative from Sir Malcolm Delevigne and Sir Gerald Bellhouse, Chief Inspector of Factories.

When George reported for work as an unpaid factory inspector on 12 April it might have served as a tremendous boost for national morale. At that time, in the midst of an unemployment crisis, it presented a perfect opportunity for Baldwin and the King to reveal that at least one member of the Royal Family was breaking with tradition and moving with the times. Yet no publicity whatsoever was given on the first day he arrived to study at first hand industrial conditions and administration. Some days later, and with the full backing of the Prime Minister and George V, the Home Secretary sent a 'personal and confidential' letter to members of the powerful Newspaper Proprietors' Association and the Newspaper Society, requesting 'that there should be no reference in the Press to individual visits by His Royal Highness in the letter press or by photographs'.

As a result of private conversations with the Home Secretary, the newspaper owners agreed to play down the great royal adventure. It would have taken an extremely conscientious reader of *The Times* in the issue of 26 April 1932, eight days after George had started work, to note the few short single-column paragraphs, with a single-column headline, which announced that George had joined the Home Office Factory Inspectorate. The *Morning Post* had a small single-column headline, 'Prince George and Industry', while the *News Chronicle* in a similar small space reported: 'Prince George – Inspection Tour of Factories'. This last headline was totally misleading.

It has to be remembered that in 1932 there were no high-powered public relations officers either in business or in industry. The exchange of memoranda at the time between the Home Office, Downing Street and Windsor Castle reveals that there was only 'a Mr Mitchell' described as 'the publicity expert at Buckingham Palace'. It was no better at Downing Street, where 'a Mr Steward' was somewhat disparagingly referred to as 'the Number Ten liaison officer with the Press'.

The Home Secretary was on sure ground when he further informed newspaper proprietors that he felt sure he could 'rely on your co-operation in preventing any embarrassment being caused to His Royal Highness and to ensure that Prince George's desire to be treated as a private individual on the occasions of his visits of inspection should be respected'. George did not receive a salary and factory inspectors did not wear uniforms.

It is hardly surprising that journalists were greatly excited about George's new career. Their interest grew to such an extent that the Home Office was soon inundated with requests to be allowed to take pictures of George at work. Unaware of the connivance of the Home Office with the proprietors, Fleet Street wanted to make as much as possible of one of the most dramatic royal news stories of the decade. Every application to take photographs was turned down. No news photographer in 1932 would have dared to attempt a 'snatched' picture of the prince. The price would have been the immediate loss of his job and, what is more, the 'snatched' picture would never have been published. This subservient attitude on the part of newspaper proprietors towards the establishment was to continue for only a few more years. Soon afterwards they were to turn a deliberate blind eye to a royal matter of grave national importance: they kept news of the affair between David and the American divorcee, Mrs Wallis Simpson, from the British public.

George certainly wanted to be able to go about his new job without hindrance or interference. He felt his request for anonymity to be a valid one and in this he had the full support of his father. He wanted above all to be accepted as an ordinary factory inspector and not as a royal prince. It should have been obvious to Baldwin that this would never work, but for his own reasons the Prime Minister kept silent.

By taking off his jacket and putting his back into the job, to paraphrase the Prime Minister's memorandum, George's bold step could have served to identify the Royal Family more closely with working men and women. The monarchy was held in respect and affection by the public but there was no sense of personal contact between the family and the public as there is today, when the Queen goes on frequent walkabouts with her relatives and meets all manner of professional people at regular lunches at Buckingham Palace. George V could never accustom himself to being the focus of popular attention. As Kenneth Rose observed in *King George V*, 'He was a man who, when urged to display in public some of the geniality which delighted his own table, told his private secretary, "We sailors never smile on duty." ' Little was known about the private lives of members of the Royal Family before the war, and if more information had been released about George's job with the inspectorate the gulf between the palace and the public would have been narrowed. Relatively few people, even to this day, ever knew of George's personal triumph in breaking down barriers that had never been attempted by a royal prince. One of the outcomes of his service with the factory inspectorate was that, on many of his official visits to factories later in the decade and during the early days of the war, he was able to discuss factory-floor problems with workers on an easy, man-to-man basis. From personal experience he was often able to recognize when complaints were justified. Quite minor matters were sometimes righted by the adept way in which he cut through red tape.

Because of his royal background and experience of public engagements, George displayed a well-bred, unaffected, easy manner in the factories he inspected. For the workforce and owners alike this was often in marked contrast to the sometimes dour or truculent inspectors they were accustomed to meeting.

Those who met George during 1932 and 1933, when he openly discussed problems about conditions with the workers themselves, are now mostly long since dead. It is only in fading Home Office documents of the time that it is possible to piece together this most important part of his life. Dressed as inconspicuously as possible, George gained an extraordinary insight into working conditions, many of them leaving much to be desired in the way of safety measures. Men who had no idea of his true identity poured out their troubles and grievances and found a sympathetic and eager listener. George wanted to see everything for himself. He clambered over ladders and scaffolding, came to understand the monotony of assembly lines, made his way up and down dimly lit staircases and tramped across concrete floors until his feet ached. He seized every opportunity to study the way in which some factories had changed their products in order to combat shortage of orders. A Home Office report dated 11 November 1932 reads,

Although not strictly within the provisions of the Factory Act, the Prince wanted to visit the extensive Gift Department of the cigarette factory of J. Wix & Sons Ltd, 210 Old Street, EC1, where a large variety of attractive gifts are exchanged for coupons enclosed in the cigarette packets. Since some £40,000 – £50,000 is spent annually amongst British manufacturers on these gifts, it was felt that the time was not wasted.

Many of the buildings he inspected were in poor shape, as he discovered when he went to Henry Howell and Co., a walking stick and umbrella factory in London. The Home Office report states:

This is a very old firm and the premises are rambling and in some cases, not well lit. It was explained to His Royal Highness how essential adequate lighting is, but at the same time how difficult it is for the Inspector, in the absence of legislation, to secure good lighting in some cases. In consequence of the decrease in sales of walking sticks, the firm have sought out new lines, and the manufacture of enamelled bedroom furniture for nursery use, and of ashtrays, gong stands out of briar, provides means of keeping a number of staff employed.

Throughout the summer months George spent long days going to firms making lift equipment, paint, fine chemicals, photographic materials, wirelesses and clothing. He was learning all the time, and when he got back to York House at night prepared long reports ready to present to his superior the next morning. At the fine chemical works of Burroughs, Wellcome and Co., in Dartford and Temple Hill, George watched the manufacture of drugs throughout different stages, from the raw product down to the finished tablet. A Home Office report for 3 June 1932 ends, 'The preparation of Insulin, in particular, was explained, and the extreme care taken in the maintenance of aseptic conditions was noted. Few irregularities were observed. In the afternoon he visited the United Dairies in Streatham.' On 4 June he went to the brewery of Watney, Combe, Reid and Co. at Mortlake, where he discovered 'certain irregularities in the cooperate'. Home Office records show that 'these were indicated on the spot, and the correct form of guarding indicated'. As often as possible he worked on Saturdays, and early in his career ardently supported the call for a five-day week.

George had one or two grim experiences. When he was inspecting a large flour mill at Charles Brown and Co. there was an accident. A temporary stoppage had occurred in the feed of flour, so one of the workers opened a cleaning slide in the casing of a new type of conveyor and inserted his hand to investigate. The machine was running and the man was badly cut. George went quickly to the spot, only to be told that the man would probably lose his finger. He inspected conditions in bottle factories, and watched waste materials like paper, rags and scrap iron being collected, sorted and baled. For a man used to the formal manners of court circles, life on the factory floor must have seemed very raw. When he turned up at D.G. Somerville's at New Cross to inspect the manufacture of concrete telephone and police boxes, the whistle blew for the lunch hour just as he entered the premises with a senior inspector. The foreman, anxious not to lose any precious minutes of his break, nevertheless briskly provided George with the information he wanted, simply confirming that mealtimes were in accordance with regulations.

The Prince became utterly absorbed in his job but it was inevitable that he would be recognized. The owners of relatively small firms were at first taken aback and then overjoyed to discover that the handsome young man inspecting their premises was none other than the King's youngest son. Immediately he was pounced upon and hustled away into offices marked 'Private'. Managing directors and their colleagues could not believe their luck in being so unexpectedly honoured by a royal visit. George did his best to ease his way out of this unwanted hospitality, but his protests were never of any avail. Brought up to display good manners, he did not possess the knack of escaping from his delighted hosts in order to get back to his job. Such unwanted hospitality began to affect carefully timed schedules for visits to other premises. The senior inspector accompanying George was often left tapping his feet in a cold yard as he waited for the royal trainee to release himself from employers who were bombarding him with questions. The situation became so difficult that on 21 September 1932 one inspector, concerned about the restrictive influence that recognition was having on George's work, reported to his superiors in the Home Office,

The Prince can only get any real benefit from the scheme by sticking with the Inspector during his visits and following the Inspector closely in his work and refusing to be tempted by the well-meaning but tiresome attentions of Managing Directors and the like. Up to now the Prince's attention has been to a very great extent diverted from the inspection work in this way. It rests, of course, with the Prince himself to stop it as he could quite easily by explaining that he has to remain with the Inspector.

This was easier said than done. George did his best to charm his way out of these situations, but found it extremely difficult to do so without giving offence. Sometimes he was able to extricate himself in ten minutes, but there were other times when he was held up for more than an hour.

Other problems faced him, too. His public engagements were increasing in number and, as Baldwin had privately feared, he soon found it increasingly difficult to give the maximum number of hours to the job. George V, while apparently fully agreeing to his son being given all the time he needed for Home Office duties, baulked when it was suggested that some royal engagements would have to be sacrificed. George's colleagues in the factory inspectorate, who not only liked but admired the prince with the common touch, were fully sympathetic about his conflicting pressures. His father, however, was not. George tried to make the best of a bad situation, but in autumn 1932 senior officials at the Home Office felt that the time had come when the King should allow his son to choose his own priorities. They did not know the King!

That September the Home Secretary received this memorandum from a senior inspector:

There has been no regularity about the Prince's visits. Social and other functions have been allowed to take precedence over his inspection work with the result that in some weeks the latter was entirely or almost entirely crowded out. The scheme can only be really useful to the Prince if it is pursued with regularity – certain days in the week should be set aside for inspection (say, Monday, Wednesday, Friday, if *three* days only are to be given) and other engagements which would interfere with those days should be declined on the ground that his work at the Home Office prevents acceptance.

By early 1933 George was in a dilemma. He had every reason to look forward to promotion in the not too distant future, and no man could have been prouder of his work. How could he overcome the problems that his duties as a royal prince presented? They were to be resolved by the hauntingly beautiful Princess Marina of Greece.

4

Marina

From the accession of George V in 1910 until his death in January 1936, Queen Mary developed an image which, in my opinion, was a poor reflection of her real self. Those who are still alive to remember her, and those who see her in photographs and old films, and who read of her behaviour, particularly perhaps after the abdication of her eldest son, Edward VIII, receive the impression of a rigid, stern lady, critical, without compassion and remote. But years dedicated to her own conception of the role of a Queen had put a heavy restraint on her natural warmth, her abundant interests and intelligence. The character of the young wife, mother and mother-in-law was not shown to many people and might well have been forgotten, even by members of her close family. But some remembered.

The most important person in the lives of both Princess Marina of Greece and Georgie, the man she was to marry in November 1934, was the so often misunderstood and misinterpreted Queen Mary. Perhaps in no other aspect of her life was her kindliness and understanding more powerfully expressed than in the great love she felt for these two extroverts. Over many years she was instrumental in bringing them together without ever appearing to have made a move. Georgie was Queen Mary's favourite son and Marina was her favourite godchild. She loved both when they were babies and saw that each was gregarious and profoundly inquisitive. Their individual intellectual potentials were apparent from a very early age.

Queen Mary often appeared stiff and uncommunicative with adults. Even relations criticized her apparent cold and undemonstrative manner, particularly with her own sons, but she seldom failed to establish an immediate rapport with bright children. Queen Mary was at her best with young, inquiring minds like those of Marina and Georgie. When she told them stories, as she often did, they nearly always had historical themes into which were woven the lives of royal personalities. Her faculties of observation, combined with a remarkable memory, led Queen Mary to find one of her great outlets in stimulating and encouraging young royals. She strove to help them to think to some purpose and to be aware of their heritage. Just as she had always been a highly self-disciplined person, she sought to develop this quality in young members of royal families.

Marina, with her puckish sense of humour and intelligence, was not unlike Queen Mary as a child. Both were quick, clever and musical. They each possessed a strong streak of obstinacy. Both women derived their greatest pleasure and fun in the company of their siblings. Marina and her sisters, Olga and Elizabeth, were frequently reproved for giggling by their nanny, Miss Fox, and it was noted by James Pope-Hennessy in *Queen Mary* that on more than one occasion when Queen Mary and her three brothers visited relatives, 'they were noisy and giggly over their tea and did not mind what they were told'. Both were shy outside the family circle, Queen Mary infinitely so. Yet Marina and her future mother-in-law could be high-spirited and mischievous when they got to know other people well. Once, at Henley Regatta, Queen Mary snatched off the new blue silk sash another child was wearing and hurled it into the Thames. Marina, however, was never as bold as Queen Mary, who was quite capable before her marriage of taking part in such fashionable country house romps as sliding down the staircase on a teatray. However, from a relatively youthful age Queen Mary had always shown perfect self-control over important issues. Nothing exemplified her complete dedication to her own birthright more than her unquestioning acceptance of a proposal of marriage from the Duke of York, the future George V, after the death on 14 January 1892 of his elder brother and her fiancé, the Duke of Clarence and Avondale, from influenza complicated by pneumonia. Queen Mary had known the Duke of York since childhood and had always been fond of him, but there were many who doubted that she was in love with him. Yet shortly before her wedding she wrote to her fiancé, 'I am very sorry that I am so shy with you, I tried not to be so the other day, but alas failed, I was angry with myself. It is so stupid to be stiff together and really there is nothing I would not tell you, except that I love you more than anybody in this world, and this I cannot tell you myself so I write it to relieve my feelings.'

From personal experience, therefore, Queen Mary believed that arranged marriages between royal houses not only should, but could, work. It would have been extraordinary and quite out of character if she, with her background and shrewdness, had not recognized, even when they were children, that Marina might one day prove a suitable partner for one of her sons. The favourite son, Georgie, must surely have been in the forefront of her mind.

Many researchers and scholars, perhaps better informed than I, may not share my own conception of the essential character and influence of Queen Mary. However my own studies have aroused in me a wish to present the material I have in such a way that a different aspect of the personality of this remarkable lady may be revealed.

When Princess Marina of Greece was born, on 13 December 1906, her life promised to be both enchanted and happy. Relations who attended her splendid christening in the Old Palace of Athens arrived with great entourages and travelled by private train or yacht. They came from vast royal estates in Russia, Germany, Austria, Spain, Bulgaria, Romania, Hungary and Denmark. Queen Mary, then Princess of Wales, could not make the long journey from London but was only too delighted to accept an invitation to be one of Marina's six royal godparents. She sent her youngest goddaughter a gift of a silver mug, porringer and spoon which were to see daily use in the nursery. Marina's christening brought together kings, emperors, princes, grand dukes and archdukes, all wearing full-dress uniform and accompanied by their bejewelled wives in glorious gowns and tiaras. Though of different nationalities, they were all related, and a christening, like a wedding or funeral, was an important occasion since it provided ample time for everyone not only to catch up on the gossip in the courts of Europe, but also to exchange political views and news. Amid the throng at the celebratory luncheons, receptions and dinners was one special royal godfather, Marina's uncle, Prince Andrew of Greece, a tall man of distinguished military bearing who wore a monocle. His main preoccupation was his beautiful young wife who was already, like her great-aunt Queen Alexandra at the same age, prematurely deaf. Four decades later their fifth and last child, Philip, the only son of the marriage, who was born on the island of Corfu on 10 June 1921, was to marry the future Queen Elizabeth II of Great Britain. Like his four sisters, Margarita, Theodora, Sophie and Cecile, as Philip grew up he was to regard Marina as one of the people closest to him.

At these royal social gatherings, where very few people spoke Greek and the common language was French, there was an air of confidence in the future. Members of the comparatively new House of the Hellenes, established in October 1863 after an eruptive period following four centuries of servitude under the Ottoman Turks, were aware of growing rumours circulating in the Greek capital. Balkan anarchists and nihilists were said to be plotting in back streets against the monarchy. However, neither the Greek Royal Family nor their relatives paid serious heed to these sinister tales that once again raised the spectre of republicanism. Marina's relatives were a privileged group who lived their lives to the full at a time when sovereigns never doubted the security of their thrones, their opulent courts and the continuity of powerful, inter-related family ties. These had been carefully forged and maintained over generations by skilfully arranged marriages which had, except in a few rebellious cases, never been questioned. Possible future partners were often discussed when they were only children. Had smouldering Balkan unrest not erupted in 1912 when she was only seven years old and again in 1917, Marina might also have grown up prepared to accept her parents' choice of a husband. She would have been fortunate indeed if she had been seriously attracted to the man; love would have been an extraordinary bonus.

One woman was relegated to a comparatively minor place at Marina's christening. She had a good view of the Greek Orthodox Church ceremony but as an elderly Greek Mistress of the Robes carried the baby to the font where she was to be named after a Greek saint this Englishwoman waited, anxious to gather Marina into her arms and carry her back to the nursery. She was ready to speak her mind to any royal personage who dared to make an ill-timed remark about her methods of bringing up children. Miss Kate Fox was a Norland Institute-trained nanny who had never liked 'foreign places', and Greece, with its hot climate, poor cuisine and questionable standards of hygiene found no favour with her.

Apart from the doctors and Marina's Russian-born mother, Princess Nicholas of Greece, Miss Fox was one of the few people who knew that, because of a difficult and complicated confinement, the baby had been born with her left foot twisted to one side. Princess Nicholas remained ill for many months after the birth of her baby daughter. Despite a limited knowledge of orthopaedics, Miss Fox recognized that it was up to her to try to temper the deformity which could well leave Marina handicapped for life. The nanny spent long, patient hours massaging the tiny foot, but it was never to be completely right and as an adult Marina always had to wear different-sized shoes. However, by the time the child began to walk Miss Fox discovered that her efforts had not been in vain. She no longer needed to warn Marina's two sisters, Olga, three, and Elizabeth, two, to be careful with 'the little one'.

It was Kate Fox, more than anyone else, who moulded Marina's early life. The baby travelled all over Europe in her care, sometimes but not always accompanied by Olga and Elizabeth. Miss Fox remained cool and unperturbed no matter where she found herself, in the Tsar's Winter Palace overlooking the River Neva in St Petersburg or at Buckingham Palace. Nearly forty years later, as a bent old lady, she was still at Marina's side at a moment of terrible tragedy.

Foxy, as the children called her, was to become Marina's friend for life. With her dark brown hair swept back over the right temple of her heart-shaped face, immaculate in her high-necked blouses edged with crisp white lace and moving gracefully in long, sweeping linen skirts, she possessed all the qualities that the Norland Institute wanted in a children's nurse. She was adaptable, efficient, and above all never overawed in the presence of her royal employers or their even more august royal relations. Just as Miss Fox was competent and firm with the three little princesses, she would brook no interference in her nursery domain. Marina's paternal grandfather, King George I of Greece, was convinced that the complexions of his granddaughters were being ruined for ever because Foxy allowed them to spend so much time in the sun. The nanny put the King firmly in his place by quietly informing him that sun bonnets provided more than adequate protection. The King was even more horrified when he discovered that Miss Fox allowed them to play almost naked on the beach when they spent holidays on the Greek islands. Foxy sweetly assured the King that no harm would result, stressing that she regularly sponged the three children with cold seawater and dosed them with camomile tea. The King was calmed.

Prince and Princess Nicholas were a singularly enlightened couple, well ahead of their time in their attitude towards the upbringing of children. They merely exchanged wry smiles when the nanny insisted that Monkey brand soap was brought over from England because she was not satisfied with the way the Greek servants cleaned the nursery bathtub; she did the job herself. The couple accepted Foxy's dictum that only English should be spoken in the nursery, and Marina was four before she began to use Greek words with any fluency, although by then she had a good smattering of Russian and German too. With her sisters, Marina always said her prayers in English despite the fact that she belonged to the Greek Orthodox Church, and the only nursery rhymes she ever learned were English. They ate plain, simple, English nursery food prepared by Foxy, who dismissed the help of the royal kitchen staff by complaining, according to Stella King's *Princess Marina, Her Life and Times*, 'It is impossible to get just what I want for the babies when there are so many cooks about. . . .'

Foxy was fortunate in her employers, who disliked formality and unnecessary pomp. Both were fine conversationalists and gifted linguists who surrounded themselves at evening salons with the most stimulating company they could find in Athens. They had time for their children and it was Prince Nicholas, whose exceptional artistic talent was later to solve some of his pressing financial problems, who first kindled Marina's interest in painting. As a child he had studied drawing under Monsieur Gillieron, a Swiss artist whose greatest claim to fame was his series of watercolours of the Byzantine frescoes of the churches of Mistra near Sparta, commissioned by the Marquess of Bute. Because of his other passionate interest, archaeology, Prince Nicholas was well placed to judge Marina's childish drawings with a more than usual degree of parental detachment. He appreciated her potential at the age of six when his youngest daughter presented him with a well constructed and easily recognizable drawing of the Acropolis. He decided to teach Marina himself. Soon the little girl began to use paints. When Prince Nicholas was working before his easel his daughter was either sitting beside him and watching his strokes or attempting to copy him. Prince Nicholas was an indulgent father and there were few nights when he did not join in the fun at bathtime. When his daughters became over-boisterous, as they often did, the only reproof they ever received from him was a mild spank from a rolled-up copy of the *Times*. Princess Nicholas, a niece of Tsar Alexander III, who bore the title Grand Duchess Helen before she married, fully accepted that Foxy's basic discipline, with its emphasis on good manners and regular hours, was right for daughters who could easily have been spoiled.

Marina's early years were almost totally free from any form of protocol and, like her sisters, she was never addressed as 'Your Royal Highness'. Every morning Foxy pushed the trio in a large black pram out of the palace gates and into a nearby park. Each time the little group made their exit Greek guards in their traditional skirted dress presented arms and blew a bugle. For Marina and her sisters this was always a source of great hilarity. Foxy admonished them, but failed to stop their shrieks and giggles.

Marina grew up in a relatively informal home that was more a very large house than a palace, although it was always known as Le Petit Palais. The new house was Tsar Alexander III's wedding present to her parents, and with Prince Nicholas's keen architectural eye, combined with his insistence on perfection, it took nearly three years to complete. The house became one of the showpieces of Athens and in 1905, when the family moved in, hot and cold running water, several bathrooms and full central heating had been installed. No member of the British Royal Family was to enjoy such luxury until after World War II.

As a little girl Marina, daughter of a royal prince, granddaughter of a king and a kaiser, and great-niece of a tsar, belonged to the last generation to witness and participate in the climactic years of European royalty. Later she was to watch as one by one, over the years, great royal houses were banished or destroyed, her relatives often revealing a tenacious will to survive even when stripped of their possessions. Although Marina was to know the bitterness of exile, she had one advantage from birth – the close relationship established before she was born between her own family and the British Royal Family. In earlier years, when both were bachelors, few relatives from the Continent were more welcome at Buckingham Palace, Sandringham and Windsor Castle than her father, Prince Nicholas, and his brother, Prince Andrew.

On his first visit to London, in 1895, Nicholas stayed at Marlborough House with his uncle by marriage, Edward VII, then Prince of Wales. The worldly future King found Nicholas amusing and entertaining and adopted an almost fatherly attitude towards the twenty-three-year-old. Unimpressed by Nicholas's suits, which had been made in Athens, the Prince of Wales packed him off to his own Savile Row tailor. He also took him on shooting parties at Sandringham and urged him to extend his stay in London when it was time for his return to Greece. It was at Sandringham that Nicholas first met and made an extremely favourable impression upon the future Queen Mary, then Duchess of York. At a time when her first son was less than a year old, and five further pregnancies were still ahead of her, Mary established a close rapport with Nicholas who would gaily recount his adventures . . . seeing

London from the top of buses, and going to museums, art galleries and exhibitions. He would describe how, in his newly acquired expensive suits (paid for out of his own pocket), his bowler and cane, he listened, fascinated, to orators at Speakers' Corner in Hyde Park. The artist in Nicholas, who often went around with a small sketchbook in his coat pocket, intrigued Queen Mary. She continued to take a special interest in the young man who, encouraged by Edward VII, made regular visits to London. It is, therefore, not surprising that Queen Mary later showed unusual enthusiasm about becoming Marina's godmother. Prince Andrew became equally close to his British relatives, and when he married Princess Alice of Battenburg his wife was always proud to point out that she had been born in Windsor Castle.

In order to escape the vagaries of the Greek climate, cold in winter and uncomfortably hot in summer, Prince and Princess Nicholas and their three daughters always spent much of the year away from Greece. Like members of other European royal families, when they were away from home they always stayed with relatives who, for the most part, had far grander lifestyles than that of the House of the Hellenes. When Edward VII died on 6 May 1910 Prince Nicholas and his wife were both griefstricken. The following August they went to see their bereaved relatives in England, where they were warmly welcomed by George V and Queen Mary at Buckingham Palace, their new official residence. Accompanying them were Foxy and her three young charges, Olga, Elizabeth and Marina, who were given splendid suites overlooking the Mall where the children played, tumbled, jumped and enjoyed themselves in the vast palace grounds with its lake, great lawns and honeycomb of winding paths.

It seems unlikely that the three little Greek princesses did not at some time encounter George V's sons, Edward, Bertie, Harry and Georgie, who was then eight years old. Throughout her childhood Marina visited England and this pattern continued into adulthood. Yet what is extraordinary is that when she became engaged to Prince George, in 1934, few people outside immediate royal circles knew anything about her. When the official announcement of the betrothal was issued from Balmoral, newspaper editors found they had only meagre references about the future bride of the King's youngest son. Baffled, they asked one another, 'But who *is* she?' They had no idea that Marina had met her future mother-in-law, Queen Mary, when she was only three years old.

The British court was still in mourning, but there were grouse shooting parties when Marina's parents accompanied George V and Queen Mary to Balmoral. Instead of joining them in Scotland, Marina and her sisters were sent to Kent in the care of Foxy. The quartet stayed in a small hotel in Margate enjoying the simple but well-regulated holiday life followed by so many middle-class English children. They paddled in the sea, built sandcastles and rode on donkeys. They made day trips to London to lunch at Buckingham Palace with George V's favourite sister, Princess Victoria, who became as deeply attached to Marina as she was to Georgie. Miss Fox wrote to her father in a letter quoted in *Princess Marina, Her Life and Times*, 'Last Friday we motored with my princesses to Buckingham Palace. We went straight in by the Privy Purse door and went up in the lift. . . .' They were ushered into a dining room where Queen Alexandra, her son George V, and Queen Mary were all at lunch. For Miss Fox this was an ordeal, as she had to 'dress my babies with all the royalties looking on'. It was not long, however, before the nanny became utterly at ease at Buckingham Palace. Over the years, coming to England often with Prince and Princess Nicholas, she was enchanted by the fun and warmth extended to the children, especially Marina, by Queen Alexandra and her unmarried daughter, Princess Victoria. Queen Mary paid regular visits to their nursery and read stories to the sisters. Marina came to be almost as familiar with Buckingham Palace as she was with Vladimir Palace, the magnificent home in St Petersburg of her maternal grandfather, the Grand Duke Vladimir.

Once a clash of temperaments occurred. Foxy was challenged on her own nursery ground by two formidable matriarchs, Queen Alexandra in England and the Grand Duchess Vladimir in Russia. Queen Alexandra totally disapproved of the way in which Marina was allowed to sleep alone in her bedroom without a nursemaid present. 'Your Majesty, the baby is used to it. She sleeps better by herself,' said Miss Fox. Queen Alexandra retreated, unable to achieve any sort of victory. In the Grand Duchess Vladimir, however, Foxy made a lasting enemy. At Vladimir Palace Marina and her sisters were given a nursery suite of eight exquisitely furnished rooms, ante-rooms, and even their own dining room. It was freezing cold outside but the entire palace had special glazed windows and was beautifully heated. When it was time for the children to go to bed, Miss Fox opened the carefully sealed windows to let in fresh air. This incensed the Grand Duchess, who stormed into the nursery and closed the windows herself. Miss Fox again stood her ground and reopened the windows, proving herself to be more than a match for the Grand Duchess. A true Norland nanny.

Her years in exile made Marina a cosmopolitan person who was, ultimately, to intrigue and captivate Prince George. By the time she was seventeen, in 1923, she and her family had already experienced three banishments from their homeland. The first was in 1912, on the outbreak of the first Balkan War, when Marina was six. That lasted a year. Marina's first experience of some degree of deprivation began on 4 July 1917, when she was eleven. With her parents and sisters she then had four years of unsettled life in Switzerland, where they stayed in apartments in St Moritz, Zurich, Lucerne and Lausanne. Prince and Princess Nicholas, bereft of their private fortune, had to manage for the most part on borrowed money. Marina's education, however, continued uninterrupted, with emphasis on languages under the guidance of experienced tutors.

But it was Prince Nicholas's determination to earn extra money by his own efforts that was to prove an important turning point in the development of his youngest daughter. Her father decided to paint seriously and, signing himself with the pseudonym of Nicholas le Prince, did well enough to hold several modest exhibitions. The sales of his watercolours were sufficiently successful to provide a considerable boost to his income. Encouraged, Nicholas often worked at his easel for six hours at day with Marina frequently at his side. Her father took Marina with him on sketching expeditions and, impressed by her enthusiasm, bought her an easel and paints. Marina was to become a talented artist and, later in life, dependent very much upon her own resources, painted some very fine portraits. She became a skilled draughtswoman in oils and pastels.

After a plebiscite in Athens on 5 December 1920, which overwhelmingly supported the restoration of the monarchy, Marina's family once again returned to Athens. The pro-royal mood was short-lived, however, and in the spring of 1922, when Marina was in England with Foxy, her family went into permanent exile in France. Marina was at an impressionable age. She was sixteen and the atmosphere of a small, nondescript hotel not far from the Bois de Boulogne in Paris was an unhappy contrast to Le Petit Palais in Athens.

Marina's father longed to take his family to live in England where his family had their closest links, to a country they all regarded as their second home. For political reasons, however, the exiled Greeks were not wanted on the other side of the English Channel: the British Foreign Office were not anxious to open doors to a flood of royal refugees from Greece, who could have proved a political embarrassment. Prince Nicholas was made aware that he and his family must manage as best they could in Paris.

This presented George V and Queen Mary with a difficult situation, one which could have proved to be highly charged had it not been dissipated by plain commonsense. They were in very much the same position as their granddaughter, Queen Elizabeth II, after World War II.

Anti-German feeling ran high in Britain for many years after the war. Even in the 1950s the Queen was advised that it was desirable for Prince Philip's close links with his German relatives to be played down. As a result his sisters and their families used the greatest discretion, almost furtiveness, whenever they came to London. At first they stayed in hotels, sometimes Claridges. When it was finally decided that it was safe enough for them to stay at Buckingham Palace, they kept discreetly in the background and their names were never mentioned in any court circular. It is worth recalling that the legacy of World War II was so bitter that it was not deemed wise for the Queen to pay a state visit to Germany until 1965, twenty years after the end of the war, and it was not considered opportune for her to make a private visit to Germany to see Philip's relatives in their German homes until as late as 1967.

What Queen Elizabeth did under the circumstances was to follow the line taken by George V and Queen Mary in the case of Marina's Greek family after their exile in 1923. Prince Nicholas and his family, especially Marina, paid regular visits to England, visiting and staying with royal relatives without the British press or the general public being any the wiser. George V and Queen Mary followed the only sensible course open to them.

In October 1923, the year that saw the end of the Greek monarchy, Marina's sister Olga married the twenty-nine-year-old former Oxford undergraduate, Prince Paul of Yugoslavia, in Belgrade. They had met and fallen in love at the races during Ascot Week. For Bertie, who had married Lady Elizabeth Bowes-Lyon the previous April, the wedding in Belgrade, where he represented his father, was a happy reunion with Marina. When Marina 'came out' in London in the summer of 1924, Lady Cynthia Colville, Queen Mary's lady in waiting, writing about her at that time and quoted by Stella King in *Princess Marina, Her Life and Times*, said she was 'struck by her charm and good looks'. She added that she could 'see her now in the King's box at the Royal Tournament in a most becoming blue chiffon dress'. Lady Cynthia added, 'Many people thought what a happy opportunity this might be for the Prince of Wales . . . though this did not materialise.' David and Marina displayed no interest in one another.

After a series of parties and balls, Marina stayed on at White Lodge in Richmond Park, loaned by George V and Queen Mary to Olga and her husband, who were expecting their first child. Queen Mary was always a welcome visitor. This quiet, secluded house with its pillared portico was, as she would explain to Marina, so full of memories. Here Mary had spent her formative childhood years, and left it to marry George V when he was Duke of York.

On her return to Paris Marina observed great poverty, which would probably otherwise have escaped her if she had not been exiled. While her family were more than comfortably off, able to afford four servants and a part-time chauffeur, thousands of refugee Russian aristocrats and their families settled in Paris in a state of penury. Because her grandmother, the Grand Duchess Vladimir, had managed to smuggle securities and jewels out of Russia, Marina's family had a private income and were able to support others less well off than themselves. In May 1924 Princess Nicholas, appalled by the plight of the Russian émigrés, opened a home for Russian children which was run by an émigré Russian couple. Marina worked with a will at the side of her mother, helping to teach, feed and clothe fifty children between the ages of two and ten. Later she organized social functions – fêtes, bazaars and balls – to raise money to keep the home going.

Great thought was given by both parents to Marina's education. She went to a top finishing school run by Princess Metchersky, an old friend of the family, where she specialized in French history and literature; she always spent Sundays at home. At no point were her art studies neglected. She attended classes and continued to receive expert tuition and guidance from her father. Since there was no financial necessity for Marina to take a job, her life unfolded in a leisurely manner. She broadened her knowledge of painting in museums and art galleries, travelling widely in Europe.

When George and Marina were in their twenties they were both highly cultured, and different in outlook and temperament from their royal siblings. They had much in common. Both had presence combined with striking good looks. They were equally stimulated by the companionship of men and women of distinction in the world of the arts and the theatre. Where they differed fundamentally was in their individual lifestyles. Marina, apart from supporting her mother's social work, led a more or less indulgent life. Painting was for her own pleasure – for Marina the pursuit of culture was an end in itself. George, however, while he was still at sea, was earnestly intent upon establishing himself as a person in his own right and not only as a royal prince.

Their choice of friends reflected quite different attitudes and approaches. Marina's closest ties were with her family – she was always very close to her sisters – and other near relations of her own age. The home which she shared with her parents, Prince and Princess Nicholas, meant so much to her that the prospect of living in an apartment of her own would have been anathema. People who joined the intimate circle of Prince George, however, never entered the orbit of the Royal Family, and even when he lived at York House with his brother David he preferred to meet his friends and acquaintances on their home ground. Some of his highly charged, short-lived and somewhat dubious friendships were established with people he had met abroad either in the Royal Navy or on official tours.

George never had what might be termed a best friend. That role from childhood until marriage was filled by David, at once his alter ego and his mentor. It was, perhaps, because of his inability to enter into deep relationships that, after he left the Royal Navy, George was prone to moods of depression. He could be mercurial and notoriously impatient. One man who knew him well was the diarist, Sir Henry (Chips) Channon, who said that George 'had drunk deeply from life'. According to J. Bryan and Charles J.V. Murphy in *The Windsor Story* a royal equerry said,

'Self-esteem was a strong trait in the whole royal family, especially in Kent. He had more brains than any of the other brothers and more taste, and was more interested in intellectual affairs, but he was a scamp. He was always in trouble with girls. . . . Whenever I heard about a new caper of his, I was reminded of Jingle's remark in *Pickwick Papers*: "Kent, sir – everybody knows Kent – apples, cherries, hops and women." '

Referring in *The Heart Has Its Reasons* to her visits to Fort Belvedere with her then husband, Ernest Simpson, in January, February and March 1933, the Duchess of Windsor recalled,

. . . Prince George . . . I found on closer acquaintance to be altogether as attractive as his brother. He played the piano very well, knew all the latest jazz and loved to bang away at the keys while the rest of us danced after dinner in the Octagonal hall. Saturday evenings at the Fort were usually a little livelier when Prince George was on the scene; he was a natural mimic and loved to do caricatures of people he knew well, and often the Prince of Wales joined in. I had the distinct feeling, as I watched them together, that the older brother was at times a little worried, even anxious, about the younger, perhaps because he was too lighthearted.

Before they became engaged the names of neither George nor Marina had ever been seriously linked with anyone else. Had either of them so wished, they could have taken their pick in the marriage stakes since each was a superb catch. All the evidence available indicates that at some level Marina and George were aware that the great hope of both their families was that one day they would marry. Her sisters, Olga and Elizabeth, believed that Marina was in love with George years before he proposed: she had the wisdom to bide her time. As a regular visitor to England where she occasionally stayed in royal residences and was received almost like a daughter by Queen Mary, Marina was privy to royal gossip. She knew one of the great preoccupations shared by George V and Queen Mary was the urgent need for David to marry. It was also important in their eyes that Georgie should find a 'suitable' bride too.

There is good reason to suppose that Queen Mary advised Marina to be patient. In some ways the situation in which George and Marina found themselves can be likened to that of the modern-day Prince Charles and Princess Diana. Lady Diana Spencer had been a familiar figure to Prince Charles since her childhood days when she had lived with her parents at Park House on the Sandringham Estate: she, too, seemed to engage the attentions of a royal prince with extraordinary suddenness. Like Marina's, Diana's parents had always been extremely close to the Royal Family, and she had also grown up to be accepted by the royal children as part of a closely knit circle of intimate friends.

George and Marina had known one another since they were children. When they grew up and George was on leave in England from the Royal Navy, it was no surprise for him to find Marina at Buckingham Palace or one of the other royal houses. Yet it was not until September 1933, when George was thirty and Marina twenty-six, that there was any sign of real interest one for the other. They grew closer when Marina stayed with her sister and brother-in-law, Princess Olga and Prince Paul, at Claridges. For the best part of two weeks George sought out Marina's company, taking her to theatres and cinemas: several times they went dancing with friends at the fashionable Embassy Club. But when Marina returned to Paris there was no indication of a deepening relationship, and in January 1934 George left for South Africa, the first official tour he had carried out alone. A tall figure in the white uniform of a lieutenant-commander, with the brilliant blue Garter ribbon across his chest, he left Southampton on the *Caernarvon Castle* with David to see him off.

Unlike other members of the family who were content to leave tour arrangements in the hands of their personal staff, George master-minded his own itinerary and set himself a punishing schedule. As a result, when he returned home after covering 10,000 miles in two months he was exhausted.

From the start, however, he revealed a new and independent style. Away from formal receptions held in big cities, he spent most of his time in short-sleeved shirts and shorts, avoiding red tape and protocol whenever possible. Travelling on the famous South African 'White Train', he had a grand piano and a 'gram radio' installed in one of the coaches. At numerous official halts on the long journey he would ride hatless on horseback in pouring rain to talk to poor tenant farmers and visit natives in their kraals. He picked up enough Afrikaans to make himself understood, and always parted with the words *Alles sal reg kom* – all will come right. George had always been a physical fitness addict. Accustomed to light meals, he was appalled when he studied the rich, heavy meals planned for himself and his entourage on the long train journey. The changes he made were dramatic. He insisted that only sandwiches should be provided at lunch, and evening meals were to be limited to three courses – fish, poultry and soufflé. It was in South Africa that a physical culture expert in the naval dockyard in Simons-town noticed that George had developed his own special technique of hand-shaking. He held his wrist loosely and not taut so that, unlike other members of his family, he never experienced painful hand strain.

When the matter of overseas royal tours arose, it was not the habit of George V's sons to question paternal decisions. Before George left for South Africa it was put to him by his father that he should sail for Australia at the end of August 1934 to attend the centenary celebrations of the first settlements in Victoria, and then tour other Australian states and New Zealand. In the very positive manner he always adopted with the King, in contrast to that of his three brothers, George refused to commit himself to the tour. He insisted that no final arrangements were made until he gave his personal approval after his return from South Africa. In the event, it was Harry who went to Australia. George V stated that, after George's exhausting trip to South Africa, 'it might be', as quoted in Noble Frankland's *Prince Henry, Duke of Gloucester*, 'rather a strain to undertake in the same year another probably strenuous tour in Australia and New Zealand'.

In January 1934, when George left for South Africa, Marina's sister Elizabeth married Count Karl Theodor (Toto) zu Toerring-Jettenbach, an English-educated Bavarian with a vast fortune derived mostly from German brewery interests, and who owned a castle in Winhorring. Marina, however, at twenty-seven the only unmarried sister, seemed very much a dreamer, and it was not until the summer after he had refused to tour Australia that George saw her with new eyes. Marina was again staying at Claridges with Prince Paul and Princess Olga when George began to devote more and more of his time to her, again taking her out to lunch and dinner, and driving her to spend days with David at Fort Belvedere.

Queen Mary's hopes of a happy ending to the increasingly close relationship developing between her youngest son and her Greek goddaughter were dashed when she heard that Marina had left London with Princess Nicholas, with no immediate plans to return to England. Mother and daughter were to spend a few weeks at a spa in the Savoie department of France before going on to join Prince Paul for three months at a shooting lodge on the shores of a lake in the Julian Alps in Yugoslavia.

In July George spent Cowes Week sailing with his parents and other members of the Royal Family, but instead of following them to Balmoral for the traditional summer holiday he asked David for the loan of his private plane. Only Queen Mary knew George's secret destination. Accompanying him on the flight, with George at the controls, was his friend and equerry, Major Humphrey Butler. After one stop for refuelling at Le Bourget in France they landed at Ljubljana aerodrome, some 50 miles from Bohinj where Marina and her family were staying.

According to Marina's uncle, Prince Christopher of Greece, and quoted in *Princess Marina, Duchess of Kent* by James Wentworth Day, on the third night, after an evening playing backgammon,

. . . everyone retired tactfully to bed until George and Marina were left sitting alone at opposite ends of the sofa. I had been in my bedroom for about half an hour when I discovered I had left my cigarette case on the backgammon table. Putting on my dressing-gown I went in search of it. The door of the drawing-room was open; George and Marina were still seated on the sofa, though no longer, I observed with satisfaction, at the opposite ends of it. I stole back to bed without my case. . . .

George proposed on 23 August 1934, five days after his arrival at Prince Paul's log cabin at Bohinj, and was accepted. The engagement was kept secret until the official announcement was made on 29 August from Balmoral where George V and Queen Mary were still on holiday. That evening the villagers, dressed in Yugoslav national costume, headed by the mayor and accompanied by men playing violins and concertinas, climbed the hill to the chalet. After showering the couple with rose petals, small children presented them each with a bouquet, red roses for George and blue cornflowers mixed with white edelweiss for Marina.

By royal standards neither George at thirty-one nor Marina at twenty-seven was old for marriage, but they had nevertheless both reached an age when their parents felt it was time for them to find partners. George was well aware that Queen Mary was most anxious for David and himself to find a 'suitable' bride. Marina was in every way 'suitable'. Discussing Marina with a friend, as quoted in *HRH Princess Marina, Duchess of Kent*, he said, 'She is the one woman with whom I could be happy to spend the rest of my life. We laugh at the same sort of thing. She beats me at most games and doesn't give a damn how fast I drive her when I take her out in the car.' The words do not have the ring of a man who was madly in love, but he was clearly very fond of the Greek princess. Marina, who had experienced all the trials of an exiled royal, could not have been oblivious to the obvious advantages of marrying a son of the King of England. Theirs was not a case of love at first sight. Perhaps Prince Nicholas, Marina's father, summed up the engagement most succinctly when he said, 'My wife and I are delighted. We are both very much attached to England and so is Marina who is delighted at the prospect of going to live there. There is nothing political in the marriage. It is one of affection.' In a letter to her husband, quoted in James Pope-Hennessy's biography of her, Queen

Mary wrote that George's engagement to a member of 'the Greek family' seemed 'highly suitable'. She said, 'I am sure we shall like Marina and that she will be a charming addition to the family.' After Marina's first visit to Balmoral with George before their marriage George V wrote, 'Marina is looking very pretty and charming and will be a great addition to the family.' In the months which followed the King often spoke of his pride in her beauty, and from the first he was a tower of strength and comfort to her.

Only one man felt lost when he received news of the engagement. That was David. The departure of George from his everyday life was the most severe blow he had yet experienced. The marriage of his youngest brother to a Greek princess only served to deepen his personal sense of loneliness and isolation. He was left vulnerable at the most critical time of his life.

5

A Wedding and a Crisis

In the weeks leading up to their wedding in Westminster Abbey on 29 November 1934, when Marina was in Paris selecting her trousseau, George spent his weekends with David in the country at Fort Belvedere. George was excited and ebullient. To other guests, who at that time always included Mr and Mrs Ernest Simpson, he talked of the hours he was spending meticulously checking the deluge of wedding presents pouring in from all parts of the world and of arrangements for the celebrations that were to last for the best part of a week before the great day. George, whose father had created him on 9 October Baron Downpatrick, Earl of St Andrews and Duke of Kent, had no reason to express surprise when David told him that he had invited Mr and Mrs Simpson to the state banquet to be held at Buckingham Palace two days before the wedding. Nor, after she crossed the Channel by special ship to Dover and arrived to cheering crowds in London, was this information of significance to Marina. She knew the Simpsons, just as she had known David's other close friends, including the discreet and charming Mrs Freda Dudley Ward, for fifteen years David's closest woman friend. Some years earlier Marina had done two fine sketches, one of Mrs Dudley Ward and the other of her daughter, Angela. Yet one glittering reception which preceded the great banquet in the white and gold State Room, at which the splendour of the Edwardian era seemed to be recreated, marked a moment in history in which neither George nor Marina played any part. It was the first and last time that Mrs Simpson, later to become Duchess of Windsor, met George V and Queen Mary. Much later she was to recall in *The Heart Has Its Reasons*, 'It was the briefest of encounters – a few words of perfunctory greeting, an exchange of meaningless pleasantries, and we moved away.'

In that splendid week George was so immersed in his wedding plans and the new life ahead of him with Marina that his eyes were, for once, not on his eldest brother. It is doubtful whether he spared a thought for the vacuum that would be left in David's life after his marriage. George had shared David's home at York House in St James's Palace for more than four years and there was little, if anything, that either brother did not know about the other. In their private lives George had pursued his own affairs while David remained faithful, for the most part, to Mrs Dudley Ward before she was replaced by Thelma, Lady Furness; otherwise their friends were mutual. It was at Fort Belvedere, an eighteenth-century castellated house that had been neglected for years when he first saw it in 1930, that David gave his weekend parties for the tightly knit circle of men and women who amused and entertained him. George was always a tremendous support. Sometimes Marina had been there too on one of her visits from Paris, accepted as always as a friend of all the Royal Family, especially of Queen Mary.

Few people seemed to observe the traumatic effect that the news of George's engagement had upon David: it was to mark the beginning of the end of the only powerful male relationship he had ever had in his life. For David there was a strange irony about the timing of George and Marina's wedding: it came when his friendship with Lady Furness had come to an abrupt end and no one had yet replaced her. The one person to observe clearly and understand David's deep unhappiness was Mrs Simpson, who, with her husband, was so often in his company either dancing at the Embassy, entertaining him in their London apartment at Bryanston Court, or relaxing at the Fort. With her shrewdness, and perhaps compassion, she alone sensed that after George's departure from York House a void would be created in David's life that would have to be filled by someone. Without George, who was always able to lift him out of moods or depression, David's loneliness could only become more acute. Looking back on November 1934 many years later, the Duchess of Windsor wrote in *The Heart Has Its Reasons*,

Because it was the first Royal marriage since that of the Duke of York eleven years before, all England was excited. But as I watched the Prince [David] during the weeks preceding it, it seemed to me that a sadness began to envelop him. He and his younger brother were very close, and the bonds of blood were strengthened by an unusual kinship of spirit. . . .

Mrs Simpson knew that David was fond of her. By falling in love with Marina, however, George had unwittingly and unknowingly presented

Mrs Simpson with the perfect opportunity to become David's closest confidante. The road that was to lead to the abdication two years later, in December 1936, began during the weeks when George and Marina, the Royal Family and the entire nation were building up to a state of fever-pitch excitement over the forthcoming wedding, the timing of which could not have been better. It had been a grim decade, and the public was in a mood for a celebration to take people's minds off the economic depression. The political climate abroad was slowly beginning to move towards its fateful conclusion in September 1939. The Austrian Socialist Party had been suppressed in February, followed by the Austrian putsch and the murder of Chancellor Dollfuss by the Nazis in July. With the death of Field Marshal Hindenburg in August Hitler, already Chancellor, became Führer of a totalitarian Third Reich in Germany. At home, although unemployment was down for the first time in ten years, there was no indication that this was a permanent trend. The only cheerful news of the year had been the launching and christening by Queen Mary of a great new liner from John Brown's yard on Clydebank. On a pouring wet day in September a quarter of a million people watched her slip into the basin that had been prepared for her. She was named the *Queen Mary*. In a bleak, grey era, the Kents captured the public imagination. The last royal wedding had been that of the Duke of York and Lady Elizabeth Bowes-Lyon on 26 April 1923. Charming though the couple were, they lacked the charisma of the handsome Duke of Kent and his beautiful Greek bride, who had the additional intriguing quality of being a foreign princess. Tension built up to almost hysterical adulation, quite different from the sheer joy that marked the wedding of Prince Charles and Lady Diana Spencer in St Paul's Cathedral forty-seven years later.

Mrs Simpson was quick to respond to David's emotional needs after the loss of George. As a sympathetic and understanding listener, she had no rival. In a revealing passage in *The Heart Has Its Reasons* she wrote,

The gap in the Prince's life caused by his brother's marriage was not easily filled. Nor did the usual round of visits that the Royal Family were accustomed to make, stays at the various country seats of the great families, do little more than politely amuse him. . . . It was curious to see a man of such dynamic qualities, a man so active and so often filled with the true joy of life, suddenly disappear before my very eyes into uncertainty. He was reaching out for something that was as yet unknown to him, something to which he could anchor his personal life. It was easy for the rest of us to change or rearrange our lives, but for him it was not only difficult, it was also well-nigh impossible.

David, George's natural choice of best man, appeared nervous at the wedding and forgot the precise moment in the service when he should have handed Marina's wedding ring, made from Welsh gold, to the bridegroom. Queen Mary saved the situation. She quickly nudged George V, who signalled an usher to draw David's attention to the lapse. It was a small incident but perhaps extremely telling. The wedding of his younger brother, whom he had loved and needed since he was sixteen, was a cataclysmic experience for him. And Mrs Simpson, sitting alongside her husband somewhere amid the vast congregation, alone knew it.

'Dull, mild and misty' had been the weather forecast for the great day, and it was fulfilled to the letter. Because of the damp atmosphere in London the bride had to wear a white ermine wrap as she drove in the glass coach to the Abbey, the bells ringing a full peal of no fewer than 5,040 changes. But nothing could dim the brilliance of this first royal wedding to be broadcast on the wireless. It was described by the Archbishop of Canterbury, Dr Cosmo Lang, who officiated at the ceremony, as 'a new and marvellous invention of science'. The service was broadcast not only at home and overseas but also by loudspeaker to the crowds outside the Abbey, so that the Archbishop was able to add, 'The whole nation, nay, the whole Empire, are the wedding guests.'

Shortly before ten o'clock, when Marina was at Buckingham Palace, George was about to put on his full-dress uniform of a commander in the Royal Navy when he discovered that he only had a few pounds in his pocket. Unlike David, he always carried money on his person. Unperturbed, he put on an ordinary suit and made his way through the dense crowds from St James's Palace to cash a cheque at his bank in Pall Mall.

When he returned to the Palace his astonished brothers, David and Bertie, are quoted by Jennifer Ellis in *The Duchess of Kent* as saying, 'But surely you could have sent someone to the bank?'

George replied blithely, 'It gave me something to do.'

Her old nanny, Kate Fox, was at Marina's side to help her as she stepped into her wedding dress of silver French brocade, woven with English roses and based on a medieval design, that was to stun the public and designers alike. Designed by Edward Molyneux, it provided the first indication that Britain might at last have a royal leader of fashion. Marina brought no dowry with her from Paris. As recorded by Kenneth Rose in *King George V*, the King cheerfully told his Prime Minister, Ramsay Macdonald, 'She has not got a cent.' Nevertheless Marina had the priceless qualities of grace, beauty and a dramatic sense of style and colour. These were to inspire a generation of couturiers, who had long since stoically resigned themselves to the tastes of Queen Mary with her inevitable toque, ankle-length coats and dresses, and parasol. The Duchess of York, today the Queen Mother, who had married Bertie in 1923, did not appear to have any special interest in fashion as such, either; clearly, however, her popularity was not affected by this.

As Marina walked slowly up the aisle of the Abbey on the arm of her father towards George in his splendid naval dress uniform, two young girls in knee-length dresses of white tulle over silver lamé were solemnly holding her long white and silver train. One of them was Bertie's eight-year-old daughter, Princess Elizabeth, who, until such time as her Uncle David married and had children of his own, was third in line of succession to the throne. That she would one day be crowned Queen of England in the same great Abbey surely crossed no one's mind. Even if David did not marry, there was still time for her parents to produce a son who, if that happened – as Elizabeth hoped – would automatically precede her in the order of succession. Bobbing up and down on a footstool near her mother was Elizabeth's four-year-old sister, Princess Margaret Rose, too young and too fidgety to be one of the six young bridesmaids, three of whom were exiled princesses from Greece and one an exiled grand duchess from Russia. A second wedding service, according to the rites of the Greek Orthodox Church, was held in the chapel of Buckingham Palace when the Greek Archbishop, Dr Strinopoulos Germanos, took the Welsh gold ring from Marina's left hand and put it on the third finger of her right hand. He also transferred the ring which Marina had given her husband during the Anglican service. As was the custom in Greece, Marina wore her wedding ring on her right hand for the rest of her life and her husband always wore his. The fog which had threatened to descend over London lifted towards the end of the wedding breakfast. As George and Marina left the Palace amidst a shower of rose petals and tiny silver horseshoes on the first stage of their honeymoon, to be spent at Himley Hall near Dudley, a solitary figure lingered until the two figures were finally enveloped by the gloom of the November afternoon. It was David.

George V, however, was far more cheerful than he had been for a long time. After the wedding and before he left London for a week's shooting at Sandringham, he wrote this letter, quoted by John Gore in *King George V*, to thank the Primate for his share in the success of the wedding ceremonies:

Buckingham Palace
1st Dec 1934

I shall never forget the beautiful service in the Abbey, so simple and yet so dignified, which greatly impressed the Foreigners and indeed all that were present. Then the enormous crowds in the streets and especially the one outside the Palace, who showed their love and affection for us and our family, by their enthusiasm, impressed us more than I can say and we deeply appreciated it. I must thank you for all that you did in arranging and carrying out the two services. The Prime Minister and Jim Thomas* both came up to me after the breakfast and said, this is a great day for England! You are one of my oldest friends and I always appreciate your kind words. Believe me, always your sincere old friend, George RI.

George and Marina received so many wedding presents that it was decided to publish an official booklet listing 1,048 names of people who had vied with one another to give the perfect present. By royal standards the couple were by no means rich, and with the prospect of finding and furnishing a home of their own when they returned from honeymoon every item was important. They received a great many more cigarette cases and cigarette boxes than they needed. On the occasions when George had been consulted in advance about wedding presents he had been practical. When he was at the Fort he asked Mrs Simpson, and she tells the story in *The Heart Has Its Reasons*, 'Wallis, what is the most expensive kind of fur?'

David said, 'What an odd question.'

George replied, 'Not at all. I'm trying to solve a problem for a very rich friend who wants to give Marina a fur coat for a wedding present. Now, Wallis, what is the most expensive fur?'

'Chinchilla,' she answered.

'Fine,' said Prince George, 'I wouldn't want my friend to make a mistake.'

'Damn it, George,' said David. 'You're beginning to sound like an auctioneer.'

---

* J M Thomas (1874–1949). British politician and labour leader. Was appointed Secretary for the Colonies in 1924, and Lord Privy Seal in 1929.

Mrs Simpson interposed, 'Prince George will suffer no such anxiety from the Simpson offering. I have already chosen two lamps at ten guineas apiece from Fortnum's. They were reduced in a sale and are not exchangeable.' Mrs Simpson was clearly not joking, since in the official list of wedding presents number 755 reads: 'Mr and Mrs Ernest Simpson: Pair of globe-shaped crackle vases on carved wood stands, fitted as electric lamps, with panelled octagonal shades painted with Chinese scenes.'

Marina was overwhelmed by the jewellery she received from the Royal Family. George V gave her a rivière of thirty-six large diamonds and Queen Mary a tiara of sapphires and diamonds; a long cluster necklace; two bracelets; a pair of drop earrings; three brooches; a rectangular diamond brooch with a diagonal ruby and diamond bow ornament; and an all-diamond oblong brooch with a square cluster centre and link ends. In addition, George V and Queen Mary joined in giving their new daughter-in-law a long diamond link sautoir forming four bracelets with a pearl and diamond regular drop pendant.

George gave his bride eight pieces of exquisite jewellery: an all-diamond scroll-pattern tiara with a brilliant cluster centre and an entourage of baguette diamonds; a ruby and diamond trellis-pattern bracelet with six oval ruby and diamond clusters; a ruby and diamond fancy oblong link sautoir with a fringe-pattern ruby and diamond pendant; a pair of diamond and ruby drop earrings; a pearl and diamond sautoir; two rows of pearls at the back and a festoon of three rows at the front joined by two diamond circle and link ornaments; a pearl and diamond bracelet; and, lastly, a pair of diamond drop earrings. Marina gave George two presents, a leather-covered gold cigarette box bearing the monogram 'G' and a crown, and a set of four ruby buttons. They were relatively simple gifts, but all she could afford.

George's old friends in the Home Office sent a pair of eighteenth-century silver sauce boats, while Noël Coward, a source of great support to Marina later in her life, decided upon twenty volumes of his own works with book ends to match. Even though she was never to see David again, Mrs Dudley Ward remained devoted to George and Marina and from her they received two wooden-handled silver milk and coffee pots stamped with the royal crest. Lord and Lady Fermoy, the present Princess of Wales's maternal grandparents, decided upon a brown leather wastepaper basket tooled in gold, while the choice of Dr

Malcolm Sargent – destined to become one of Marina's closest friends – was the works of Chopin in three volumes bound in morocco. Men who had sailed with George during his unhappy years in the Royal Navy remembered him too. From Lieutenant Pugh RN came an aeroplane mascot for his car. And towards the end of the extraordinary list was an 'engine-turned silver cigarette box with a "ribbon" edge' from the British Union of Fascists.

Of all the magnificent gifts there was one that was to have pride of place in their new home, 3 Belgrave Square: a radio-gramophone, presented by the Gramophone Company. The house, on the south side of the square, was pleasant but small – it only had one guest room – and had once been occupied for a short time by Queen Victoria's mother, the previous Duchess of Kent. It was rented from an old friend of Queen Mary, who agreed that the newly married couple could use their own furniture and change the decorations in any way they wished. Marina had always taken life at a leisurely pace, had a somewhat dependent personality, and knew nothing about cooking or household management. It is doubtful, however, whether she fully realized, on the last stage of her honeymoon in the West Indies, just how much of the domestic side of her new life would be dominated by her husband.

She saw the positive and persuasive side of George's character when they stopped off at Nassau. To their mutual delight and surprise they were invited to lunch with President Roosevelt who was cruising in the area on a friend's yacht. This was the year in which the American President, faced with the grim years of depression following the Wall Street Crash of 1929, had launched his great New Deal programme. He could be testy and at this time his courage and intellectual qualities were being severely taxed. A weakness in his make-up, if it can be described as such, was a notorious tendency to judge by first impressions. He had had no encounters with members of the Royal Family and had never expressed any particular interest in them: the invitation he extended to George and Marina was probably no more than a courteous diplomatic gesture. Roosevelt was in for a happy surprise. From the moment he shook hands with the striking couple, happy, bronzed and exuding tremendous self-confidence, he saw they were not as he had expected. George, with his habit of reading the major international newspapers from cover to cover every day, his knowledge of economics, his first-hand experience of living conditions among the unemployed at home and his fear of the growth of fascism in Europe, was able to focus

Roosevelt's attention on Britain in the manner of an experienced British diplomat. Intrigued and impressed by George and Marina's wide-ranging interests and their democratic approach to social problems, the President responded warmly. Their friendship was to grow and flourish, and the King was impressed.

George had so much confidence in Queen Mary, and their tastes were so similar, that while he was on honeymoon with Marina his mother supervised the decoration of their new home in Belgravia. On their return it was George, not Marina, who masterminded the arrangement of the furniture, which included some of his magnificent Georgian and Queen Anne pieces from York House. In his four years under David's roof George had acquired a valuable collection of drawings, paintings and lithographs and, like Queen Mary, had quietly amassed old English silver, porcelain and Chinese jade. Marina played a small part in the creation of a home which became noted for its sense of space, soft pastel colours and rejection of the dark, heavy furniture of other royal and aristocratic houses, but it was George who made all the major decisions. He dominated the Kents' domestic life in other ways, too, and soon took over the active day-to-day running of the home. It was George, not Marina, who planned meals and organized the small staff. It was George who consulted the chef and carried out all the arrangements for dinner parties, even to the point of supervising floral arrangements and deciding who would sit next to whom. Not only that, George always advised his wife on the clothes and jewels to wear for both private and public occasions. Yet Marina, far from protesting, was more than willing to accept her husband in the role of 'mistress' of 3 Belgrave Square. She confessed to Queen Mary's lady in waiting, the Dowager Countess of Airlie, who recounts in her memoirs, *Thatched with Gold*,

I am really a very bad hostess. I must confess that I didn't know what we were going to eat tonight until the food appeared. George chose the dinner and the wine – and the flowers and everything else. He enjoys doing it, and so I always leave the household affairs to him. I let him make all the decisions over furniture and decorations. He has a wonderful sense of colour and design.

Marina's submissive attitude can be better understood if one looks back on their individual lifestyles before marriage. Both of them had longed for a home of their own but their approach to fending for themselves had been utterly different. Marina had never shown any disposition for domesticity. In the Paris apartment she shared with her parents there were three full-time servants. In the affluent circles of exiled Greeks and Russians in which she moved in Europe and, above all, in the splendid homes of the royal relatives whom she visited for weeks at a time, she was accustomed to a level of personal service enjoyed only by the very rich. Her sister Olga, married to Prince Paul of Yugoslavia, who became one of three Regents when his cousin, King Alexander, was assassinated in Marseilles on 9 October 1934 during a state visit to France, offered near-regal hospitality, while her other sister, Elizabeth, married to Count Karl Theodor zu Toerring-Jettenbach, owned a large house in Munich as well as a castle, and her guests wanted for nothing. Marina had thus acquired no domestic expertise of any kind. Members of the British Royal Family had always regarded the exiled royal Greeks as the 'poor dears', a favourite phrase of Queen Mary; however, by ordinary standards Marina, like other girls in the European aristocracy, lived very well indeed. Unless they had the inclination there was no need for them to be involved in domestic matters of any kind, and Marina never had.

George, by contrast, like all naval cadets, had grown up in the tradition of the Royal Navy, so that from an early age he acquired many practical skills. He could sew on buttons and as a midshipman had mastered the basic culinary arts. Despite his overt masculinity, there was a streak of femininity in George's make-up which probably stemmed from his close relationship with his mother. He was fastidious, meticulous and passionately interested in furniture and interior decoration; he was also a born organizer and accustomed to getting his own way. Having travelled widely, he had acquired cosmopolitan gastronomic tastes, so that when it came to planning Belgrave Square menus and deciding the wines to be served he considered it only right and proper that he alone should make all the decisions. Marina not only tolerated George taking on the role of managing their home but was more than content to let him do so. It was but a continuation of the indulgent lifestyle she had enjoyed in the cocoon of her family in Paris, when she had unprotestingly allowed other people to make decisions for her. The couple were deeply in love with each other when they married. The Duchess of Windsor recalled in *The Heart Has Its Reasons* the days leading up to the wedding in Westminster Abbey, 'Prince George was genuinely in love with Princess Marina, a most beautiful woman whom I had met earlier at the Fort [Belvedere]; and he was also delighted at the prospect of at last having his own home.'

In 1935, while George was completely immersed in his new life,
David was ever more frequently with the Simpsons. He went on
holiday to Kitzbühl in February for the winter sports with Mrs
Simpson and a small coterie of intimate friends. This time Ernest
Simpson stayed behind in London. Loath to return to London, where
public duties would mean separation from Wallis, David extended the
holiday, going on to Vienna and Budapest. From time to time, when
David's holiday was over, George and Marina went to Fort Belvedere
and occasionally they entertained David and Mrs Simpson, though
always with other guests. Absorbed in married life, George regarded
David's relationship with the American woman merely as another of his
passing affairs. George had other matters on his mind. In March 1935
he was thrilled to learn that Marina was expecting their first child in the
following October. In a state of near euphoria, George, the one person
who could have influenced David, missed the early signals that his
brother was becoming more deeply involved with Mrs Simpson.
George V and Queen Mary, who for many years had dined alone
together in the majestic solitude of Buckingham Palace, were happy to
find themselves often at the dinner table of their youngest son and
daughter-in-law. Although they too were aware of David's 'latest love',
it was never a matter for family discussion. There were many other
distractions that year. On 6 May George V celebrated his Silver Jubilee
which culminated, amid great national rejoicing, with a thanksgiving
service in St Paul's Cathedral. Standing behind the King and Queen
were their four sons and daughter, and their two daughters-in-law,
Elizabeth (the present Queen Mother) and Marina. On 14 May guests
at the great Jubilee State Ball at Buckingham Palace included Mr and
Mrs Simpson, but George's attention was concentrated upon his wife,
not upon David and Wallis who danced a number of quicksteps and
foxtrots. Yet another family event served to distract King George's
attention from David that summer. On 11 August Henry proposed to,
and was accepted by, Lady Alice Montagu-Douglas Scott, the small,
shy, thirty-four-year-old daughter of the seventh Duke of Buccleuch.
Because of the death of the bride's father shortly before the wedding,
the couple were married in the chapel of Buckingham Palace instead of
Westminster Abbey. 'Now,' wrote George V in his diary that evening,
'all the children are married but David.' The Princess Royal had
married the Earl of Harewood in 1922.

Early in October David returned to London with Mrs Simpson and a party of friends who had holidayed in Cannes and cruised in the Mediterranean from Corsica to the Iles des Porquerolles. Once again, George was so absorbed in public duties and the excitement of the expected baby that he never noticed the new aura of happiness that surrounded David. Nor, perhaps because Marina's confinement was imminent, did he attach any importance to the fact that Ernest Simpson was spending increasing amounts of time in America. What George could not have known was that Mr and Mrs Simpson had already agreed to go their separate ways.

Shortly before nine o'clock on the evening of 9 October 1935 it is reported that a sleek black cat walked slowly up the steps of Belgrave Square and stayed outside the door. Some five hours later, in a second-floor bedroom, Edward George Nicholas Paul Patrick was born. He was seventh in line of succession to the throne. Apart from Prince Albert, who was with Queen Victoria at the birth of each of their nine children, George was the first royal father to be at his wife's side for the birth. When Victoria's first child, Princess Victoria, the Princess Royal, was born on 21 November 1840 Albert was present throughout the twelve-hour labour. Later the Queen wrote in her journal that it was 'a great comfort' to have Albert there to hold her hand.

One of the first people to see the baby was George V's favourite sister, the unmarried Princess Victoria, who had known Georgie from birth and Marina from the first time she visited England. Less than two months later, on 3 December, the old Princess died, leaving George V so distressed that for once he could not face up to his official duties and cancelled the State Opening of Parliament. In his grief he wrote in his diary, 'How I shall miss her, and our daily talks on the telephone. No one ever had a sister like her.' For George and Marina, however, their own sadness was partially eased when they learned that in her will Princess Victoria had left them her home, Coppins, a large, rambling Victorian house in the sprawling village of Iver in Buckinghamshire. It had the relaxed air of a holiday villa with its bay windows and stone mullions, and had no claim to architectural distinction. Yet it could not have come at a better time in the lives of the young Kents. Neither of them was dismayed by its rather ordinary exterior or dark rooms filled with heavy old furniture and crowded with unimaginative pictures. That the grounds were stifled by too many huge trees and shrubs did not perturb them.

That Christmas, spent as it always was at Sandringham in Norfolk,

George and Marina enthusiastically described their plans to transform Coppins. Now frail and stooping, George V delivered his Christmas broadcast, and one of the last pleasures in his life was provided by the Kents' baby son, Edward. On Christmas night the King noted with satisfaction in his diary, which Kenneth Rose quotes in *King George V*, 'Saw my Kent grandson in his bath.' George only had eyes for his wife and son but was able to share in the happiness of Bertie and his wife and their two children, Elizabeth, nine, and Margaret Rose, five, who romped around a twenty-foot Christmas tree. Also present were Harry and his wife Alice, who waited six more years before they had a child. One person felt detached and lonely in the presence of his happily married brothers – David. George, who under other circumstances would have detected the slightest note of melancholy in his brother and tried to dispel it, remained oblivious. David later described in *A King's Story* his feelings that Christmas, 'I was caught up in an inner conflict and would have no peace of mind until I had resolved it.' He was waiting for the New Year when he could escape to join a house party at Burrough Court, Melton Mowbray, in Leicestershire, the country home of Mr Benjamin Thaw, First Secretary of the US Embassy in London, and his wife. Here he could be once more in the company of Mrs Simpson.

During that Christmas at Sandringham George might have changed the course of history. David both admired and respected him and would certainly have listened to his brother's advice, although he would not necessarily have heeded it. In the entire Royal Family there was no one else who could have broached the affair with Mrs Simpson without facing abrupt dismissal in a bitter confrontation. George V, even though he had raised the matter and discussed his anxiety with Baldwin, Lord Hardinge of Penshurst, the Archbishop of Canterbury and his own brother-in-law, the Duke of Connaught, avoided discussion with David, as did Queen Mary. Although they got on well with him, both Bertie and Harry would have regarded the matter as too personal. Despite growing unease, yet never fearing the worst, the men in the Royal Family all kept their silence. Had it not been for his total preoccupation with his own family, which gave him complete satisfaction and happiness for the first time in his life, George would definitely have sensed David's troubled state. He would have offered some sort of counsel. One can only reach the conclusion that David would have been relieved to reveal to George the true depths of his feeling for Mrs

Simpson. One thing is quite certain: if there had been any sort of intervention on George's part, David would have given it his consideration. Over the years George had always been a sympathetic listener, acting as a sounding board for his elder brother. Given a free exchange between the brothers, during the family Christmas at Sandringham when they had every opportunity to be alone together, George would have tried to show the way for David to find a compromise in his relationship with Mrs Simpson well before he embarked upon the road that was to lead to the abdication the following December.

Throughout the holiday George V was failing and sick, and no one was under any illusion that he had long to live. Early in January, as is recounted in *Prince Henry, Duke of Gloucester* by Noble Frankland, he wrote to the Duchess of Gloucester from Sandringham saying that he regretted the departure of 'George and Marina and their sweet baby. . . .' A few minutes before midnight on 20 January 1936 the King died peacefully in his sleep and, with David the new monarch, George became fourth in line of succession. His royal duties increased and Marina, though nervous in the early days of her marriage, soon revealed a natural ease in public life; after decades of royalty wearing fussy, frilly or dowdy clothes, she became the first royal fashion trend setter of the century. She had flawless taste and whatever she wore was copied by women all over the country. She introduced simple, classical lines and appeared in so many shades of blue, George's favourite colour, that a subtle light turquoise became known everywhere as Marina blue. So great was public interest in her day and evening dresses, suits and hats that London couturiers and milliners vied with one another to secure her patronage. Brought up in exile to be relatively careful with money, she did not hesitate to become the first royal duchess to accept a special price from haute couture houses. During the depression she popularized cotton dresses in order to boost ailing Lancashire mills, and bought clothes off-the-peg to boost the flagging retail industry.

It was as a team, in both their social and working life, that George and Marina became famous and were always described as 'that dazzling pair'. They were the first to tour unemployment areas in the North and the Midlands, where they avoided the traditional formal approach and instead talked to whoever happened to be nearest to them. George fought hard for the establishment of occupational clubs in good premises and well equipped for both men and women. In the meantime

Coppins was being transformed into one of the most elegant royal homes, with George once again masterminding the alterations. All that remained inside the house, as a reminder of old Princess Victoria, was a marble bust in the entrance hall of her father, Edward VII. Among the guests who came to Coppins to enjoy witty, stimulating conversation in the light, spacious rooms with their gay chintzes and pastel walls lined with fine pictures were Noël Coward, Malcolm Sargent, Somerset Maugham and, from time to time, either for tea or dinner, David and Mrs Simpson. Both George and Marina still saw Mrs Simpson as no more than a passing fancy of David's, and quite liked her. In May 1936, the beginning of a splendid summer, Marina told George that she was expecting their second child. Because of the pregnancy they did not join the family at Balmoral in August and September and had no opportunity to resent, as Bertie and his wife did, the almost abrasive manner in which Mrs Simpson was acting as David's hostess at the castle.

The Kents' baby was to be a robust and healthy girl, Alexandra Helen Elizabeth Olga, but her birth on 25 December 1936 was to prove to be, in the words of Queen Mary, 'the only nice thing to have happened this year'.

Wallis was granted a decree nisi at Ipswich, on the grounds of her husband's adultery, on 27 October 1936. 'To ensure that the press continued to behave with discretion', wrote Frances Donaldson in *Edward VIII*, 'the King had come to an arrangement with Lord Beaverbrook [*Daily Express*], Esmond Harmsworth [*Daily Mail*] and several other newspaper proprietors, whereby they all agreed to play down the Simpson divorce as well as "limiting publicity after the event".' The result was that an unsuspecting British public knew nothing whatsoever about David's love affair with Wallis – although the American press suffered no such constraints.

On the morning of 1 December a relatively obscure cleric, the Bishop of Bradford, Dr A.W.F. Blunt, forced the hand of the British press when he delivered an address before a diocesan conference in which he discussed the religious meaning of the approaching coronation service, which had been set for 12 May 1937. If Dr Blunt had kept to generalities his words would have had no impact. Instead, wrote Frances Donaldson in her biography, he asked the conference to commend the King (David) 'to God's grace which he will so abundantly need . . . if he is to do his duty faithfully. We hope that he is aware of his need. Some of us wish that he gave more positive signs of his awareness.' On 2 December these remarks passed unnoticed in the London papers but the *Yorkshire Post* and several other provincial papers commented on it. On 3 December the long silence was broken to the public in sensational Fleet Street newspaper headlines. Press and people were divided. The *Daily Express* and the *Daily Mail* spoke up in favour of the King but *The Times*, the *Morning Post* and the *Daily Telegraph* were for abdication. Late that evening Wallis Simpson fled to the South of France, convinced, wrote Frances Donaldson, 'that the solution to the problem was for her to remove herself from the King's life. She did not, of course, intend to be believed.'

George immediately cancelled all engagements in order to be with his brother. But David shunned every member of his family. Twenty-four hours of torture for George were finally broken by a telephone call from David inviting him to dinner with his brothers and saying that he was going to marry Wallis Simpson.

On 13 November the King told Baldwin that he hoped to marry Mrs Simpson and that, if he could not do so and remain king, he was prepared to abdicate. When the news of his relationship with Mrs Simpson was revealed in the British press and Parliament on 3 December, David had to make a decision rapidly. The possibility of a morganatic marriage had been raised and rejected. There was talk of the formation of a 'King's Party'. Aware that the public, Parliament and the Dominions were split in their support for him, and unwilling to divide the nation, David told Baldwin on 5 December that he could see no future for himself as King. In a matter of days the crisis was over. On 10 December David signed the Instrument of Abdication witnessed by his three brothers, Bertie, Harry and George. The next day, introduced as His Royal Highness Prince Edward, he made his famous farewell broadcast from Windsor Castle in which he said, ' . . . you must believe me when I tell you that I have found it impossible to carry the heavy burden of responsibility and to discharge my duties as King as I would wish to do without the help and support of the woman I love. . . .' At Portsmouth that night, 11 December 1936, David boarded the destroyer *Fury* which carried him across the Channel into exile. At his accession council on 12 December, Bertie, the new King, George VI, created his elder brother Duke of Windsor.

'He is besotted by the woman,' George exclaimed angrily to Stanley Baldwin, the Prime Minister. 'One cannot get a word out of him.' Baldwin had admired and respected George ever since he had first met him on the tour of Canada with David in 1928. In this national crisis and the uncertainty about the effect David's abdication would have on the monarchy, Baldwin could only compare the vigorous, intellectual George with his shy, introverted elder brother Bertie, beset with a terrible stammer and supported by a wife whose distress had kept her confined to her room with what was publicly described as flu. The comparison between the two brothers was striking – and a throne was at stake. What might have crossed Baldwin's mind as he listened to an angry but lucid George who felt so bitterly let down by the brother he loved?

Sources close to the Prime Minister felt at the time that Baldwin considered George for kingship. Not only was George the father of a male heir – his son Edward was a year old – but he was in every way more impressive, gifted and accomplished than Bertie. Moreover, Marina was of royal birth and a princess in her own right, elegant and sophisticated in comparison with Bertie's wife. There were grave doubts about Bertie's health and there were equal anxieties about his wife, Elizabeth. She lacked a commanding presence and with her retiring manner and almost total dedication to a quiet domestic life she gave little indication of being suitable to become a queen. According to the historian Theo Arenson, though, Baldwin's idea that George could have succeeded Edward, instead of Bertie, 'is an unlikely story'. Arenson goes on,

Neither the British constitution nor royal tradition allowed for any such cavalier treatment of the order of succession. The Abdication had been traumatic enough; this was not the time for tampering with dynastic rights, not only of the Duke of York [Bertie] and his two daughters [Elizabeth and Margaret Rose] but of the Duke of Gloucester. In any case, for all his apparent shortcomings, the Duke of York was a far worthier man than the lightweight Duke of Kent.

Some senior statesmen who were alive at the time, and contemporary constitutional experts, did not share Arenson's views. Had Baldwin acted at the right psychological moment, they believed that both Bertie and Harry might well have relinquished their own rights of succession in favour of their younger brother, a far from lightweight man. On 9 December, the day before the Instrument of Abdication was signed, Bertie was terrified at the prospect of becoming King and Harry was in despair. Bertie, without the support of his wife who was ill at their own home, 145 Piccadilly, saw Queen Mary and 'broke down and sobbed like a child', wrote James Pope-Hennessy in *Queen Mary*.

Only George, hurt and angry, kept calm until David returned after the abdication broadcast to Royal Lodge, Windsor, to say goodbye to his family. Frances Donaldson wrote,

It was late and his mother and sister Mary left quite soon, but the four brothers and Walter Monckton [adviser to the King] sat on until midnight when the Duke of Windsor and Monckton left to drive to Portsmouth. As he took leave of his brothers he bowed to the new King, a gesture which led the Duke of Kent to cry out: 'It isn't possible. It isn't happening.'

George had good reason to be hurt since David had kept his decision to give up the throne secret from him for as long as possible. It may be that David *and* Baldwin were playing for time, in the hope that a way could be found to ensure that the succession went to George. The historian Dermot Morrah wrote in 1950 in his book *Princess Elizabeth, Duchess of Edinburgh*, 'It was certainly seriously considered at this time, whether by agreement among the Royal Family, the Crown might not be settled on the Duke of Kent, the only one of the abdicating King's brothers who at that time had a son to become Prince of Wales, and so avoid laying so heavy a future burden upon the shoulders of any woman.'

Morrah went further eight years later. In *The Work of the Queen*, published in 1958, he revealed that the idea *had* been seriously considered inside the Royal Family, without making it clear when and how.

Morrah wrote,

Since Parliament must be asked to alter the laws of succession so as to transfer the Crown from the heir designated by the Act of Settlement to some other person, it was not a legal necessity that the person selected should be the next in hereditary order; and there are veteran officers of the Household who remember how much persuasion had to be brought to bear upon the Duke of York [Bertie] in order to persuade him that he was the man that the nation and Empire overwhelmingly desired to see at their head. Excessively modest though he was, he would never on his own account have repudiated the new load of responsibility; but he shrank from imposing the burden eventually on his daughter [Elizabeth]. At that time the only prince near to the line of succession who had a son was the Duke of Kent, and the draftsmen preparing the Abdication Bill at least tentatively considered what to do if his two elder brothers asked to stand aside in his favour.

On 20 December George was thirty-four. At 11.30 a.m. on Christmas Day 1936, after an easy confinement, Marina gave birth to Alexandra Helen Elizabeth Olga. Upstairs in the second-floor nursery of 3 Belgrave Square, her fifteen-month-old brother Edward was playing with his presents. He did not learn until many years later that the moment had passed when his father might have become King and he Prince of Wales.

6

Togetherness

Unsuspected qualities nearly always emerge in men and women after they have married into the Royal Family. Marina was no exception. Unassuming and essentially reserved, she came not only to accept but actually to enjoy public adulation. She discovered that she possessed a charisma hitherto unsuspected by her. The pleasure and pride that George derived from her success were what mattered most to Marina. However, at the coronation of Bertie and Elizabeth in Westminster Abbey on 12 May 1937, Marina concealed the fact that she had firm principles when moral issues were at stake. Sitting opposite her husband in an open carriage, waving and smiling to cheering crowds as the procession made its way from the Abbey to Buckingham Palace, she appeared relaxed. Nothing indicated that she was about to take a much tougher line in her private life. Religion had always been important to her, and at thirty-one she was deeply moved by the ancient service in the Abbey.

On that chilly, showery May day, Marina was one of three sisters-in-law who, until then, had had little in common except that they had all married one of George V's sons. Each of them had experienced great stress since David's abdication the previous December, which allowed only five months to prepare for his brother's coronation instead of the usual year. Since Queen Mary had decided to break the unwritten but old tradition that a dowager queen never attended the coronation of her successor, a new crown had had to be hastily made for Elizabeth. The sisters-in-law had all carried heavy emotional burdens throughout the winter and spring of 1936–7. Elizabeth, former Duchess of York, for whom a closely knit family life with Bertie and their two daughters, Elizabeth and Margaret Rose, had always been of paramount importance, was now Queen. Alice, married to the conscientious but unambitious Harry, Duke of Gloucester, whose natural inclinations would have been to enjoy the life of a gentleman farmer, worried about the extra responsibilities that would fall on him. Should anything happen to George VI, Harry would have been appointed Regent until the eleven-year-old Elizabeth reached her royal majority at the age of eighteen. In her turn, Marina had had to cope with George's deep distress over the virtual loss of David and his anxiety about the whole family. Her husband's unhappiness forged in her an iron will.

It was not manifested until later that summer when she went with George on a short holiday to Austria. She anticipated relaxing; as it happened, she could do nothing of the sort. The Windsors, who had married at the Château de Candé in Touraine, France, on 3 June 1937 without any member of the Royal Family present, went on to Austria to stay at Schloss Wasserleonburg near the Wörther See in Carinthia, loaned to them by Count Paul Munster. With enthusiasm George told Marina that, since the Windsors were not far away, they must visit David and his wife. This was the third year of George's marriage to Marina and he was accustomed to a devoted and acquiescent wife, always willing to follow his lead. He was in for a shock: Marina adamantly refused to meet David and his wife. There were two reasons why her husband wanted to see David: he wanted to re-establish contact with the brother who meant so much to him and, secondly, he wanted to be in a position to brief Bertie about David's future plans. But despite all George's pleas Marina flatly refused to make the journey to Schloss Wasserleonburg. In desperation, her husband telephoned George VI at Balmoral for advice. The message he received was that Marina must go with him, and it was stressed that she should be told this was a personal directive from the new King. Marina still would not change her mind. George then telephoned David with a suggested date and said that he would visit his brother alone, offering the excuse that Marina would be visiting members of her own family. To this David replied, 'Well, put off your visit for a day or two and bring her with you. . . .' In the end neither George nor Marina went to Wasserleonburg. Not until after the death of her husband, on 25 August 1942, was this inflexible side of her nature to re-emerge.

The following year, in October 1938, Marina again failed to share completely in her husband's enthusiasm when George VI revealed that he was going to appoint George Governor General of Australia. The plan was that the couple would go there in November 1939 and make Government House in Canberra their official residence. The prospect of spending at least three years in a job where he felt sure he would make his mark as an individual appealed to George. Not only would he be the personal representative of the new King, but he would have an opportunity to introduce a new and perhaps far more relaxed style into what had always been a very formal office. The announcement caused tremendous excitement in Australia and it was hailed at home by Winston Churchill as 'a master stroke in Imperial policy.' What troubled Marina was separation from her mother and two sisters. There was hardly a month in the year when one of more of her relatives from the continent was not staying at Coppins, or when Marina and George did not cross the Channel to see them. Family and childhood ties were of vital importance to Marina and even Foxy, her old nanny, spent a great deal of time at Coppins. Foxy was still often inclined to exercise the same forthright nursery manner that she had adopted with Queen Alexandra and the Grand Duchess Vladimir of Russia, and this did not always please George. Marina had always been particularly fond of her youngest cousin, Philip, a dynamic, handsome boy for whom she had great hopes. She and her family had watched him grow up under the scrutiny of his parents, Prince and Princess Andrew – Marina's uncle and aunt – in a large, rambling Parisian house not far from the St Cloud racecourse. Philip came to live in England in 1929, and after the Kents' wedding in 1934 he was a frequent visitor to Belgrave Square and Coppins. In July 1939, with his sights set on a career in the Royal Navy, Philip told Marina that he had met the future Queen Elizabeth for the first time when she visited the Royal Naval College at Dartmouth with her parents and sister: Elizabeth was then thirteen and Philip eighteen. The importance of that first encounter was not lost upon Marina, who was later to play an important role in convincing an uncertain and possessive George VI that Philip was the right suitor for his elder daughter.

In August 1939, however, when Elizabeth was being educated by a governess in Buckingham Palace, George, full of ideas which he hoped would have great impact on the Australians, accompanied Marina on a short holiday to Yugoslavia so that she could bid farewell to her relatives, most of whom had long since married and, like herself, acquired new nationalities. The Kents, with Marina gradually coming to terms with a new way of life, had already made moves to sell Coppins. Many of their finest pieces of furniture were in crates and on the high seas, bound for Australia. Their Buckinghamshire home, however, was not sold and the couple were destined never to reach their new home waiting for them in Canberra.

Britain declared war on Germany on the mild Sunday morning of 3 September 1939, and much to his sadness George's appointment as Governor General of Australia was postponed. Marina wanted to play her part in the war effort and, after initial training at the cottage hospital at Iver, she became a voluntary auxiliary nurse at University College Hospital in London. As Nurse Kay she worked there for weeks, with only a few members of the senior medical staff knowing her real identity.

Miss J.M. Bond, a former sister at the hospital, talked about this period to J. Wentworth Day, who quoted her in *HRH Princess Marina, Duchess of Kent*:

She did all the ordinary jobs. Mrs Jackson, who was then Matron, sent for me one day and told me that the Duchess of Kent was to work on my ward (No.16) as an auxiliary. She was to be known as Nurse Kay and her identity was to be a close secret. The Registrar and Senior Surgeon obviously knew what was afoot but the news didn't leak out for the first few weeks.

The Duchess was escorted up to the ward on the first day by the Matron. She was neat and smart in a plain, well-cut white coat. Not the ordinary uniform – blue coats, as worn by the auxiliaries, nor the striped dress and white apron worn by student nurses. The Duchess came and went much as she liked – or as official commitments would permit. She took part in all routine activities on the ward – surgical dressings, bedmaking, washing patients, doing hair, tidying lockers, plumping up pillows, feeding and handing round meals on trays. She assisted in the pre-operative preparations of patients who were due for the theatre but I don't remember her attending an operation. She saw them on to the table and the removal of tubes after the operation was also part of her job.

The Duchess never visited a shelter [air raid] during her spell at UCH. Nobody bothered much about sheltering as we were all too busy! She nursed lots of bomb victims as most of the inmates of the ward were emergency cases. The ward was extremely busy . . . as we were desperately short of staff.

One day a registrar visited a patient on the ward. At luncheon that day he remarked, 'One of the VADs in No. 16 looks the spitten image of the Duchess of Kent.'

'How extraordinary,' remarked our senior registrar, who, of course, knew all about it. 'What a coincidence.' It was two weeks later before the other registrar realised that the VAD was, in fact, the Duchess.

One day Marina went to the Sister in dismay. She had heard that George, as President of the Hospital, was making an official visit. A few seconds later George walked into the ward. Nurse Kay was presented with the rest of the nurses and gave him the most polished curtsey. He acknowledged it without the flicker of an eyelid. Then the Matron and the Sister conducted him round the ward with Marina following well in the rear as an obscure nurse. The secret of Nurse Kay was finally out when she was recognised by a patient who was a dressmaker's assistant and read all the fashion magazines. She announced, 'I've seen her picture dozens of times. Nobody is going to tell me it isn't her.'

Her anxieties about her own family had taken a new and distressing turn. Her brother-in-law Toto, Count Toerring, Elizabeth's husband, was an officer in the German Army, so they were officially enemies. Her three favourite cousins, Philip's surviving sisters, Margarita, Theodora and Sophie, were also married to Germans. Marina's other sister, Olga, was in Belgrade with Prince Paul, later to be taken a political prisoner under British jurisdiction in Kenya for his part in signing a tripartite pact between Yugoslavia, Germany and Italy.

Because of his close friendships with influential people throughout Europe and especially in neutral countries, George was enlisted as a source of valuable information by British intelligence. He had been one of the first to recognize the early menace of the growth of fascism in Germany and Italy, and in July 1939 there was still some hope among British politicians that war might be averted if Hitler could be convinced that Britain would meet force with force. Earlier in the year George had been in Italy where he had held long conversations with his cousin, Prince Philip of Hesse,* who had served as a personal liaison officer between Hitler and Mussolini and was still thought to retain the Führer's confidence. Who better than he to convey such a confidential message to Hitler? Briefed and encouraged by his brother, George VI put the proposal to the Prime Minister, Neville Chamberlain, who then discussed it at length with the Foreign Secretary, Lord Halifax. Though the project was eventually shelved, it is an example of the way in which George was to initiate ideas and play a vital and often secret role in the war.

He carried out the first of a series of delicate and important missions in June 1940, when German troops had overrun France and the Low Countries and Britain was facing a threat of invasion. It was imperative for the British wartime coalition government, led by Winston Churchill, to secure reliable and accurate information about Portuguese intentions, since high-level German secret service agents were attempting to pressurize the neutralist dictator, Dr Salazar, into openly committing

* On his father's side he was a great-great-great-grandson of George II of Engalnd, and also of George III on his mother's side. He was killed during an Allied air raid in 1944.

himself to support Hitler. German propaganda was attempting to convince the Portuguese that England was a lost cause, and Churchill's problem was to find the right envoy to meet Salazar and gain his confidence. The man he picked was George. A perfect cover was found: he was to lead the British delegation attending the seven-day celebrations in Lisbon to commemorate the 800th anniversary of Portuguese independence. Churchill knew that George had many friends in Portugal who would help him, including a powerful and influential international banker, Dr Ricardo de Espiritu Santo e Silva, who lived at Cascais, a fashionable resort a few miles west of Lisbon. It was an operation of the utmost importance and Churchill had great faith in George, who spoke Portuguese and would, as ever, be well served by his charm. Three days before George arrived in Lisbon, on 24 June, Salazar wrote to the Portuguese ambassador in London saying how pleased he was 'that the mission should be headed by His Highness'. The two men established rapport, and when George returned to London he was able to report to the government, only weeks before the Battle of Britain, that Salazar was completely dedicated to the British cause. He flew home from Lisbon on Tuesday 2 July 1940: that same day, after nine days in the Spanish capital, David and the former Wallis Simpson left Madrid and set out by car for Lisbon. The two brothers had not seen each other for three years and were never to meet again.

Opportunities for George and Marina to be at Coppins were rare. Transferred to the RAF as an air vice marshal, George flew thousands of miles inspecting bases in Britain and overseas. On 29 April 1940 he reverted to the rank of Group Captain at his own request so that he would not be superior to officers under whom he had to work. On 29 July 1941 he was promoted Air Commodore. George often drove home across London during air raids and seemed exhilarated by danger. Once a time bomb exploded within yards of his car, and when he stepped out, covered in debris, his only comment to his driver was, 'That was a near thing. . . .' Marina brought so much glamour into her job as Commandant of the Wrens – the Women's Royal Naval Service – that it became the most popular of the three women's services. She was quaintly unorthodox about the matter of uniform, wearing white gloves and carrying a handbag, both strictly against regulations. Sometimes she wore earrings and bracelets and high heels, all of which were forbidden. Her private nightmare, it is said, was learning to give a proper naval salute. Her tendency was to let her right hand droop, a charming habit which persisted despite the efforts made by her husband and teasing children to correct it.

It was a relief for the Kents that in November 1940, when Coppins lay beneath the direct flight path of German bombers heading for London, Edward, six, and Alexandra, nearly five, were able to spend most of the time at Badminton House in Gloucestershire. But neither George nor Marina had ever anticipated the influence that Queen Mary, now seventy-two, would have upon another generation of royal children. On 4 September 1939, the day after war broke out, Queen Mary had left Sandringham followed by a cavalcade of twenty cars piled high with luggage, and a retinue of servants, bound for Badminton where she was to stay with her niece, the Duchess of Beaufort, for the next five years. At first Queen Mary was bored with country life, but the presence of her two young grandchildren soon engaged her. Determined to save petrol, she often rejected her old green Daimler; with Edward and Alexandra in the back, she would travel across the vast estate sitting in a basket chair in a farm cart drawn by two horses. Edward and Alexandra were far more exuberant than either of their parents had been at the same age, and at Badminton, *in loco parentis*, Queen Mary instilled a new sense of decorum into these two grand-children. Alexandra, whose curtsey had sometimes left much to be desired, learned to perform to perfection. Under the old Queen's tuition, both children started to read easily and listened entranced, just as their parents had, to stories about their heritage. The influence that Queen Mary had on Edward and Alexandra was to be lasting. Marina saw her children whenever she could, travelling from London in crowded trains and sometimes in the blackout. Because he was often in the West Country on tours of inspection, George was able to see his children and his mother fairly often.

As Queen Mary's official biographer, James Pope-Hennessy, observed,

Members of Queen Mary's family visited her whenever their war-time duties allowed. The most frequent, and perhaps the most welcome of these family visitors was [her] youngest son, Prince George, Duke of Kent. They had in common a passion for collecting, and they would together make expeditions to the antique shops of Bath. The Duke of Kent was able to go to Badminton more often than other members of his family, for, as Air Commodore in charge of the welfare of Royal Air Force units, he made several tours of inspection in the West Country. To Queen Mary his visits to Badminton were a source of sparkling joy.

No gift, however, was received at Badminton with greater

enthusiasm than a box of oranges and bananas (both unobtainable in Britain throughout the war), given to George as a present for his children by President and Mrs Roosevelt when he stayed with them in the White House. George had left London in July 1941 on a fact-finding mission to Canada and the United States, the first member of the Royal Family to fly the Atlantic. Ostensibly he was first to study the Commonwealth Air Training Plan, a system whereby British pilots trained in the peaceful skies of Canada before returning home for action, and then go on to inspect aircraft factories and assembly lines in the United States.

On 4 July 1942 Marina gave birth to her third child at Coppins. He was Michael George Charles Franklin – Franklin after his godfather, President Roosevelt. One of the first people to visit the new baby was Dr Jacob Snowman, a scholar and physician who was well known to members of the Royal Family but whose connection with them had been a carefully guarded secret. Dr Snowman, who practised in Hampstead as a general practitioner for over fifty years, had a great reputation as a 'surgeon mohel' – and his expertise in circumcision was sought both outside as well as within the Jewish community. All royal sons are circumcised. He had first called on Marina in 1935 after her son Edward was born, at 3 Belgrave Square. On that occasion Dr Snowman wrote in his diary, 'On my attendances on that occasion there appeared to be so much coming and going to visit the patient, I had no opportunity of meeting her.' Dr Snowman found circumstances different after the birth of her second son, Michael. This time he was able to record in his diary,

On this second occasion, she [Marina] explained to me how in her view, a mother should prepare a young child for the advent of an infant brother or sister. It was a really cordial conversation and all the association of that visit remains the more impressed on my memory by the tragedy that occurred a few days afterwards – the death of the Duke in an aeroplane disaster. The genuine welcome I seem to have received appeared to justify a personal letter of condolence. . . .

7

Tragedy

It was a perfect weekend in high summer and as the seventy-three-year-old Foxy fussed over Marina and her seven-week-old baby at Coppins, George, now thirty-nine, spent as much time as possible working in the garden, where his favourite carnations were in glorious full bloom. In the seven years since the house had been left to him by his aunt, Princess Victoria, George had acquired the same passion for gardening as George VI and David had in their thirties. George's task, however, was greater than that of either of his brothers. In August 1942 he had no full-time gardener, as so many men had been called up in Iver, and he personally had to make the upkeep of the small estate as simple as possible. The exercise did him good. Often he returned home exhausted from travelling in difficult wartime conditions and, under stress, though normally a fluent speaker, he stumbled over the name of an RAF base when he gave a talk to airmen at Hawarden. But on 13 August Queen Mary had been driven over to Coppins and found the good-looking couple happy and full of vitality. In her diary that night she wrote these words, quoted in James Pope-Hennessy's book, *Queen Mary*, 'The baby is sweet . . . had luncheon and tea there . . . walked in the garden . . . Georgie looked so happy with his lovely wife and dear baby. . . .'

Queen Mary, George and Marina happily recalled Michael's christening thirteen days earlier at a quiet family ceremony at Windsor Castle, then a wartime fortress, where highly trained commando units guarded Elizabeth, sixteen and recently confirmed, and Margaret Rose, twelve, against attempts to kidnap them. Edward and Alexandra came over from Badminton for the day and Queen Mary had voted the christening 'a successful day' when she had seen 'lots of old friends, servants, etc.'. On the other hand King George of Greece, one of the godfathers, murmured according to Agnes de Stoeckl in *Not All Vanity*,

'I do not seem to know anybody here today. . . .' This was not surprising since many of the guests were servants from Coppins and staff from Buckingham Palace transferred to Windsor Castle, and close friends were away at the war: they had known George since his childhood. George stood proxy for President Roosevelt. The christening service was followed by an austere wartime tea party. The new baby flourished and during the weekend Baroness Agnes de Stoeckl, a close friend of the Kents, who lived in Coppins Cottage in the grounds, commented, again in *Not All Vanity*, 'The ducks quacked, the turkeys laughed, the cocks crowed . . . and the whole of Coppins seems a mass of flowers.' George kissed his wife goodbye on the morning of Monday 23 August and waved to her from the wheel of his car as he set off on another RAF welfare tour, this time to Iceland. The couple were accustomed to partings, and both were fully aware of the element of danger that faced George as much as any serviceman. He spent many hours in the air and was always a target for enemy planes. Only the previous week German planes had bombed and strafed a south coast town when he had been on official duties there. George told Marina that he expected to be back home in about a week or ten days. He never wanted special treatment when he visited RAF stations, and would arrive unannounced and sometimes unrecognized at the wheel of his own car.

On the evening of 24 August George and his party arrived at Invergordon, a flying boat base on the Cromarty Firth which had been chosen because it was easily accessible by rail from London. It had been an operational station early in the war but, when the main U-boat activity switched to the north-west coastal approaches, the base had reverted to being a training school for No. 4 (Coastal) Operational Training Unit. Leading an experienced crew was Flight Lieutenant Frank Goyen, a twenty-five-year-old Australian who had amassed nearly one thousand operational hours on ocean patrols. Late in the evening he and his crew of nine learnt that George was to be among the passengers on the 900-mile flight to Iceland that would take about seven hours. There were to be fifteen people on board the Sunderland flying boat and depth charges were to be carried. This was standard practice on transit flights, in case enemy submarines were spotted.

The following morning, the twenty-fifth, the weather was poor but the Cromarty Firth was fairly clear with a cloud base of about 800 feet, and the forecast was for improvement when the seaplane reached open sea. At 1.10 p.m. the aircraft lifted off. Flight Lieutenant Goyen had been briefed to follow the coastline in a north-easterly direction for 85 miles, keeping out to sea, and turning through the Pentland Firth with John O'Groats on the port beam. The more obvious direct route across Sutherland was out of the question because of the poor rate of climb of the heavily loaded aircraft and the high ground, which rose up to 3,000 feet in places. Just past the Dornoch Firth the cloud base began to lower, and some height was lost so that Goyen could maintain visual contact with the coastline. Now things began to go very wrong.

On a hillside, just inland from the village of Berriedale, a farmer, David Morrison, and his son Hugh were rounding up their sheep. They heard the sound of an aircraft overhead but could not see it because of the mist. Then came the sound of two explosions. The flying boat had just cleared the summit of a 900-foot hill known locally as Eagle's Rock, but the Sunderland did not clear the deep, narrow valley which separated it from the next rise and crashed into the heather on the Duke of Portland's Langwell Estate. Young Hugh Morrison ran as fast as he could downhill to the stony track where he had left his motorcycle. He raced to Berriedale and alerted the police, the local physician, Dr Kennedy, estate workers and crofters. This was in the days when volunteer searchers, when necessary, had to scour the high ground. Eventually thick mist and approaching darkness forced them to give up. The next morning they discovered the wreckage and Dr Kennedy recognized one of the victims: George. The watch that Marina had given him as a birthday present had stopped thirty-two minutes after take-off. It was not until the evening that telephones began to ring in royal homes.

George VI had spent the day on the moors at Balmoral and was having dinner with Elizabeth, Harry and Alice and other members of the household. Halfway through the meal a servant entered the room and whispered something to the King, who rose immediately and went to the telephone. At the other end of the line was the Secretary of State for Air, Sir Archibald Sinclair, who broke the news. George VI returned to the dining room, looking grave, and for some moments said nothing. Alice, who had been sitting next to him, thought something must have happened to Queen Mary. The King then cancelled the next course and, with his wife, Harry and Alice, withdrew to another room. Then he told them that George was dead. They all left for London the same evening.

In his office at Government House, Nassau, in the Bahamas, where he was now Governor General, David was listening to the BBC Empire Service when he heard a news broadcast about his youngest brother. He refused to believe that George had been killed.

At Badminton House Queen Mary had spent a long, wet afternoon with her lady in waiting, Lady Cynthia Colville, arranging photographs in her huge scarlet folio albums. After tea Lady Cynthia read aloud to the Queen, who was concentrating on her famous needlework. Shortly after the two old friends had finished dinner, there was a telephone call from Balmoral. George VI tried to break the news to his mother as gently as possible. Queen Mary was so stunned that for a time she too could not believe it. Yet her extraordinary stamina enabled her to think immediately of her daughter-in-law. 'I must go to Marina tomorrow. . . .' she said.

At Coppins, Marina had gone to bed early. Her seven-week-old baby son was sleeping quietly in the next room and when Foxy, still downstairs, went to answer the telephone she hoped it had not awakened the child. . . . Foxy stumbled up the stairs. She fumbled as she tried to open the bedroom door, ran over to the bed and took Marina in her frail old arms.

When Queen Mary arrived at the house early the following morning she found her daughter-in-law in shock, either weeping uncontrollably or sitting motionless and staring into space. In spite of her own anguish, Queen Mary's extraordinary personal resources, often tested before beyond the limit of endurance, once again did not fail her in a moment of tragedy. Never in her life did she display greater self-control than she did in those hours when she gently talked to Marina.

At George's funeral on 29 August in St George's Chapel at Windsor Castle, Marina, heavily veiled, was inconsolable. As she entered the choir stalls and saw on the coffin the circlet of summer flowers she herself had picked in the garden of Coppins, the royal widow stumbled. It was only quick action on the part of Queen Elizabeth that saved her.

What had George meant to his family? In his diary, quoted in *King George VI*, by John Wheeler-Bennett, George VI recorded, 'I have attended very many family funerals in the Chapel, but none of which have moved me in the same way. Everybody there I knew well but I did not dare look at any of them for fear of breaking down.' To his close friend, Group Captain Sir Louis Greig, he wrote, 'I shall miss him and his help terribly.' Two weeks later George VI drove from Balmoral to Berriedale and the site of the crash. He talked for a long time to the farmer, David Morrison, and his son Hugh and wrote in his diary, 'I had to do this pilgrimage.'

A memorial service held for George in the cathedral at Nassau on 29 August plunged David into despair. His equerry, Captain Vyvyan Drury, recalled, as is quoted in *The Duke of Windsor's War* by Michael Bloch, that David 'broke down at the beginning and wept like a child all the way through. It was the only time I saw him lose his self-control like that.' The death of George was the most terrible loss of his life and in his grief he only wanted to be left alone for days. Even his wife could not console him.

According to Noble Frankland in *Prince Henry, Duke of Gloucester*, Queen Mary's other sons knew that George was her favourite and Harry, Regent designate and the only remaining brother to support George VI, wrote to his mother, 'Even now I do not realise I will never see him again. . . .' His wife, Alice, recalled 'how easily fate might have selected him rather than the Duke of Kent . . . a son without compare to Queen Mary'.

There was grave concern amongst the Royal Family about the way in which Marina would cope without the husband she not only deeply loved but upon whom she had always been so dependent. George VI had voiced his fears almost as soon as he had learned of his brother's death, when he expressed the view that she simply *must* have someone with her. Foxy was too old and too distressed to be relied upon. But who among the family was close enough to Marina to help at that critical stage in the war? George VI and Queen Mary came up with the answer, but it was one which presented problems and had political overtones. Their choice was Marina's sister, Olga, who was in Kenya with her husband, Prince Paul, where he was a political prisoner under British jurisdiction. For his collaboration with the Germans when he took part in the tripartite pact signed by Yugoslavia with the Axis powers, he was regarded by many at Westminster as a traitor. But after receiving priority signals sent out on behalf of George VI, Olga travelled via Uganda, the Cameroons, Nigeria, Portugal and Ireland and finally arrived by destroyer at Poole harbour, where she and Marina had spent happy childhood holidays. On her arrival at Coppins the two sisters flung their arms around each other and burst into tears. Marina's recovery began. Even so, it was four years before she could bring herself to look at the heather-clad hillside in Scotland where George had crashed to his death. A wooden stake then marked the site.

What happened to the Sunderland flying boat with George as a VIP passenger on board has never been satisfactorily resolved. An official inquiry held by the Air Ministry into the causes of the fatal accident appeared to reach a clear-cut conclusion. In a statement to the House of Commons Sir Archibald Sinclair, Secretary of State for Air, said:

The aircraft, which was proceeding from a Royal Air Force Station in Scotland to Iceland, was airborne just after one o'clock in the afternoon of 25 August. Before departure, the correct procedure for briefing the captain to the exact route to be followed, and for providing full information about the weather conditions likely to be encountered, was complied with. Local weather conditions were not good, but the general indications showed a likelihood of improvement to the westward.

The captain of the aircraft had long experience on the particular type of aircraft which he was flying, and was of exceptional ability. About half an hour after take off the aircraft was heard approaching land from the sea at what appeared to be a low height, and shortly afterwards it was heard to crash into the hills.

Sinclair went on to report the court findings which were:

First, the accident occurred because the aircraft was flown on a track other than that indicated in the flight plan given to the pilot, and at too low an altitude to clear the rising ground on the track.

Secondly, that the responsibility for this serious mistake in airmanship lies with the captain of the aircraft. Thirdly, that the weather encountered should have presented no difficulties to an experienced pilot. Fourthly, that the examination of the propellers showed that the engines were under power when the aircraft struck the ground.

Because of wartime censorship a restricted account of the crash appeared in the press. But was there more to know?

In 1982, aviation expert David J. Smith published an article called 'The Death of the Duke of Kent' in a quarterly review, *After the Battle*. He wrote:

The spectre of high ground lurked at the back of every pilot's mind [in the war]. The importance of safety height was drilled into him from the beginning of his training and yet an experienced captain, apparently with the support of his CO, deviated from his route straight into the hills. The Court of Enquiry failed to find any explanation, the self-evident conclusion being that the accident occurred because the aircraft was flown on a track other than that indicated in the flight plan given to the pilot and at too low an altitude to clear the rising ground on the track. The opinion was expressed that the responsibility for the mistake in airmanship lay with the captain. Until more enlightened times, this verdict of 'Pilot error' was a common one when no one lived to tell the tale. The only other published finding was that an examination of the propellers had shown that all four engines were under power on impact, which implied that there was nothing wrong with the aircraft. Over the years there have been several attempts to explain what misled the crew so disastrously.

Smith rejected a theory that the plane was in effect brought down by German operators sending fake messages, saying,

Simulating radio beacons was a British pioneered device but it was not until much later in the war that the enemy began to practise such deceptions in order to lead astray aircraft on the trans-Atlantic ferry routes. An *outbound* flight would obviously not require homing bearings and any back bearings for position fixes would be treated with caution.

He also rejected the idea that 'magnetic rocks' affected the Sunderland's compass; 'There is no geological evidence to support this,' he wrote.

Smith's researches led to two strange discoveries. An examination of the operations record books for the nearest RAF stations to the crash – Tain, Evanton, Wick and Invergordon itself – showed that the first three did not even record the accident. Secondly, there was unusual haste in clearing the wreckage after the crash. Smith observed:

To No. 63 Maintenance Unit at Inverness, the unit responsible for the salvage of crashed aircraft in the north of Scotland, went the task of clearing the debris. The Maintenance Unit's ORB reports, 'Salvage of Sunderland W4026, Duke of Kent's aircraft. Squadron Leader D.A. Harrison visited the site and made arrangements for the wreckage to be completely cleared and all traces of the accident to be removed. Salvage operations were completed on September 14 1942.'

This was three weeks after the event. Smith goes on, 'This is in direct contrast to several other crash sites in the area which were partially cleared and left with an untidy collection of scattered metal, some half-buried.' On the Scaraben, the long ridge which rises just to the west of Eagle's Rock, he found the remains of four crashed aircraft: Whitley P5070 of No. 612 Squadron, Wick (1 May 1941); Anson DJ178 of No. 20 OTU, Lossiemouth (18 August 1942); an unidentified Barracuda

(December 1944); and Canberra WT531 of No. 80 Squadron, which had crashed on 2 February 1966 when flying from Bruggen in Germany to Lossiemouth. A few miles down the coast on the moors behind Helmsdale he came across the partly buried remains of Liberator BZ724 of No. 59 Squadron and another Sunderland, DP197 of No. 4 OTU, which had crashed on 15 August 1944.

David Smith summarized his investigations in these words:

My own theory on the cause of the Duke's crash was triggered whilst I was driving up the A9 road from the south past Berriedale and Dunbeath. Both villages are set in inlets and, from a few hundred feet as the coast road climbs and dips, both locations look very similar. I believe the captain decided to cut the corner across Caithness, thus saving more fuel for a possible diversion. Provided the aircraft did not turn on to the new track until passing abeam of Dunbeath, it would be clear of high ground and could begin a gentle climb in cloud to allow for the low hills on the northern coast.

Flying visual contact with the coast in poor visibility, perhaps the crew misidentified the correct turning point and changed course over Berriedale instead of Dunbeath, straight into the hills. We shall never know for sure.

Earlier, in 1966, in his book *Great Mysteries of the Air*, Ralph Barker described the crew of the ill-fated Sunderland flying boat:

The Sunderland pilot, Flight Lieutenant Frank Goyen, a twenty-five-year-old Australian from Victoria, of exceptional ability, athletic, steady and dependable, had been specially chosen for the task. Giving up an office job in Australia in 1938 to join the RAF he had spent the first two years of the war patrolling the Mediterranean and the North and South Atlantic, amassing nearly a thousand operational hours in the process. Once in June 1940, when shadowing the Italian Fleet, he had alighted on the sea when his petrol ran low, keeping the ships in sight all night without being spotted and then taking off next morning and flying back to his base with a detailed report. He was the Sunderland pilot par excellence.

With him Frank Goyen had his regular crew, equally trusted and competent. They numbered ten in all and included a second pilot, two radio operators, three gunners, a navigator, an engineer and a fitter. The second pilot, too, was an Australian, and another crew member was a New Zealander; the others were British.

In addition, as a courtesy and to mark the importance of the flight, the squadron commander, Wing Commander T.L. Moseley, also an Australian, was aboard. Moseley was a former Cranwell cadet who had been on flying boats since 1934. Before taking over 228 Squadron he had been on the staff of the

Deputy Director of Training (Navigation) at the Air Ministry.

After describing the crash, Barker continued,

What could have gone wrong? How was it that this highly experienced Sunderland crew, reinforced by their commanding officer – a navigational expert – could have made the sort of mistake that even the rawest beginner was trained to avoid?

'Beware of high ground. High ground is a killer.' Phrases like this were dinned into every wartime air force crew. It thus seems extraordinary that Goyen could have risked a shortcut across such terrain, should have descended amongst the very hills that his briefing and flight plan had warned against.

It didn't make sense. If he had been at a thousand feet or so higher, he might have been suspected of taking a short cut. Mount Morven, a few miles further inland, was almost the only point above 2,000 feet in Caithness. But at 900 feet and descending – it was the act of a madman. And Goyen was not flying alone. He had a second pilot, a navigator, and his commanding officer on board. They must all have been aware of the course the plane was flying.

Yet, none of them apparently raised any objection to it. Indeed they must all have approved it. Clearly there had to be some other explanation. Yet a full court of enquiry failed to find out. . . . The pilot was a man of long experience on Sunderlands and of exceptional ability. Yet the pilot, concluded the court, was to blame.

The court's main findings were that the accident had occurred because the aircraft was flown on a track other than that indicated in the flight plan given to the pilot, and at too low an altitude to clear the rising ground on the track. This, of course, was self-evident; there was no attempt to explain how such a tragic aberration could have occurred. The court went on to express the opinion that the responsibility for the mistake in airmanship lay with the captain. In cases like these, when an aircraft is lost through some baffling mistake that on the face of it looks like an error of judgement, and none of the responsible officers survives, the captain almost invariably gets the blame. But surely in this instance such a facile solution is insupportable, and at this distance ought to be rejected.

What about the weather? Does the court's statement that local weather conditions were 'not good' hide a belief that the Sunderland should never have flown that day? Could this even be yet another case of a wartime VIP's impatience over-ruling the better judgement of the crew? Those who knew Frank Goyen will scoff at this one.

One of the men who served on 228 Squadron with him wrote afterwards that

Goyen had a pet retort whenever it was suggested that he might be persuaded to undertake some near lunatic task. 'I wouldn't do that,' he would say, 'if the King told me.' Neither would he have done it for a Duke. Although the phrase was said in fun, no one doubted that he was capable of meaning it. Whatever may have been hinted to the contrary, no one who knew anything about the Duke himself or Frank Goyen would countenance such a solution. And in any case, the court in its findings gave the opinion that the weather encountered should have presented no difficulties to an experienced pilot.

Barker ends,

Having regard to all the circumstantial evidence, and with due respect to the official court of enquiry, one is bound to demur at the place of blame in this case on any one man. In that 32 minutes between take-off and oblivion, something went wrong in Sunderland W4026, something that confused or misled the crew, something that would have confused or misled any other crew at that particular moment in the history of the flight. That much one feels is certain. What it was will almost as certainly remain a mystery.

In 1982 barrister and historian Michael Bloch compounded the mystery. Bloch was given authorized access to the official archives of the Duke of Windsor by the distinguished Paris lawyer, Maître Suzanne Blum. In his book *The Duke of Windsor's War*, Bloch wrote that '. . . he [the Duke of Windsor] heard that his youngest brother Prince George Duke of Kent, not yet forty, had been killed *when the plane he was piloting* crashed into a Scottish mountainside.'

There was one survivor from the fatal crash, Sergeant Andrew Jack, the tail gunner. When he recovered consciousness he had searched for survivors and, finding none, had made a slow and painful way across the moors hoping to reach habitation. With nightfall, badly burned and injured, he slept in the bracken, and resumed his wanderings at daybreak. It was not until late in the afternoon, his clothes torn to ribbons, that he found a cottage and safety. Jack was subsequently commissioned, but retired from the RAF on 20 June 1964. He died on 22 March 1978, leaving no record of the short flight and fate of the Sunderland seaplane which had ended the life of Marina's husband.

The youngest of five children, he grew up in Grangemouth, Stirlingshire. His surviving sister, Mrs Nancy Blows of Hackney in London, went to Lybster Hospital in Sutherland and saw her brother twenty-four hours after he had been admitted. She was accompanied by her mother, Mrs Agnes Jack, who died in 1960, and her brother, Robert

Jack, then a sergeant in the Scots Guards, who died in 1974.

In June 1984 Mrs Blows recalled,

Andrew was the baby of the family. Our father died in 1938 and our mother brought us up single-handed. Andrew went to Grangemouth High School and stayed there until he was eighteen. When the war broke out he volunteered for the RAF.

He owed his life to the toss of a coin. Before the flight he flipped a coin with another rear gunner to decide which one would fly. Andrew lost the toss and went into the rear turret, the most dangerous place on a flying boat since the Germans always tried to knock out the rear gunner first.

Andrew was a member of a hand-picked RAF crew who flew VIPs. Frank Goyen was always the pilot, the man who was blamed for the crash. They flew Winston Churchill to Gibraltar in a Catalina called *The Golden Fleece*, and Sir Stafford Cripps to Moscow. For a time they were based in Cornwall on U-boat patrol runs.

On the day of the crash I was a leading aircraftwoman (WRAF) stationed at Moreton-in-Marsh and working on supplies for dinghies. I was given immediate leave and went to Grangemouth. My brother, Robert, my mother and I were taken by a chauffeur-driven RAF car to Lybster. I was still wearing my battledress and the first night, because there was no other accommodation available, I was given a bed in the hospital.

Doctors at the hospital told us that the next forty-eight hours would be critical for Andrew. They were afraid that he would get pneumonia. The three of us put up in a small commercial hotel in Lybster. It was the only place to stay and we spent quite a lot of time with two intelligence officers (RAF) who came from London. They gave Andrew various papers to sign – even though his hands were badly burned – one of which was an oath of secrecy about the crash.

According to the doctors, Andrew owed his life to his good health. He was only twenty-one at the time. The doctors told my mother in my presence, 'Your upbringing saved your son. You brought him up a fit lad and that is why he managed to survive.' Our mother was a wonderful person. She did everything possible for all her children. We had plenty to eat and received all the encouragement and kindness in the world.

This is what Andrew told us about the crash. He said that his turret broke away from the body of the aircraft and was thrown clear. The plane had not yet burst into flames when he found himself on his feet with no serious injuries. He said that his teeth were temporarily jammed and that the third finger on his right hand had been twisted. Then he saw the Sunderland on fire.

He got terrible burns trying to save seven of the men who were on the plane. He pulled out seven bodies including that of the Duke of Kent. Only one of the seven men was alive, the flight engineer, who was bleeding badly. Andrew said he knew he couldn't help the flight engineer and his only thought was to go for help. First, he covered the bodies with tarpaulin.

Andrew's main burns were on his hips and hands from carrying the hot and burning bodies. He described the utter desolation of the scene of the crash. He was surrounded by mountains, did not know where he was and felt terrible.

He remembered that when he was trying to make his way to find help he paused by a bank and found 5s 7½d in his pocket. He later said, 'I put it on the edge of the bank and thought, I hope someone finds it because I shan't live to spend it.' Someone did find the money and it was later sent to my mother.

Before Andrew left the wreckage to seek help he lay down and rested. He couldn't remember for how long. He spent the night in the bracken. The next day as he stumbled along he saw a white crofter's cottage ahead of him surrounded by a wire fence. In order to reach the cottage he had to somehow climb up a grass bank. He said he thought he would never reach the wire fence but he managed to get up the bank and under part of the fence by using his elbows. A woman of eighty-three found Andrew. He told her that he had to contact the observers' post and get help.

The Duke of Kent's body was taken to Duarobin Castle. Andrew was sent to the Bangour Hospital near Edinburgh where the famous surgeon, Sir Archibald Macindoe, performed skin graft operations on his hips, hands and face. King George VI went to visit him there and spent quite a time with Andrew. At my Hogmanay wedding on 31 December 1942 Andrew was well enough to be our best man. At first he didn't think we would want him because of his facial disfigurements – but of course we did.

Mrs Blows said that when her brother was fully recovered he was first posted to Invergordon and was later commissioned. With the rank of flight lieutenant he was then attached to the deputy provost's department in Paris.

She went on,

The RAF were very kind to my brother. They knew what he had gone through. The most moving thing happened just after the end of the war. My mother received a letter from the father of Frank Goyen. Mr Goyen asked my mother if he and his wife could come to Grangemouth and talk to Andrew. They flew over from Australia.

Andrew and I were with my mother when Mr and Mrs Goyen came to our home. They were very quiet and nice people and we could see that they were very upset.

They began to talk about the crash and when Mr Goyen began to ask questions, my mother said to him, 'I think perhaps it would be better if you and your wife went into the front room and talked to Andrew alone.' She turned to my brother and said, 'Tell Mr and Mrs Goyen exactly what happened. . . .'

The parents of the dead pilot spent a long time with Andrew, perhaps an hour or so. They came out of the front room looking much better. Mr Goyen turned to my mother and said, 'I came here feeling the most depressed and unhappy man in the world. My wife and I are going home happier than we could ever have believed possible.'

All the family knew about the court of inquiry was what we had read in the newspapers.

The family rather hoped that Andrew would have received some sort of decoration after the crash but he never did.

In the 1950s Andrew Jack was posted to Malta with the RAF and attached to the ground controller's staff.

Mrs Blows said,

He was once on duty when a plane carrying the Queen Mother was guided in. Some time later, about 1955, he was on duty when a plane with Princess Marina came in. Somehow or other she knew that Andrew was there and asked to meet him. They spent quite a time together and after that she always arranged to meet Andrew whenever she touched down in Malta.

In 1961, with her eldest son Edward and her daughter, Alexandra, Marina returned to Eagle's Rock and saw for herself the simple granite cross she had arranged to be erected in memory of George and those who had died with him.

Among the fifteen names carved in the granite were those of two men who had been very close to George. One was that of his secretary, John Arthur Lowther, buried at the church of St John the Baptist, Campsea Ashe, Suffolk. For his work and devotion to George he had been made a Member of the Victorian Order by George VI – only awarded 'for personal services to the sovereign'. Another was George's valet, Leading Aircraftsman John Walter Hales, buried in the churchyard of Holy Trinity at Ingham in Norfolk.

The death of the third man was overshadowed by that of George. He was his ADC, twenty-seven-year-old Pilot Officer the Hon. C.V. Michael Strutt, son of Lord Belper and the Countess of Rosebery and a brother of the Duchess of Norfolk, now Lavinia, Dowager Duchess of Norfolk, CBE. He is buried in St Wilfrid's churchyard at Kingston-on-Soar in Nottinghamshire. George, at his express wish, was buried in the private royal burial ground at Frogmore in the grounds of Windsor Castle.

8

The Widow

Marina's fundamental personality was revealed by the way in which she worked through her bereavement and emerged stronger. Up till now, in childhood, youth and marriage, she had been content to let others make decisions for her. The only time she had ever taken a strong personal stand was after the abdication when, despite the strong pressures imposed by her husband and the King, she refused to meet David and his wife. A devout Christian, Marina never forgave David his dereliction of duty, not only to the state, but also to the church. By her acceptance of a dominant husband who dictated almost every aspect of her life she gave the impression of being docile, but she proved stronger than she seemed. For instance, George had mercurial moods which would have evoked highly emotional responses from a less secure and relaxed person. Marina, however, coped by simply ignoring these outbursts. This was one of the reasons why she was so admired by members of the Royal Family, who were convinced that she was the only woman who could ever have understood George and made him happy.

But it was not until she was widowed at thirty-five and forced to carry on alone that her full potential became apparent. After living in George's shadow in her private life she became a personality in her own right, a development which gained great momentum within a year of his death. Whenever the Royal Family were together – Easter at Windsor Castle, summer holidays at Balmoral and Christmas at Sandringham – in-laws tended to seek her out as a confidante. Smoking a cigarette from a long holder, she had offered the same undivided attention to her father-in-law, George V, as she later did to young children such as her nieces, Elizabeth and Margaret Rose. To the royals she was charmingly 'different'. Her slight Greek accent, which she retained to the end of her life, her sophistication and her warmth were tremendously attractive to what was, inevitably, an insular group of people. Although she belonged to the junior branch of the family, her own children being preceded in line of succession by her brother-in-law Harry, Duke of Gloucester, and his children, William and Richard, she nevertheless exerted a great influence over many of them, most especially when personal issues were at stake.

Her background had given her close connections with almost every royal house in Europe and stood her in great stead. She had either heard of first hand, or seen for herself, so many emotional dramas played out in royal courts that at times she understood the actions of her British relatives better than they did themselves. She was thus able to play a vital role in a royal love story which could have proved more difficult without the skilful diplomacy that she exercised. By gentle persuasion she enabled George VI to recognise the potential in Prince Philip and accept him as a suitor for Elizabeth's hand in marriage.

As a Greek royal exile before her marriage, Marina had lost her financial security, as had someone else who, even more than herself, was to become a central figure in the family. As a small boy Prince Philip of Greece had lived with his family not far from her in Paris. When George and Marina moved to Coppins in March 1936 Philip was already in his second year at Gordonstoun, the famously tough school set amid pines and Sitka spruce overlooking the Moray Firth in Scotland. During the holidays he regularly stayed at Brook House, the Park Lane home of Lord and Lady Mountbatten – Uncle Dickie and Aunt Edwina – but he also spent a great deal of time at Coppins, where he was free to drop in as and when he pleased. Philip could talk for hours to his cousin, always certain of a kind and sympathetic ear. George also established an excellent rapport with the tall, handsome, fair-haired boy.

When they were little girls both Elizabeth and Margaret Rose loved the rambling house at Iver, conveniently close to Windsor Castle, where George chased them round the gardens and indulged in all kinds of practical jokes with them. Margaret Rose had a childish adoration for her Aunt Marina and nothing pleased her so much as to be allowed to sit before a mirror and try on her hats. It was November 1934 when Marina first met Elizabeth: the eight-year-old stepped forward rather shyly on a red-carpeted platform at Victoria Station to greet her Uncle George's bride-to-be, arriving from Paris for her wedding. As a bridesmaid, Elizabeth threw her normal reserve to the wind when she stood on tiptoe and spontaneously hugged Marina. They were to establish a powerful bond that was to last for the rest of Marina's life.

In these early formative years both Philip and Elizabeth, separately and for different reasons, were drawn to Marina, George and Coppins. No one really knows when Philip and Elizabeth first met. They were both at the Kent wedding in Westminster Abbey in November 1934 and attended family parties afterwards. It has often been said that they first encountered one another during the coronation of George VI and Queen Elizabeth in May 1937, possibly at one of the family celebrations given for the younger royals at Buckingham Palace after the great service was over. However, between 1936 and 1939 both Philip, and Elizabeth and Margaret Rose, separately visited Coppins so often that it is improbable they were never there at the same time. If their paths did cross it would have produced little comment because of the disparity in their ages. In any case, the house was usually so full of visitors and guests that few people present knew everyone there. The first time either Philip or Elizabeth can remember taking notice of each other was at the Dartmouth Royal Naval College in July 1939. But as early as 1941 Marina, Lord Mountbatten and his wife, Edwina, were among those who privately shared hopes that one day the couple might marry. Royal gossip circulating at the time reached the Kents' friend Sir Henry 'Chips' Channon, whose diaries of the London social scene in the twenties and thirties became famous; he kept these diaries continuously for nearly forty years until his death in 1958. Channon reported that on 21 January 1941 he went to 'an enjoyable Greek cocktail party. Prince Philip of Greece was there. He is extraordinarily handsome. . . . He is to be our Prince Consort, and that is why he is serving in our Navy.' This was an amazing prophecy for Channon to make but, unlike some of his fanciful observations, this one was based on a source upon which he felt he could rely. His informant was Marina's mother, Princess Nicholas of Greece, who had, in fact, been indulging in wishful thinking. At that time neither Princess Nicholas, nor anyone else in royal circles, had any reason to believe that Philip would ever be regarded by George VI as a possible suitor for Elizabeth. The romantic road that lay ahead for the couple was beset with problems, not the least of which lay in the character of George VI himself. As his elder daughter began to grow up he became increasingly possessive and in 1945, without the discreet and quiet intervention of Marina, who understood the King better than most people, things might well not have turned out as they did. Like George, her late husband, he was a man easily prone to irritability and his flashes of quick temper made many uneasy in his presence. To Marina, whom he had always admired, he adopted a protective attitude which made it relatively easy for her openly to discuss family matters with him in a way that would have been impossible for others. After the death of her husband George VI regarded himself very much *in loco parentis*, and when they met he showed every concern about his two nephews, Edward and Michael, and his niece, Alexandra. Given this warm relationship with the King, Marina could not have been better placed to help the young Philip and Elizabeth.

In the summer of 1943, when Marina was gradually beginning to pick up the threads of her life, she was Philip's closest confidante. On the few occasions when he was on leave in England he always spent as much time as possible at Coppins. With the cousin who was so much older than he was he could discuss his visits to Windsor Castle where he entertained the King with accounts of his adventures at sea. Although the relationship between Philip and Elizabeth was clear, the King chose to ignore it and offered no encouragement. In a letter to Queen Mary, quoted by John Wheeler-Bennett in *King George VI*, he wrote, 'We both think she is too young for that now, as she has never met any young men of her own age. . . . I like Philip. He is intelligent, has a good sense of humour and thinks about things in the right way. . . . Philip had better not think any more about it for the present.' George VI had no other suitor in mind for Elizabeth and appeared to dismiss her relationship with Philip as little more than puppy love experienced by a girl who had few opportunities of meeting members of the opposite sex, compelled, as she and her sister were in wartime, to stay in the safety and security of Windsor Castle.

Marina, on the other hand, was aware that Elizabeth was developing a mind of her own. Her affection for Philip went far deeper than a crush. Philip frequently spent long hours with his Greek cousin expressing his exasperation at the situation in which he and Elizabeth found themselves – hardly ever alone and nearly always in the company of the King and Queen, and Margaret. Coppins offered the ideal solution. It was clear to Marina that if the couple were ever going to get to know one another better the ideal place for them to meet was in her home, where she could be a discreet chaperone. She recalled the carefree days in 1933 and 1934 when she and George had been able to move freely about London and the countryside, able to discover their feelings for one another without constraint.

The arrangements were simple. When Philip was on leave she arranged tennis parties and small informal dances for young people to which she also invited Elizabeth. Elizabeth and Philip often lunched alone together at Coppins, and Marina made sure that they were never disturbed by her boisterous children. The relationship soon became more intense and it was with Marina that Philip first began discussing the possibility of marriage. She promised to discuss the matter first with her older cousin, King George of Greece, who was in England, and together they would consider the most sensible way to approach George VI.

In her book *Prince Philip, A Family Portrait*, Marina's niece, Queen Alexandra of Yugoslavia, writing about Philip and Elizabeth, disclosed,

We used to see them holding hands, disengaging themselves sometimes until we came closer and they could see it was only us. Few people wandered in the [Windsor] Great Park and it formed an idyllic setting.

'I only hope Philip isn't just flirting with her . . .' I once told Marina. 'He's so attractive and he flirts without realising it.'

Marina said soberly, 'I think his flirting days are over. He would be the one to be hurt now if it was all just flirtation or if . . . if it is not to be. One thing I'm sure about, those two would never do anything to hurt one another.'

'Well let's touch wood they don't have to wait so long for their engagement and wedding as we did,' I replied.

'They will probably have to wait much longer than you did,' said Marina. And she added with a smile, 'I won't be able to influence Uncle Bertie for Lilibet nearly as easily as I did for you.'

On 14 May 1945, six days after the surrender of Germany, the King addressed both Houses of Parliament, and when he spoke of 'those who will not come back' and mentioned the death of his brother George, his voice faltered and broke. Whilst sharing his bereavement, Marina continued her delicate mission on behalf of Philip and Elizabeth just as she had done for Alexandra and Peter of Yugoslavia. Alexandra told her future husband, 'Marina has been more wonderful than I can tell you. She has helped us in every way possible, and I know that Uncle Bertie sees things from our point of view now since Marina talked to him about us. . . .' It was not until September 1945 that Marina was convinced that George VI had finally accepted Philip as his future son-in-law. The engagement, however, was not announced until 10 July 1947.

King George VI was godfather to King Peter of Yugoslavia who lived in exile in Britain during the war. When Peter fell in love with Princess Alexandra of Greece he was only nineteen and the King considered him to be too young to marry.

As John Wheeler-Bennett explained in *King George VI*,

Like his father and grandfather before him, King George was keenly aware of his loyalties and obligations as a member of the Guild of Sovereigns, which he regarded in the sense of a 'Royal Trade Union'. Being himself so conscious of his own responsibilities he was ever sympathetic with the burdens and difficulties of his fellow monarchs. It was in a great measure this guild loyalty – over and above the ties of kinship and the bonds of common humanity – which prompted the warmth and hospitality with which he received King Haakon of Norway, Queen Wilhelmina of the Netherlands and King George of Greece during their temporary wartime exile; which induced the sympathy he displayed with King Peter of Yugoslavia. King George offered his godson much wise advice in the conduct of his political affairs and was of no small assistance to him in the somewhat complicated arrangements of his marriage. To this both King Peter and Queen Alexandra have paid tribute in their respective memoirs.

King Peter and Alexandra were married on 20 March 1944 when the bridegroom was twenty and his bride five days short of her twenty-second birthday.

That the widowed Duchess of Kent was able to devote so much thought and effort to the emotional dilemmas of her young relatives so soon after the death of her husband was remarkable. Many people close to her, including the King himself, had feared that even coping with her three children would prove too much for her, and it was thought that Edward, Alexandra and Michael might for a time have to be put in the care of some member of the family. On 23 November 1942 Sir Henry Channon described the gloom at Coppins.

The Duchess has rearranged her sitting room, kept the Duke's just as it was, and has shut up the music room. . . . Went up to bed about midnight, and I was haunted by the spirit of the Duke. Every room and object is so inspired by him, the house, in fact, is him. I met him on the staircase, saw him sitting at the end of my bed, as he so often used to do, and was constantly aware of him. The house still vibrates with his vivacious personality.

What no one had counted on was the powerful influence that Queen Mary would have on her bereaved daughter-in-law. The old lady, who had experienced so much personal tragedy, including the death of two sons and her husband, and the virtual loss of another son by abdication, still possessed extraordinary inner resources, even at the onset of old age which she resented so much. She was able to share her insight with Marina and give her some of the courage she herself had always found in times of despair. Her therapy, which began the moment she saw Marina ten hours after George's death, was over and over again to impress the word 'duty' upon her daughter-in-law. It worked. Within ten weeks of being widowed Marina made her first public appearance in London, solemn but composed, visiting a Wren training centre on 4 November 1942. Almost immediately she had decided to take on as many of her late husband's public duties as possible, and by the end of 1943 had replaced him as an active patron of more than thirty charities and other organizations. She became President of the All England Lawn Tennis and Croquet Club; President of the Chest and Heart Association; Patron of the Derwen Cripples' Training College, Oswestry; an Honorary Freewoman of the Glaziers' Company; Patron of the King Edward Memorial Hospital, Ealing; Patron of the Merioneth Nursing Association; an Honorary Freewoman of the Musicians' Company; Patron of the National Benevolent Institution; Patron of the People's Dispensary for Sick Animals; Patron of the Robert Jones and Agnes Hunt Orthopaedic Hospital, Oswestry; President of the Royal Air Force Benevolent Fund; Patron of the Royal School for the Blind, Leatherhead; Patron of the Royal Wanstead School; and Patron of the Shaftesbury Homes and *Arethusa* training ship.

Adversity brought out in Marina other unsuspected qualities. She became practical. George had always dealt with their financial affairs and was meticulous over household accounts, about which Marina knew little. When she was offered an RAF pension of £400 a year as the widow of an air commodore she refused it, thinking she did not need it. It was not until March 1943 that she realized she had made a mistake. She was shaken to discover that, far from having a comfortable fortune, the monies available to her were so limited that she feared she would not be able to make ends meet. George had received £25,000 a year from the Civil List, money voted by Parliament to cover the working expenses of members of the Royal Family and allocated to individuals by the sovereign. On George's death this allowance automatically ceased. By an unhappy oversight, when the Civil List had been drawn up at the start of George VI's reign in 1937 no provisions had been made for the widows of the previous monarch's younger sons. In peace time the Civil List was reviewed every ten years, but at that critical stage in the war Marina was advised that it was an inopportune moment for her to apply for a special grant from Parliament. She was forced to wait until hostilities ceased.

Royal wills are never made public, but it is widely accepted that when George V died, in January 1936, two-thirds of his personal fortune went to Queen Mary and the remainder was divided equally among his four sons, David, Bertie, Harry and George, and his daughter Mary. It is unlikely that any of the children received less than £300,000, and some estimates put the figure much higher. Marina's parents, Prince and Princess Nicholas of Greece, could not provide her with a dowry at the time of her wedding in 1934, but even then George was regarded as being well off. So where did his wealth go? All his adult life he had spent enormous sums on antique furniture, porcelain, paintings and other objets d'art. After his marriage he may have overspent his income, but had no reason to be anxious about his financial future. When the war broke out in September 1939 he was thirty-six and expected to receive a substantial increase from the Civil List in the years ahead. He was not worried about money: indeed, he had discussed the sale of Coppins in the spring of 1940 with a view to buying a much larger house in the Home Counties for his growing family. In his will George left Coppins to Edward, his eldest son and heir, and the rest of his money was placed in trust for his children. This was not a large sum, and when they grew up none of them was even remotely wealthy. It had never occurred to George that he needed to make special provision for his wife: he had assumed that Marina, as a royal duchess, would be looked after by the state.

When the war was over, in May 1945, Britain was plunged into several years of austerity, and the King still did not consider it the right time for the Duchess of Kent to make any official move to apply for a special allowance from Parliament. In private Marina made her feelings known: she was one of the most popular members of the Royal Family and had worked tremendously hard, yet it never seemed to be the right time for her to receive an official income.

Eleven years of widowhood were to go by before any move was made to redress the situation. When the Civil List was reviewed for the first time after the war, on the accession of Elizabeth II in February 1952, a select committee of the House of Commons established a fund of £25,000 for members of the Royal Family who undertook public duties but for whom no financial provision had been made. From this fund Marina received slightly less than £5,000 a year. It did not solve her problems, but it helped.

At intervals over the years, in order to remain solvent, Marina sold many of her husband's art treasures, nearly all of which had proved to be wise investments. In November 1943 she discovered a small treasure trove of furniture which had been left to George by his great-aunt, Princess Louise, Duchess of Argyll, who had died in December 1939. Early in the war George had carefully sorted out the articles he did not want and stored them in royal residences until a more propitious time came for their disposal. This collection raised nearly £20,000 and helped to fill a pressing need for liquid cash. In March 1947 she was again forced to sell more treasures which had been stored in Windsor Castle and Fort Belvedere, David's former country home in Berkshire. Vans nosed their way through miles of snowdrifts during that hard winter in order to transport the heirlooms to the salerooms of Christie's, the famous auctioneers, where a three-day sale raised a total of £92,341. Amongst the most prized items were a Queen Anne walnut chest with five drawers, which went for £483; eighteen Chippendale mahogany chairs, 2,200 guineas; a Sèvres dessert service of 267 pieces for £609; and two eighteenth-century silver-gilt tea caddies for £900. Three paintings by the French artist Claude Lorrain, which George had wisely bought for £3,885 in 1940, went for £8,930. Although Marina publicly insisted that she only disposed of the treasures because there was not enough room for them at Coppins, the impression that her finances were at a low ebb gained such strength that she was inundated with requests from business organizations in the United States to promote their goods.

In comparison with other members of the Royal Family, Marina was in a desperate financial situation. By ordinary standards, however, she was able to lead the life of a relatively wealthy woman. She continued to maintain a staff which consisted of a butler, a footman, a personal maid, a housemaid, a cook, an assistant cook, two daily women and two part-time gardeners. Whenever she travelled by road she was driven in her black Rolls Royce, YR11, and Coppins remained, if anything, more crowded than ever with visitors, who included RAF friends of her late husband to whom she offered warm but simple wartime hospitality.

The great difference between Marina and her royal in-laws was that she was generous almost to a fault.

In pre-war days the Kents had enjoyed an extravagant lifestyle, entertaining lavishly and travelling widely on the continent, in sharp contrast to the modest, unexciting domestic pattern of King George and Queen Elizabeth. Surrounding themselves with amusing and gifted men and women from the world of the arts, music and show business had no appeal for this royal couple. Not for them were splendid dinner parties lasting until the early hours of the morning. Although they lived in magnificent homes and could command the services of scores of servants, the King and Queen's home life was run on very simple lines, not very different from that of ordinary middle-class families. Their pleasure came from evenings spent listening to the radio, playing games with Elizabeth and Margaret Rose, and reading by the fireside. Like other members of the family they had been bemused and bewildered by the pace of the Kents' social life, which differed so much from their own.

One aspect of the Kents' relationship which the couple never comprehended was the equanimity with which Marina had accepted the friends whom George shared with his cousin Dickie Mountbatten and his dazzling wife, whose great wealth did not prevent her from holding socialist views. In outlook, the quartet were in advance of their time: they welcomed into their midst homosexual and bisexual men and women, and their friends' religion, political persuasion or colour was of no consequence to them. Their only criteria for acceptance were wit, great talent and brilliant conversation.

Marina's photograph was constantly in the newspapers and on the covers of glossy magazines, which published every detail of the clothes she wore. Even in wartime, when the size of newspapers was drastically reduced, her presence at any function remained a source of permanent interest to journalists. Any conviction the King may have harboured about an immediate change in her lifestyle on widowhood was soon destroyed. She simply could not keep old friends and relatives at bay, and this was a cause of real concern to him. As soon as he realized the extent of Marina's financial problems, at a time when she had three young children to bring up, he went to her rescue and provided her with an allowance out of his own purse. This was not given without words of advice against any form of extravagance. Members of the Royal Family have been notoriously careful with money, some of them extremely tight-fisted, especially over domestic economies. Edward VII was an exception to the general rule, but even he could be parsimonious at times and the family trait has been handed down to the present generation. Queen Elizabeth II is against any form of waste. She makes certain that when sheets begin to show signs of wear they are turned 'sides to middle'. New furnishings, like lampshades, are never bought when old ones can be repaired. To save electricity, notices inform the last person to leave a room to turn off the lights.

Faced with a sister-in-law whose sense of money was so different from his own, the King, in a kindly way and with Marina's own interests in mind, urged her to be both cautious and careful in her expenditures. He was satisfied that the allowance he made to Marina was generous. Shortly afterwards, however, Marina sold the lease on Belgrave Square, realizing that she could no longer afford the upkeep of two homes. She also received occasional financial help from the immensely rich Queen Mary but, kind as she was, she too had a reputation for watching her pennies and enjoyed few personal indulgences in her private life. Only to a handful of Greek relatives did Marina reveal her acute sense of humiliation at not being in receipt of an income from the state. There was no substitute for an independent income.

It was altogether a shabby business. As Sir Charles Petrie observed in *The Modern British Monarchy,*

In view of their tireless services to the country one would have thought that Parliament might have voted an annual sum to the Duchess of Kent and Princess Alexandra instead of leaving them dependent on the bounty of the Queen and what they can raise by selling trinkets at Sotheby's. They should each of them surely receive at least the same treatment as Princess Margaret.

At the time when Petrie was writing, in 1961, Princess Margaret was carrying out relatively few duties and yet received an annual income of £15,000 from the Civil List. Marina's allowance was still only £5,000.

At invervals Marina went into the red. This was not the result of personal extravagance but because she had three children to bring up and educate and a large house and estate to maintain. Her fundamental problem was that, as the widow of a royal duke, she felt she must maintain royal standards even though she did not have the money to do so. By paying low salaries to her staff and limiting entertainment she dramatically cut down her expenses, but in the process acquired a reputation for meanness. The alternative would have been to move into a much smaller house, but this she could not do as the estate had been left to Eddie by his father and was in trust until he became of age. Despite her financial difficulties, Marina nevertheless managed to give small sums to impoverished relatives who could always rely on her to help them out and never breathe a word about it. Marina's treatment remains a serious black spot in the record of the modern Royal Family. Eventually she was provided with a small office and a secretary in Marlborough House, Queen Mary's London home in peacetime, and from there she dealt with her vast mail in a highly efficient manner. Even dictating letters was new to her. At Coppins she turned her attention to the big walled kitchen garden and soon the family were self-sufficient in vegetables. There were other economies. Instead of sitting round a mahogany table in a dining room which overlooked the lawns and a meadow beyond, guests, who often included the Prime Minister, Winston Churchill, helped themselves to rationed wartime dishes placed on hot plates on a side table.

Members of the Royal Family adhered strictly to wartime rationing. When Mrs Eleanor Roosevelt, wife of the US President, stayed at Buckingham Palace in September 1942 she was struck by this identity between King and people. The plain 'utility' meals 'might have been served in any home in England', wrote John Wheeler-Bennett in *King George VI*, although they did repose upon gold and silver plates. And though the bedroom she was assigned, the Queen's own, was enormous, recounted Robert Lacey in *Majesty*, its windows were totally without glass because of the bombing and were blocked with small casements of wood frames and isinglass. Queen Mary, who ate strictly according to the ration book, agreed to the appearance of bourgeois napkin rings at the table to avoid the need for laundering after every meal.

With her children evacuated to Badminton under the eagle eye of Queen Mary, Marina devoted all her energies to royal duties. George, with his background as a Home Office factory inspector, had first awakened her interest in factory visits. Her natural curiosity always established an easy rapport with people she met in shipyards or light engineering shops. It was strange that this totally feminine woman could have become so immersed in highly specialized industrial projects, but it was the direct result of an enthusiasm passed on to her by George. As a result, during the war she visited more factories than any other member of the Royal Family, intent upon convincing workers,

especially women, that their jobs were just as important as those of
people who were in one of the services.

In December 1946 the Royal Family gathered at Sandringham for
their first peacetime Christmas. There had been many changes, and
there were new faces too. One of them was Group Captain Peter
Townsend, a wartime RAF pilot with a distinguished record who had
been appointed temporary equerry to the King in 1944. His talents
were great and he fitted in so well that this good-looking man with
charming manners rapidly climbed the Royal Household ladder to
become Deputy Master at the age of thirty-six. He was at hand at all the
most intimate and informal gatherings and that Christmas, as he
recorded later in his book, *Time and Change*, he met Marina for the
first time. He wrote,

The Duchess of Kent, Aunt Marina, completed with her three children, the
inner family circle. Princess Marina's face was of an exquisite, almost tragic
beauty, with a permanently wistful expression. She was sensitive, artistic and
sympathique, going straight to the depths of a subject. Her husband, an
airman, had been killed in an aircrash only a few years earlier; perhaps it was
because I was an airman, too, that I found areas of common ground with the
beautiful, bereaved Duchess.

I longed to know this gifted woman better, but felt too shy to insist in face of
the sophisticated company with which she often surrounded herself. I believe
that wit and brilliance were more effective at buoying up her spirits than the
searching, nostalgic conversations I had with her.

For all her sophistication, the Duchess of Kent was a devoted mother,
presiding at her children's tea parties at her house, to which my children were
sometimes invited. Prince Eddie, her eldest son, was diffident and hypersensi-
tive; Princess Alexandra easy and enchanting, with unmistakeable signs of
becoming a great beauty; Prince Michael a plump little boy with the charm
already, of his father.

Marina's main preoccupation was the future of her children. Her first
step had been to engage a governess, Miss Catherine Peebles, a small,
spry Scotswoman in her early thirties. She had no formal training, no
university degree and no revolutionary ideas on the upbringing of
children, but Alice Gloucester had highly recommended her to Marina
because of her mixture of commonsense and kindly strictness. Alexandra gave her the nickname of Bambi because of her large brown eyes.
When she was later employed by the Queen in 1954 as governess to
Prince Charles, her five-year-old charge called her Mispy. In com-

parison with the 1980s media pressures were almost non-existent, and the young Kent children were able to travel about London, in the care of Miss Peebles, without attracting attention. The firm line she adopted with the boisterous Alexandra reminded Marina of her beloved Foxy, who died in Iver Hospital in November 1949. After making various bequests, including, to Alexandra, an aquamarine pendant which Marina had given her on her wedding day in November 1934, Foxy left her entire estate to her former charge. Many valuable gifts which she had received during her lifetime were returned to the original donors.

At Balmoral in the summer of 1947 Marina voiced her anxieties to the King about the education of her children. She received surprising advice. He had been saddened by the restrictions imposed on Elizabeth and Margaret Rose, who had always been in the care of a governess. With hindsight he regretted their sheltered existence, and the limitations of their education in the hands of Miss Marion Crawford – Crawfie – who had joined the family in September 1932 for a month's trial and stayed for seventeen years. She had taken over full-time responsibility for the daily activities of the two sisters and was given an astonishingly free hand. Later she wrote, in *The Little Princesses*,

No one ever had employers who interfered so little. I often had the feeling that the Duke and Duchess [later George VI and Queen Elizabeth], most happy in their own married life, were not over concerned with the higher education of their daughters. They wanted most for them a really happy childhood, with lots of pleasant memories stored up against the days that might come, and, later, happy marriages.

Miss Crawford was right in her assessment of the King's attitudes towards Elizabeth and Margaret in the 1930s, but the end of the war heralded a break with past traditions in all walks of life and there was a dramatic change in his own outlook. On 8 May 1945, when London celebrated VE Day, he had allowed a group of young officers to take his daughters out to mingle with the throngs of merrymakers in the streets. His last entry in his diary for VE Day was, 'Poor darlings, they have never had any fun yet.'

In a bold and imaginative move, the King now urged Marina to send Alexandra to school. While royal princes had been enrolled as cadets at the Royal Naval College at Dartmouth and the Military Academy at Sandhurst, this was unprecedented; no other princess in the family had ever been to school before. Marina visited various famous girls' schools, including Cheltenham Ladies' College with its fine record of scholastic achievement. It was Alexandra's good fortune that her mother's final choice was a much smaller establishment, Heathfield School, near Ascot, run by one of the youngest and most forward-looking headmistresses in the country. Miss Kathleen Dodds, then thirty-one, had joined the school in 1945 and her reputation was now attracting wealthy parents from all over the world. Academic attainments were not her main objective. She was more concerned with the overall development of individual personalities, whose goal was not necessarily to go on to university. The King was delighted that the only daughter of his late brother was blazing a new trail, one which, had he known it, was soon to become firmly established for all royal children.

Two-year-old Prince George (the future Duke of Kent) in the arms of his grandmother, Queen Alexandra, in 1904

Princess Marina of Greece (centre) and her two elder sisters, Princess Olga (*left*) and Princess Elizabeth (*right*) with their beloved Norland nanny, Miss Kate Fox

The future King George V and Queen Mary with their six children. *Front row, left to right*: Princess Mary (later Princess Royal), Prince Henry (later Duke of Gloucester), Prince George (later Duke of Kent), Prince Edward (known as 'David', later Edward VIII, finally Duke of Windsor), Prince Albert (known as 'Bertie', later George VI). *Back row, left to right*: Duke and Duchess of York (later King George and Queen Mary) holding Prince John who died in 1919

Above: The most dazzling couple of the thirties. The Duke and Duchess of Kent attend a gala performance of *Me and My Girl* at the Victoria Palace Theatre, London, 1939
Below: The Duke of Kent with Prince Edward and the Duchess of Kent with Princess Alexandra at Coppins, their country home in Buckinghamshire, 1940

Prince Michael celebrates his first birthday in July 1943 at Coppins, with him are his elder brother Prince Edward and Princess Alexandra.

Right: The Duke of Kent leaving York Minster with his bride, the former Miss Katharine Worsley, on 8 June 1961 *Below:* The Duke and Duchess of Kent with their young family in 1975. *Left to right*: George, Earl of St Andrews, the Duchess of Kent, Lord Nicholas Windsor, the Duke of Kent, Lady Helen Windsor

Left: A radiant Princess Alexandra and her husband, Angus Ogilvy, on their wedding day in April 1963 **Right:** The Ogilvy family at their home in Richmond, Surrey in 1980. With Princess Alexandra and the Hon. Angus Ogilvy are their two children, James and Marina, both titleless

Left: Princess Michael of Kent *Right:* Prince Michael of Kent

Prince and Princess Michael of Kent at their home in Gloucestershire, in 1983 with their two children, Lord Frederick Windsor and Lady Gabrielle Windsor.

9

The Making of a Princess

Shortly after the wedding of the Queen, then Princess Elizabeth, and Prince Philip in Westminster Abbey on 20 November 1947, the Duchess of Kent carried out a delicate royal mission. On behalf of George VI she flew to Germany to placate Philip's German relatives, who had not been invited to London for the great occasion. Hostilities in Europe had ended on 8 May 1945, but as anti-German feeling was still running high in Britain two years later the King's closest advisers considered it unwise for the bridegroom's relatives, former enemies, to receive invitations.

In 1927 Philip's sister, Princess Sophie of Greece, had married Prince Christopher of Hesse, who subsequently became dedicated to Hitler's cause and helped to make the Nazis respectable in pre-war aristocratic circles in Germany. He was appointed head of the Abhördienst in Goering's Luftwaffe research office. As Denis Judd wrote in *Prince Philip: A Biography*,

This job was even more sinister than it sounded. The Geheimer Abhördienst (secret telephone tapping service) was charged with the 'supervision' of telephone calls and correspondence of foreign embassies and diplomats, but soon extended its activities to Germans in sensitive and prominent positions. It was, alas, the nucleus from which grew the Geheime Staatspolizei, or Gestapo. At the time of Hitler's rise to power, it ought to be stressed, Philip was twelve years old. Still, the connections were potentially embarrassing.

According to Richard Hough in *Mountbatten: Hero of Our Times*, Prince Christopher 'became an ardent Nazi and Luftwaffe pilot, and in the middle of the war recanted and was killed (almost certainly assassinated) in an air crash'.

In the 1930s Philip's three other sisters, like Sophie all Marina's cousins, each married Germans. At twenty-six Margarita became the wife of Gottfried, Prince Hohenlohe-Langenburg; Theodora, one year younger, married Berthold, Margrave of Baden; and Cecile, twenty, married George Donatus, hereditary Grand Duke of Hesse. In 1937 Cecile and her children were killed in an air crash near Ostend.

At the time of his marriage Philip had many German relatives, including ten nieces and nephews, and others whom he did not know and had never met. Long before the royal wedding list was being drawn up Lord Mountbatten, then in India as Viceroy, was the only person in a position to provide the King with accurate information about them. Mountbatten's private hobby was royal genealogy. He was President of the Society of Genealogists and in 1947 he had produced, for private circulation only, a 235-page book called *Relationship Tables – compiled for his children*. It was dedicated to his five grandchildren 'of the 43rd generation' and printed by the Viceregal Press, New Delhi. Mountbatten pointed out that the Hesse family tree had so many branches that a considerable number of Germans might be in a position to claim relationship to Philip and thus expect to be invited to England. A decision was made – an unhappy one for Philip – that his German relations should not attend the wedding.

While the Queen and Prince Philip were on honeymoon, first at Lord Mountbatten's home, Broadlands, in Hampshire, and later at Birkhall on the Balmoral Estate, Marina carried out the task of placating the Germans, some of whom she had known since childhood. Her private visit to Germany was supposed to be a well guarded secret but it was inevitable that some of her closest friends knew of her mission. One of them was Sir Henry Channon; married to Lady Honor Guinness, he had become an MP in 1935 and, in the crucial years 1938–41, served at the Foreign Office as Parliamentary Secretary to R.A. (later Lord) Butler. Members of the Royal Family and internationally distinguished people attended his famous salon in Belgrave Square. After the royal wedding Channon gave a big dinner party on 25 November 1947. He wrote in his diary (*Chips: The Diaries of Sir Henry Channon*),

Noel Coward arrived first . . . and everyone was in gala dress – white ties and the women dripping with jewels. The Queen of Spain arrived punctually and I was on the doorstep to meet her. Five minutes later the Queen of Romania drove up with her sister in a taxi. . . . It was four o'clock before they all left. 'A great, great success,' as he left, Willy Maugham whispered to me, 'This is the apogee of your career.' In a way it was, and I am sorry that Queen Freddie [Crown Princess Frederike of Greece, later Queen] and the Duchess of Kent could not come too (they are on a secret visit to the affronted German relations, to tell them about the wedding).

Marina had always been close to George VI and she was one of the first members of the family to learn in December 1951 that he might not live long. After the removal of a lung the doctors had made it clear to the King himself, without going into all the details, that his expectation of a full and moderately active life might be a matter of only a few years, or even less. The King, however, remained unconcerned. On the morning of 31 January 1952 he waved goodbye to Elizabeth and Philip from the tarmac of London Airport as they embarked on an ambitious tour of East Africa, Australia and New Zealand. Some time in the small hours of 6 February in his bedroom at Sandringham his heart stopped beating.

With the entire Royal Family distracted by their own adjustments to the King's death, at the early age of fifty-six, Marina began to formulate a bold course of action over the future of her daughter. Alexandra had left Heathfield School at the end of the winter term in December 1952, and when she celebrated her sixteenth birthday on Christmas Day the Royal Family was facing a crisis that could not be resolved for several years. The new Queen, Elizabeth, absorbed in the time-consuming and difficult task of taking over the reins, was faced with an acute shortage of experienced relatives to carry out public duties. At eighty-five Queen Mary was sick and ailing and in April she fell ill and remained in bed for five weeks. The new Queen Mother was still in a state of shock over the loss of her husband and could not be taxed further. Princess Margaret, for the most part, was a moody twenty-two-year-old who had still not come to terms with the death of her father and had neither the will nor the interest to concentrate on official duties or to leave London. With arrangements for the coronation, to be held on 2 June 1953, well under way and detailed planning at a critical stage, the Queen had only three stalwarts upon whom she could rely: Marina, and the Duke and Duchess of Gloucester. Prince Charles, born on 14 November 1948, and Princess Anne, born on 15 August 1950, were toddlers, and the only person available and as yet uncommitted to royal duties was Alexandra. To Marina she was not yet endowed with the poise, sophistication or knowledge necessary for an efficient working princess. The task of training her daughter was a daunting one. The easiest answer would have been to send Alexandra to a finishing school, possibly in Switzerland, the traditional course for most girls from wealthy and aristocratic homes. This line of action, however, offered no guarantee that at the end of a standard two-year period Alexandra would be any better equipped to take on a royal role, which would demand far more than any traditional educational establishment could provide.

Marina had to think of something more effective and practical. There were no royal precedents to help her, so she relied upon experience and commonsense. No guidelines had ever been drawn up for the training of a modern working royal princess. The names of the daughters of Queen Victoria and Queen Alexandra were scarcely even remembered. The only British-born princess of Marina's generation was her sister-in-law, the fifty-eight-year-old Princess Royal, only daughter of George V and Queen Mary, who on 28 February 1922 had married the Earl of Harewood, a rich Yorkshire businessman and landowner fifteen years older than herself. Her brothers, Edward VIII, George VI, the Duke of Gloucester and the late Duke of Kent, had always taken on major royal duties, and the Princess Royal only entered public life when it was absolutely necessary. She was shy and reserved and, like her mother, disliked all public royal duties. It was sometimes with grim determination that she carried out her allotted number of functions, and she was always relieved to find herself at home once more in the quiet of Harewood House near Leeds. Widowed since 1947, she lived unostentatiously with her two sons, George, who had inherited his father's title, and the Hon. Gerald Lascelles. Only three royal princesses had been born in the Royal Family since the birth of the Princess Royal in 1894. They were Elizabeth of York in April 1926, Margaret of York in August 1930 and Alexandra of Kent in December 1936. Elizabeth and her sister had been made fully aware of their status since childhood. As little girls they had been accustomed to instant recognition as they were driven around Hyde Park with their nanny in an open landau. Until they reached their late teens both had led sheltered lives, companions of their own age being either friends of their parents or senior members of the Royal Household. Their training as princesses had amounted to little more than an emphasis on perfect manners and good behaviour.

Marina had brought up Alexandra on different lines. Alexandra had a strong personality, and even though, at sixteen, she was much younger, she had a far greater knowledge of the world than either of her cousins. She had enjoyed some freedom and had had a taste of normal life. Any restrictions as had been imposed upon her were no different from those experienced by any other boarder at a relatively small public school for girls. She travelled by coach to London with fellow schoolgirls and a teacher on organized outings to museums, theatre matinees, the Houses of Parliament, the Law Courts and other places of general interest. The fact that she was a royal princess meant little to her. At school she regarded it, if anything, as a handicap. When Miss Dodds, the headmistress, met King George VI at Windsor she was told that he 'wanted Alexandra to have the broadest possible education and to learn how to rub shoulders with the world and keep up with it'. Alexandra received no preferential treatment and if she got into mischief, as she frequently did, she was 'kept in' like other girls. When she was chosen as one of the eight bridesmaids for the wedding of Elizabeth, her cousin, and Philip, she kept the news a secret until the official announcement was made. However, when Alexandra returned to Heathfield after the wedding and the traditional appearance of the Royal Family on the balcony of Buckingham Palace she was mobbed by schoolfriends plying her with questions. Alexandra had already learned the art of royal discretion and refused to be drawn except to say that the food at the wedding breakfast had been splendid. The following week, when the school attended a special showing of the wedding film at an Ascot cinema, Alexandra asked to be excused on the grounds that she would be 'too embarrassed'. An understanding Miss Dodds gave her permission to remain behind at school.

Only a small part of her summer holidays was spent with the rest of the Royal Family. Marina preferred to distance her children from palaces and castles and took them instead to the south coast resorts she had known as a child, places like Poole in Dorset and Clymping and Bexhill-on-Sea in Sussex, where they stayed anonymously in small, comfortable, middle-class hotels. Marina and her two sons and daughter were seldom recognized, and the simple pleasures of riding donkeys, building sandcastles and queuing up for icecreams were the highlight of their childhood. When the children were at school, Edward at Eton, Michael at a prep school and Alexandra at Heathfield, the fatherless family made a few half-term trips abroad, once to Paris and also to Grasse in the South of France where the quartet, always staying with Marina's relatives, explored the French capital and then Provence without any sort of entourage. There was nothing in their appearance to distinguish them from other upper middle-class English children.

It had always been Marina's goal to ensure that Edward, Alexandra and Michael grew up on lines as ordinary as possible despite their background, and developed, during early years, in relative anonymity. What neither she nor any other member of the Royal Family had envisaged was the early death of George VI, which dramatically changed the lives of them all – especially Alexandra, who would otherwise not have been called upon to carry out royal duties until she was much older.

It is, perhaps, remarkable that Marina, with her cosmopolitan European background, was the most modern mother in the British Royal Family in 1952. She harboured no sense of nostalgia about the past. She foresaw some of the post-war changes in lifestyle that younger members of the family would later have to face. One of her greatest triumphs was the training which resulted in Alexandra becoming the most efficient working princess in the world. Alexandra was and is the reliable, stable all-rounder of the family, and even after her career had spanned thirty years she had only ever made one recorded mistake, as a gawky newcomer: when she was fifteen and accompanied Marina to a Red Cross reunion she was so absorbed in a conversation that she dropped her cup and saucer. She stooped down and immediately began picking up the broken pieces herself. Alexandra laughed, but her mother made a mental note that this sort of thing must not occur again.

The Duchess of Kent's strength as a mother was that she allowed Alexandra to grow up with a minimum of restraint while at the same time instilling into her old-fashioned virtues that were to become second nature. Alexandra was never distanced from her mother by nannies or governesses, so that an intimacy unknown to other royal children flourished from babyhood. As a child, Alexandra was impulsive, mischievous and often naughty, but Marina tempered her rebukes with mildness so that a potentially unruly girl responded without resentment. Although Coppins was an elegant house run on efficient lines, for the young princess it was a home, a relaxed place where she could play with toys whenever she liked provided she put them away in the proper place at the end of the day. Witty and amusing with adults, Marina could also enter into the spirit of her daughter's games, and they shared a similar sense of humour.

Marina was fortunate in that the second powerful influence in Alexandra's life had been that of Queen Mary, with whom she had been evacuated to Badminton in 1939. Apart from occasional visits to

Coppins, Alexandra was constantly under the devoted scrutiny of a grandmother whose sense of duty to the family and to the crown had not changed since her youth. Although mellowed by the years and far more indulgent towards her grandchildren than she had ever been towards her own children, she was still obsessed with basic discipline, standards of behaviour and good manners. There were many times when the grandmother saw flashes of temperament that reminded her of Alexandra's father. She had inherited his spontaneity, his infectious laugh and an ability to make a quick retort in the face of minor adversity. There was little evidence that Alexandra had inherited any of her father's intellectual qualities, but she was quick and eager to learn.

Sometimes, even at Badminton in the peace of the West Country, there were air-raid warnings. One bomb fell in the grounds of the estate, landing in a cabbage patch. When a warning sounded, royal evacuees and Badminton servants all descended into underground shelters, a sleepy Alexandra and her brother Edward wrapped in blankets and carried in the arms of a maid. Queen Mary busied herself with knitting – Philip of Greece was on her list for socks and balaclava helmets – or *The Times* crossword. She was frequently interrupted by Alexandra pleading with her grandmother to tell her a story. The words Alexandra heard may have changed over the decades but the themes were much the same as those of the stories told to both her parents when they were small, with heroes and heroines drawn from real life in the royal houses of Britain, Denmark, Greece and Russia, of whom, as Queen Mary was careful to emphasize, Alexandra was a direct descendant.

Queen Mary was also fond of Alexandra's more subdued brother, Edward. She regarded all members of the Royal Family with some objectivity. Even in wartime she focussed her attention on the traditional future her grandchildren could expect. Edward, because of the royal dukedom he had inherited on the death of his father, faced a pre-determined career. His schooldays would automatically be followed by a period in one of the branches of the services and not until marriage, or even later, would he be available for regular royal duties. A similar future would face his brother Michael. Alexandra, on the other hand, might be ready to join the royal rota towards the end of the 1950s, when she would be in her early twenties. Queen Mary could not have foreseen the death of George VI which meant that Alexandra would enter public life at sixteen, younger than any other member of the family.

Marina was confident that she could train Alexandra to a high standard, perhaps within a year, but it meant hard work and supreme effort on the part of mother and daughter. Miss Dodds had greatly encouraged Marina when she had described Alexandra in an end-of-term report as a girl 'with all the lovable qualities of quick sympathy, affection, generosity, laughter and total honesty'. These were the qualities most needed in a royal princess, not only in 1953 but at any time in history. Princess Anne did not begin royal engagements until she was almost nineteen and went to Pirbright in Surrey to present traditional leeks to the Welsh Guards on St David's Day, 1 March 1969. She proved a good and reliable trooper, but it took her a long time to acquire some of the warmth and charm of the young Alexandra. Had Marina failed to draw out all Alexandra's potential, the Queen would have found the early years of her reign more difficult. Marina's success seemed effortless. She provided the Royal Family with the right sort of princess at the right time. As later generations were to prove, this was much easier said than done. While Elizabeth was to be blessed with a dedicated son and heir in Charles, she had real problems with the two extrovert and resistant younger children, Anne and Andrew, who both, for different reasons, failed for a long time to adjust to the pressures of a media age. They reacted badly as teenagers to what they regarded as intrusion into their private lives and did not come to terms with their status until they reached adulthood. Alexandra, on the other hand, accepted her responsibilities in the same way that her mother had done two decades earlier and was never involved in public tantrums or scenes of any kind. She registered only enthusiasm at the prospect of following in her mother's footsteps. Alexandra was too young for the death of her father to have had any real impact on her life, and her first experience of bereavement came in 1953 when an icy February gave way to an overcast and windswept March.

She had always paid regular, happy visits to Marlborough House to see Queen Mary, and early in February she had listened to her grandmother's proud account of a drive in Hyde Park to look at stands being erected along the processional route for the coronation. The last day Queen Mary ever left her home was 9 February 1953. She died during the evening of 24 March at the age of eighty-five, having previously let it be known that should she 'no longer be there to attend the Coronation, this solemnity must on no account of mourning be postponed'. For Marina, the loss of a mother-in-law who was also her oldest and closest confidante was a shattering blow. Queen Mary's death also provided Alexandra with an important early lesson: at the funeral her grief-stricken mother and other relatives remained dry-eyed, while Alexandra failed to keep back her tears. Soon she too was able to exercise the same extraordinary self-control and never reveal her personal emotions in public.

Alexandra's début as a working princess could not have come at a more testing time – the year of a coronation. In the months leading up to the great day, she accompanied her mother on a range of engagements culminating in state banquets, receptions and family celebrations. In the spring of 1953 Marina's simple but clear advice to her daughter was to keep close to her side and observe all that was going on around her. When they returned to Coppins, often exhausted after spending hours on their feet, mother and daughter would take off their shoes, curl up in easy chairs and over a cup of tea quietly discuss the events of the day. In the early days Alexandra was over-excited by all that she had seen and Marina listened attentively without voicing any criticism. As the coronation drew nearer Alexandra's crash course in deportment, behaviour and royal protocol began to change. Marina pointed out mistakes. She impressed upon Alexandra the need to walk more slowly, not to slouch, to stand with her shoulders well back and to avoid wriggling and criss-crossing her legs when she was sitting down. On 17 May 1953 Alexandra walked up the aisle of St Paul's Cathedral two steps behind her mother when they were attending an Empire Youth Sunday service. Accustomed to wearing flat-heeled shoes and trying to adapt to more elegant footwear, Alexandra tripped and only just managed to avoid stumbling. Mother and daughter exchanged rueful glances but there was merriment in their eyes. Marina knew that she had an apt pupil, but there were still hurdles to be overcome before Alexandra could earn her royal wings. One of Alexandra's great joys at Heathfield School had been energetic country dancing, but when she attended a glittering ball at Hampton Court given by officers of the Household Brigade she wished herself miles away. She was in the strange position of being with an outstandingly beautiful mother of forty-six who had greater appeal to most of the dashing officers than she possessed at sixteen. Alexandra was already as tall as her mother, but the classic features she had inherited and which were later to make her a beauty had not yet emerged. She was still on the plump side, her movements were sometimes ungainly, and when she felt nervous she had a habit of resting heavily on one leg. Dutiful officers invited her to dance, but Alexandra knew that the most attractive woman at the ball was her mother.

On 2 June, as the coronation ceremony began with all its pomp, splendour and pageantry, all eyes were on the Royal Family as they majestically proceeded to their royal stalls. When Marina entered the Abbey, closely followed by Alexandra, it was the mother not the daughter who caught everyone's eye. Alexandra, however, in a robe of white lace and tulle threaded with gold, and her train borne by the Hon. Katherine Smith, at last revealed a new dignity that was not lost on astute observers. She was learning fast. Few people except those well versed in the symbolism of heraldry noticed that Alexandra was not wearing a coronet: she was not entitled to that privilege of birth until she reached her royal majority at the age of eighteen. She watched her seventeen-year-old brother, Edward, kneel in homage before their cousin, the newly crowned Queen Elizabeth. He made one small error – he forgot to remove his gloves.

Alexandra looked stunning in the Abbey in her dress designed by Norman Hartnell, one of the great couturiers of the 1950s, but she was still unable to wear everyday clothes with style. She was growing up at a time of great changes in fashion, when the New Look which followed the end of the war had been replaced with an equally unbecoming line. The trend was for unflattering ankle-strap shoes, heavy flared skirts to mid-calf and tight, close-fitting hats which could only be worn to real advantage by women of natural elegance like Marina. They were of no help to Alexandra. Perhaps Marina's one failure at this time was an inability to recognize that, rather than follow the more rigid and staid ideas of designers like Hartnell, Alexandra needed youthful clothes more suited to her own age group. It was ironic that in 1953, when the mother remained a leader of fashion in Britain and her taste was followed and copied by women in France and America, the daughter by her side often appeared dowdy and old-fashioned.

It was unfortunate that, when Alexandra made her first royal tour starting on 13 October 1953, which took the party through the heart of industrial Lancashire, no one was impressed by the dull chestnut brown beaver-trimmed coat that she wore. Only her gay, red, head-hugging hat aroused any favourable comment. Marina had hoped that the two-day tour, which included visits to print works at Accrington, five cotton mills at Padiham and Nelson, and dyeing and bleaching machinery at Broad Oak, would give Alexandra a happy experience of royal duties. But she was bitterly disappointed. The tour, which had been organized by the Cotton Board, did little to boost Alexandra's hoped-for new image. Because of bad planning they arrived late for every function, and in an attempt to keep to the official schedule Marina and Alexandra were often driven at speeds of up to eighty miles an hour to keep all their appointments. For mile after mile, as Alexandra and her mother sped through cobbled streets, aproned housewives and rain-soaked children who had braved the drizzling weather to cheer them on their way hardly caught a glimpse of the royal party. Individual managements and organizations had been given a free hand to choose the people who were to be presented to the royals, but although there were more than eighty official presentations on the first day, no workers were ever introduced to the royal couple. Despite last-minute cuts in the programme and the rush between appointments, the schedule could not be completed in time. At Nelson Alexandra and her mother were, through no fault of their own, an hour and a half late arriving at the Valley Mills. It was hardly surprising that on the last day, when they visited a research institute at Didsbury, they both looked pale and tired. Late that afternoon, at a reception given in Manchester Town Hall, the gauche Alexandra turned to her mother and, in a voice that echoed round the mayoral chamber, said, 'Are all engagements like this?' But the tour was not the unmitigated disaster that it had first seemed to be. Important people such as Lord Derby, the Lord Lieutenant of Lancashire, and Sir Raymond Streat, Chairman of the Cotton Board, had been deeply impressed by Alexandra's cheerfulness. In those two days she had shaken hands six hundred times, visited five cotton mills, a college, three exhibitions and three town halls packed with civic heads, and had taken every opportunity to reach out and shake hands with mill girls who had been standing for hours under leaden skies in the hope of catching a glimpse of a princess. It had been a badly bungled first royal tour for Alexandra, but the outcome was that she learned another lesson she was never to forget, the necessity for split-second timing on engagements.

One thing made Marina feel uneasy. Her daughter still lacked sophistication and complete ease of manner in public. How was she to overcome this problem? Marina's thoughts turned to her own family and to her own days in Paris when she was the same age as Alexandra. She wasted no time, and two weeks later Alexandra went to stay with her mother's old friends, the Comte de Paris, pretender to the French throne, and his wife who lived with their eleven children in the Manoir du Coeur Volant, a rambling, fifteen-roomed château at Louveciennes near Versailles, on the outskirts of Paris. Marina was sure that it was essential for Alexandra to have a period of freedom to develop away from home. The Comte's sister was the second wife of Marina's uncle, Prince Christopher of Greece. Marina felt that Alexandra could only benefit from mature French and exiled Greek influences similar to those which she had experienced in Paris when she was young. Alexandra reacted with enthusiasm to the plan that she should spend three days a week at the select Paris finishing school in the Rue de l'Amiral d'Estaing known simply as Mademoiselle Anita's. For that part of each week she would also be under the scrutiny of Marina's sister Olga, who lived nearby with her fifteen-year-old daughter, Alexandra's cousin, Princess Elizabeth of Yugoslavia. In sending her to Paris, Marina knew she was taking a risk. Unless Alexandra applied herself to the strict curriculum offered by Mademoiselle Anita and her highly qualified staff, and avoided the temptations of the French capital, her objective would never be realized.

Numerous eyebrows were raised among members of the Royal Family. Wouldn't an English school have been better? Hadn't the Queen and Princess Margaret succeeded without ever going to any such school? Wasn't it more important for Alexandra to remain at home carrying out engagements with her mother? Marina sat tight, said nothing and waited for results. She had set a time limit of six months on Alexandra's stay in Paris. Aware of a tense situation that was building up within the family, she knew that Alexandra must be ready to become a fully fledged working royal within that time. It was a slimmer, poised and quite beautiful seventeen-year-old Alexandra who returned home.

She discovered that in her absence her cousin Margaret's love for Group Captain Peter Townsend had been creating a rift within the ranks of the Royal Family. Only a short time before the coronation Margaret confessed to a hitherto unaware mother and sister that the divorced Townsend, now Deputy Master of the Royal Household, was the man she wanted to marry. What was extraordinary was that, although Townsend had been part of the royal scene and an intimate of them all, not the Queen, Prince Philip nor the Queen Mother had recognized the growing intensity of the relationship. It seemed perfectly normal to them that the couple should ride together in the grounds of Windsor Great Park and disappear for hours in the hills on the Balmoral Estate.

Marina, who had come to know and respect Townsend, had had her suspicions. She had never been a gossip and kept her thoughts to herself. She knew that if Margaret married a divorced royal servant, albeit the innocent party, it would present not only constitutional problems but an outcry that could only harm Elizabeth's new reign. When the scandal did break it was handled from start to finish in a glare of publicity and so badly mismanaged that there was genuine fear in government circles that the monarchy could be damaged. In June 1953, two weeks after the coronation and with undignified haste, Townsend was banished to the British Embassy in Brussels as air attaché. The only restriction imposed on the couple was that they should not meet for a year and thereafter only in circumstances of absolute discretion. In two years' time it would be seen how strong their love remained. Margaret, hurt by Townsend's enforced departure, petulant and emotionally lost, indulged in black moods or mindless pleasure-seeking. As she endured agonies of heartbreak, she lost her will to work. It was her misfortune to be public property when she most needed solitude and privacy.

On the evening of 26 October 1955 Princess Margaret and Peter Townsend met for ninety minutes at Clarence House. This marked the end of the affair. On 31 October she issued the following statement:

I would like it to be known that I have decided not to marry Group Captain Peter Townsend. I have been aware that, subject to my renouncing my rights of succession, it might have been possible for me to contract a civil marriage. But, mindful of the Church's teaching that Christian marriage is indissoluble, and conscious of my duty to the Commonwealth, I have resolved to put these considerations before any others.

I have reached this decision entirely alone, and in doing so I have been strengthened by the unfailing support and devotion of Group Captain Peter Townsend. I am deeply grateful for the concern of all those who have constantly prayed for my happiness.

MARGARET

In her distress the Queen was anxious to know when Alexandra would be ready to join the royal rota. Her great worry was that Margaret would either fail to turn up for engagements or flatly turn them down.

Marina was able to report to the Queen, who had always been

devoted to her young cousin, that Alexandra could be relied upon to take over any of Margaret's duties at short notice. Alexandra's support at the time of this crisis earned her the sovereign's lasting respect.

10

Edward Stands Firm

The death of his father when he was only six years old was the greatest disturbance that Edward, sixth Duke of Kent, ever had to contend with. It was to influence his development lastingly. Eddie, as he was known, retains a clear recollection of his father, though Alexandra, only a year younger, has no memory of the man who crashed to his death on a Scottish hillside in August 1942.

In the spring of 1935, when Marina told her husband that she was pregnant, he made up his mind that the baby would be a boy. He insisted that blue should be the dominant colour in the large, bright nursery on the second floor of 3 Belgrave Square, only permitting a few touches of white in the chintz curtains and a rug worked in a nursery rhyme design. Weeks before the baby was due he insisted upon blue ribbons for the cot. Marina's labour began in a canopied Directoire bed on the morning of 8 October, and as shafts of pale autumnal sunlight played upon the bronzed and golden leaves on the trees in the square outside a steady stream of visitors arrived to offer a nervous George moral support. Among them were Marina's parents, Prince and Princess Nicholas of Greece, her sister Elizabeth, Countess Toerring-Jettenbach, from her home near Munich, and Foxy who, although she was no longer an employee, had become such an integral part of the Kents' life that it was unthinkable that any event of importance could take place without her presence.

For a time the father-to-be was at ease, but as the day wore on George became visibly paler and more drawn. Even the worldly Home Secretary of the day, whose presence at the residence of any royal birth was obligatory under the existing constitution, could not ease George's anxiety. Not eating, but drinking endless cups of coffee, George paced the room murmuring, 'I hope it will soon be over. I don't think I can stand much more of this.' At two o'clock in the morning of 9 October he was called to the side of his wife after she had given birth to a boy, seventh in line of succession to the throne. He was to be called Edward George Nicholas Paul Patrick.

George was devoted to his son. One of Marina's oldest and closest friends, the Polish-born Baroness Agnes de Stoeckl who lived on the Coppins Estate, often observed George with the baby. She wrote in her diary,

Every evening, instead of sitting late as usual, he leaves the table shortly after ten o'clock and carries his son to the nursery and lays him on his cot and stands watching and watching. Nanny told me that each night as he lays his son in his cot she discreetly leaves the room, but she can hear the Duke talking softly to him.

As well as a powerful and loving bond, father and son also shared an uncanny likeness. Even at Eddie's christening in the chapel of Buckingham Palace, when he was only six weeks old, relations observed that he already showed a family resemblance shared by his father and his three uncles, Edward VIII, George VI and the Duke of Gloucester. As the little boy grew older it became apparent that he had also inherited his father's mechanical mind. At four, lovingly watched by George, he could take a toy motor car to pieces and quickly reassemble it. When he was five and went to a London hospital to have his tonsils removed, he wanted to know how many bricks had been needed to construct the huge building. His mother could not provide him with a satisfactory answer and nor could the nurses. One evening, when the Matron entered Eddie's room where his father was reading aloud to him, Eddie cried, 'I know how many bricks there are in this building. My father has just told me. He knows everything!' George winked knowingly at the Matron.

No other royal child in recent generations has been deprived of a father at such an early age. George would probably have been a most modern-minded parent. He discussed putting Eddie's name down for Eton when the baby was only four months old, convinced that an education there would provide a sounder background for a royal prince than the more rigid discipline he had known and hated as a cadet at Dartmouth Naval College. He was intent that Eddie should enjoy his childhood and be allowed to develop in his own way as he grew up.

After George's death, and conscious of Eddie's position in the family as a royal duke, Marina was obviously worried about her ability to manage alone. Her greatest support was her brother-in-law, George VI, who had a deep sense of responsibility for the son of his dead brother. He had always wanted a son himself, but in 1942, when his wife was forty-two, he knew that the likelihood of an addition to his family of two daughters was remote. With the King to turn to for guidance Marina felt secure and both agreed that, with the war at a critical stage – the German onslaught on Russia was under way – there was no need to dwell on Eddie's future until he went to Eton in 1948.

The King died only months before Eddie ended his final term at Eton, leaving his mother with no strong man in the family to guide her and with a son who was more difficult to handle than his boisterous sister, Alexandra, or his happy and uncomplicated younger brother, Michael. Eddie could be a taciturn child, prone to the same sudden outbursts of temper that had been noted among male members of the family since the time of his great-grandfather, Edward VII. There were some difficult moments and Marina blamed much of this on the lack of a father and the petticoat-dominated world in which he spent so much time. Eddie missed his father and talked about him a great deal. Marina decided that her son needed occasional undivided attention from a man, preferably someone outside the family, who could handle these difficult moods better than she could. Her choice of friend and part-time tutor for her son was inspired. She approached a brilliant young history master at Eton, Giles St Aubyn, son of Lord St Leven who owned the historic and romantic castle, St Michael's Mount, lying half a mile off the coast at Marazion in Cornwall, and discussed her problem with him. It was this distinguished young academic, combining a natural empathy with a strong sense of humour, who provided Eddie with the firm guiding hand and stimulus he needed. He later became tutor to Prince Charles. During his vacations and at weekends St Aubyn took Eddie on walking holidays, arousing in him new enthusiasms and new interests. The attacks of asthma which had dogged Eddie since the death of his father became less severe. Gradually the boy became more assertive and showed a greater degree of self-confidence.

His performance at Eton, and later at Le Rosay School in Switzerland, was not outstanding. He had inherited his father's love of music, but not his brilliance. Nevertheless, Eddie was strong-willed and in his last days at Le Rosay, where the Swiss air had further eased his asthma, he made up his mind about his future. He wanted to become a professional soldier. The Army was to be the making of Eddie Kent. It turned a slouching youth of hesitant disposition into a man of bearing. Later, as a young officer, an Army posting was to bring about a chance encounter that was to change his life and mature him in a way that had never been thought possible.

When Eddie was at Sandhurst, Marina and Alexandra were jointly carrying out more public duties than any other members of the family. It was becoming increasingly difficult for them to operate with a skeleton staff from a tiny suite of rooms in Marlborough House. Coppins was no longer a practical permanent base for two working women who were travelling all over Britain and spending many evenings in London, attending functions which often did not end before midnight. The Queen, eventually, came up with a solution. Early in 1954 she suggested that the Kents should take over grace and favour apartments formerly occupied by the late Princess Louise, Duchess of Argyll and the daughter of Queen Victoria, in Kensington Palace. This would provide the London base they badly needed, and at the same time allow Marina to take over some of the official entertaining of visiting foreign dignitaries and statesmen that the hard-pressed Queen found difficult to manage in addition to her own heavy commitments. The offer of a home in the capital was long overdue and Marina was delighted. Yet this gesture, made at a time when every other senior member of the family had grace and favour residences in London, was to be clouded by public criticism.

When experts examined the Wren apartments in the south-west corner of Kensington Palace, unoccupied since the death of Princess Louise in 1939, they were dismayed. They found it so badly damaged by dry rot, death watch beetle and wartime incendiary bombs, and left in such a state of dilapidation, that restoration work would take at least a year to complete. There was doubt whether the seventeenth-century panelling, elaborate ceilings and fine wood carvings could be saved. The original estimate of £80,000 for repairs and alterations to the three-storeyed house proved totally inadequate. Restoration involved the complete relining of many rooms, a new roof, new windows, new plumbing and the installation of central heating – it had always been a cold house. Marina was deeply upset to learn that Conservative and Labour MPs were protesting about the expenditure on improvements authorized by the Minister of Works, Sir David Eccles. She, like the Queen, regarded her new home as part of the national heritage. In the

House of Commons Mr Percy Morris, Labour Member for Swansea West, wanted to know 'why the Minister is spending about £127,000 in adapting a house in Kensington Palace grounds, having regard to the urgent need for economy'. There was further criticism in the House over an Adam fireplace that the Ministry of Works had purchased the previous year, at a public sale at Halnaby Hall near Darlington, for the bargain price of £525. Marina was never mentioned by name and had no right of reply.

On 21 October 1955 it was finally announced in the Court Circular published in *The Times* that the Duchess of Kent had taken up residence in Kensington Palace. Although it was on three floors, the new Kent family home was not large by royal standards. The main living and reception rooms in the historic building were on the ground floor, and Marina and her children each had their own suites on the second floor. There were two spare rooms for guests.

Marina had always left the furnishing and decorating of her two homes, Belgrave Square and Coppins, in the hands of her late husband. Now she found herself sharing the refurbishing of Kensington Palace with Alexandra. Her daughter had inherited many of her father's artistic traits, but whereas George had made all the decisions on his own, Alexandra cheerfully encouraged her mother to make up her own mind about where to hang pictures, the kind of curtains to buy and how to arrange her father's objets d'art. From Coppins they brought most of what remained of his collection of snuff boxes, porcelain and books after so many had been sold to raise money. Marina was uncertain what to do with forty clocks of all shapes and sizes which George had bought over the years. Alexandra urged her to take most of them to Kensington Palace, where they ended up with as many as three clocks in some rooms. Each had to be wound up every day. A staff of six – a butler, a footman who doubled as a handyman, a cook and three maids – found themselves working in the most relaxed and undemanding of royal homes. Like the Queen, the Kents turned one of their sitting rooms into a family den filled with everyday clutter. Papers, magazines and books never had any special place. Occasionally Marina and her children lunched and dined off trays rather than face the formality of their fine dining room. There was a constant stream of visitors, friends of Eddie and Alexandra mixing easily with those of their mother. Over a period of many years by far the most popular family friend was the brilliant American comedian Danny Kaye, who went straight to Kensington

Palace or Coppins on his frequent visits to Britain. He was a man of
great understanding who established a close rapport with Marina.
From childhood Eddie, Alexandra and Michael had some of their most
hilarious times with Danny, who often sent them into hysterical and
uncontrollable laughter but who also played rough and tumble games
which endeared him to them all.

It may seem strange that, after the death of her husband, Marina's
name was never romantically linked with anyone. Even in the early days
of her bereavement not one member of the Royal Family thought she
would marry again. She never did. She found her stimulation in the
company of men like Kaye, Cecil Beaton, Noël Coward and Malcolm
Sargent: amusing, witty and attentive people who asked nothing more
than platonic friendship. For Marina there was no replacement for her
late husband.

It was not, however, that Marina did not receive proposals of
marriage. In April 1957 Marina turned down the chance of becoming
Queen of Norway. In a quaint and old-fashioned way she was invited to
meet Crown Prince Olaf of Norway, a fifty-four-year-old athletic
widower, specifically with a view to matrimony. In September that year
he became King Olaf of Norway. The proposal reached Marina
through royal channels reminiscent of procedures used in arranged
marriages of bygone days. Prince Olaf selected his friend, the tall,
handsome King Frederick of Denmark, to be his courier in offering his
hand in marriage to Marina. King Frederick arranged a quiet lunch
with the Queen Mother at Clarence House, where he explained Prince
Olaf's hopes and asked the Queen Mother to accept the role of second
courier. The message he gave was that Prince Olaf hoped that Marina
would be his guest for a few weeks in Norway, and over lunch a few days
later the Queen Mother passed on the message to Marina. Olaf had been
born in Britain and studied economics at Oxford, and although he knew
many members of the Royal Family he had met Marina briefly on two
occasions only, the last time at the coronation in June 1953. He had
been constantly urged to remarry after the death in 1954 of his wife,
Crown Princess Martha, and various names had been suggested to him
as possible candidates for the role of the future Queen of Norway,
including the thirty-eight-year-old Princess Thyra of Mecklenburg-
Schwerin. However, the one person to whom Prince Olaf was drawn
and to whom he felt he could offer a more fulfilling life in Oslo than
continued widowhood in London was Marina. But his offer was

graciously declined. Through the Queen Mother Marina expressed her thanks to the Norwegian Crown Prince for his proposal, but regretted that she had no intention of marrying at any time. Her children were, she said, her whole life.

As far as her children and their future marriages were concerned, Marina had an ambivalent attitude. She wanted them to be happy, but her great hope was that they would find partners of wealth and standing. In 1957 she was still having difficulty in balancing her budget, even though most of the running expenses of Kensington Palace were met by the state. She had received a small bequest and a few items of jewellery on the death of Queen Mary in 1953, and later a small legacy from her mother, Princess Nicholas of Greece, who had died from a heart attack in Athens in March 1957 at the age of seventy-five. Apart from the allowance provided by the Queen and her personal limited investments, she had no other resources. It was because she was intent upon maintaining the lifestyle of a royal duchess – as she was expected to do as a working member of the family – that she was constantly faced with financial problems. Entertaining was often a costly business when guests included Sir Winston and Lady Churchill, politicians and international statesmen and their wives.

Marina always began her day, as recorded by Peter Russell in *Butler Royal*, with breakfast served on a tray in her bedroom. Generally lunch was a very simple meal, clear consommé followed by a casserole, steak and kidney pie or fillet steak with boiled potatoes, broccoli spears, asparagus tips or baby brussels sprouts. There was always a wide selection of cheeses from a shop in Kensington or Fortnum and Mason's. Greek cheeses were very popular. Luncheon visitors were given French or German wines, but Greek guests preferred retsina and ouzo. Afternoon tea was at 4.30, accompanied by toast, croissants or crumpets. There was a silver kettle with a methylated spirit burner underneath. Sometimes Marina gave instructions, 'Just a cup of tea today.' Dinner was generally much the same as lunch. If there were guests the starter would be fresh asparagus, then fish – sole, salmon or lobster – usually followed by a roast or game, pudding, a savoury, dessert or cheese with a range of wines to go with them. For large parties Marina was obliged to hire staff from a reputable agency. During one of her economy drives Marina decided to have a picnic lunch in the palace. This consisted of ham and apple tart. Members of the Royal Family were regular visitors, and when the Queen, Prince Philip or the Queen

Mother were expected the front door was always left open so that they could walk straight into the house. All other guests, royal or not, found the door shut and had to ring the doorbell.

In the summer of 1957, when Marina was contemplating a further sale of paintings in order to raise money, she continued to instil a sense of thrift into her children. Eddie had to manage on his Army pay; Alexandra was careful over her wardrobe, and Michael was on limited pocket money at Eton. Only for state functions and special occasions did Marina and Alexandra wear clothes from haute couture houses, which were often loaned to them. Instead they often turned to Marks and Spencer's and to cheaper, popular designers such as Susan Small. They found that investment in good accessories, with the addition of dazzling brooches, clasps and pearls, transformed reasonably priced, simple dresses.

While she wanted her children to be comfortably off, Marina feared that the freedom she had given them, especially to Eddie, now permanently away from home, might backfire. She hoped their heads would rule their hearts if they made an unwise friendship. Looking back over the years, she could recall many emotional upheavals in the family. After the abdication she had watched the difficulties which beset Elizabeth and Philip during their courtship when the possessive attitude of George VI caused his elder daughter a great deal of unhappiness before he finally gave his permission for the engagement to be announced. She had also seen the development of the love affair of Margaret and Peter Townsend which had brought deep rifts and bitterness to the family, lasting long after the relationship was over. While Elizabeth and Philip were well matched and happy, Margaret in 1957 was often depressed and irritable. She showed little enthusiasm for royal duties, and while her royal lifestyle remained secure Townsend's once brilliant career had been dashed to pieces.

Like Queen Mary before her, Marina had great faith in arranged marriages. Both Eddie and Alexandra knew this. It was to be the only serious difference between Marina and her two elder children. While at home they would question any notion that they should show greater interest in distantly related people of their own age who belonged to other royal houses in Europe. They went their own independent ways, completely disinterested in Marina's notions of possible suitors. 'Breeding will out,' said Marina, but brother and sister held their ground. As it happened, Marina had little cause for concern, since her two elder children naturally gravitated towards people of the opposite sex whom they had known in childhood or who were related in some way to families close to the Royal Family. Their choice of friends was quite unlike those of the Queen's younger children, Princess Anne and later Prince Andrew and Prince Edward, who moved in circles that had no connections whatsoever with royalty or the aristocracy. Prince Andrew was just as much at ease having dinner in a suburban house in Ealing in west London, the flat of a model or a girl in show business as he was in a large house of the aristocracy.

Marina realized that, while her own marriage had been a love match, without the intervention of Queen Mary she might never have had the opportunity to get to know George well enough for her to have fallen in love with him. She longed to play the role for Eddie and Alexandra that Queen Mary had done for her, cherishing the hope that one, or both, would renew European royal links, perhaps with Greece, in a new generation. She was not successful.

At Sandhurst, and after he was commissioned as a second lieutenant in the Royal Scots Greys in 1955, Eddie's escapades and indulgences gave frequent cause for concern. Like his father he had a passion for fast cars and crashed two of them, narrowly escaping death in June 1956 when he was knocked unconscious and admitted to the National Hospital for Nervous Diseases in London. He was often seen in night clubs until the early hours of the morning and seemed set on a pleasure-seeking private life. In the summer of 1956 it came as a bitter blow to learn that he had been posted with his regiment to Catterick camp in the North Riding of Yorkshire, where the kind of social life he enjoyed was non-existent. Eddie was befriended by his aunt, the Princess Royal, who regularly invited her nephew to lunch at Harewood House near Leeds. Alexandra, too, arranged introductions to some of her old schoolfriends in the area, who were only too delighted to invite the eligible young Army officer to dinners and parties. But Eddie was bored and frustrated, and yearned for London.

It was the habit of Sir William Worsley, Lord Lieutenant of the North Riding, to invite new young officers at Catterick to lunch at Hovingham Hall, his eighteenth-century manor house set in an estate of great beech and oak trees twenty miles north-east of York. On the last Sunday in October 1956 Sir William invited ten people to lunch. The fine old dining room was filled with Hepplewhite and Chippendale furniture. Four of the guests were Army officers from Catterick, among them Eddie who, only three weeks earlier, had celebrated his twenty-first birthday at Coppins when every member of the Royal Family, including the Queen and Prince Philip, had joined in the celebrations. For Eddie the luncheon party at Hovingham was a welcome escape from tough training exercises and it seemed to pass off uneventfully. Sir William's daughter, twenty-three-year-old Katharine, the only daughter in a family of three boys, talked to Eddie about music and art and escorted him on a tour of the family's collection of old masters and contemporary drawings. When they reached the most recent portrait, a study of Katharine herself painted by Sir Timothy Eden, Eddie observed, 'Ah, but it doesn't do you justice, Miss Worsley.'

Hovingham Hall, although much larger and far more splendid, reminded Eddie of Coppins. It exuded an easy atmosphere and in the weeks that followed that first visit Eddie became a regular visitor, relaxing in a home full of chintz-covered armchairs, well-filled book-cases, fine old furniture and walls lined with family portraits. They went to dances – once to a fancy dress ball – and listened to gramophone records. Eddie knew he was in love. Later, he explained to Katharine that he would not be able to see her over Christmas: it was *de rigueur* for him to join the Queen and the rest of the Royal Family at Sandringham. Christmas Eve at the vast red-brick Victorian mansion near the Wash in Norfolk found the young army officer restless and ill at ease, nothing like his usual ebullient self. He remained preoccupied on Christmas Day, and after lunch Eddie sought out his mother. Marina knew that her son had been befriended by Sir William Worsley and his family, and was grateful for all the hospitality they had extended to him. She was, however, not prepared for what Eddie had to say. He wanted her permission to ask the Queen if he could leave Sandringham on Boxing Day in order to drive to Hovingham to see Katharine Worsley. Marina was angry. Since the early days of Queen Victoria's rule it had been an unwritten rule that every member of the family spent the festive season with the sovereign and remained there until well after the New Year. She said that for Eddie to approach the Queen with such an unheard of request would be a severe breach of protocol and quite out of the question. Marina was adamant. Eddie Kent was devoted to his mother, but times were changing. Later that afternoon, before tea was served in the great drawing room of Sandringham House, Eddie encountered the Queen. He told his cousin that he was in love and wanted to see Katharine. Would the Queen give her blessing for him to leave

Sandringham on Boxing Day? The Queen's answer was immediate.
Yes, he could go to Yorkshire and she wished him well.

Marina was not only displeased by the outrageously independent line
taken by her son, she was also alarmed. Eddie was impulsive and
immature for his age. His father had not married until he was thirty-
one, by which time he had had broad experience of life and, equally
important, established himself as a man of stature in the Royal Family.
Eddie was far less secure. He had only once been abroad in a semi-
official capacity and that had been aimed at helping to increase his self-
confidence and to mark the end of his years at Eton. Marina had asked
for Eddie to accompany her on a six-week state visit to Malaya and the
Far East in 1952 when he celebrated his seventeenth birthday at
Government House in Singapore. That was an occasion Marina preferred to forget. Eddie had been presented with a Malayan dagger with
which to cut a special birthday cake, and had been shown how to use the
knife in a Malayan manner with a swing and an overhead flourish.
Young Eddie had swung the knife and, as he did so, struck his mother in
the eye. Blood had poured profusely down her face, but by a miracle the
blade only nicked the corner of her eye and the accident left no lasting
damage. Eddie had changed a great deal since that terrible day when,
for a few moments, he thought he had either killed or blinded her. For
Marina, however, he was still immature for his age and certainly far too
young to become romantically involved with any girl. He was only
twenty-one and neither old enough nor responsible enough to consider
marriage. If Marina had any doubts about Katharine Worsley it was not
something she could easily pinpoint. Although Katharine was not of
royal rank, and did not have any experience in public life, her
background was impeccable. For Marina the problem was that the
difference in age between Eddie and Katharine threw his own
immaturity into relief. She doubted his readiness for the responsibilities of marriage.

The Worsleys could trace their family tree back to the eleventh
century, and their forbears had lived in the village of Hovingham since
1723. By a strange coincidence Hovingham had been one of the royal
stops when Eddie's father had paid an official visit to North Yorkshire
when Katharine was six years old. For a brief moment he had taken the
little girl in his arms and answered questions put to him in her piping
little voice. Marina could not fault her parents. Sir William Worsley
was a man of distinction who in his capacity as Lord Lieutenant of

the North Riding had been a guest with his wife at the Queen's coronation in June 1953.

Her education had been sound, first at St Margaret's School at Castle Howard and later at Runton Hill School, both in Yorkshire, followed by a period as a kindergarten teacher in Kensington. An early ambition to take an entrance examination for one of the women's colleges and follow her elder brothers, Marcus, John and Oliver, to Oxford had faded. At the end of two years at an Oxford finishing school Katharine's only serious interest had been assisting her arthritic mother with some of her charity work. Marina had little doubt that, with help and guidance from herself, Katharine had all the basic qualities for a future Duchess of Kent. But was she capable of coping with her young-for-his-age elder son? Marina doubted it. However, she could not bring herself to dismiss Katharine Worsley as just another of Eddie's passing fancies. Going over her head and asking the Queen for permission to leave Sandringham at Christmas was evidence of far deeper feelings. It was also further evidence of a new strength and stubbornness in Eddie, reminiscent of his father. A few weeks later, instead of spending his 1957 Easter leave at Coppins, Eddie accepted an invitation to be at Hovingham Hall with Katharine and her family. Marina pondered her next move.

She decided to invite Katharine Worsley to spend the Whitsun weekend in May at Coppins. As Eddie sat behind the wheel of his Sunbeam Talbot with Katharine at his side and headed down the Great North Road for his Buckinghamshire home, he was hopeful that his mother would see his point of view. He felt sure of Katharine. Before the short holiday was over, however, he was to become a bitterly disappointed man, let down, for very different reasons, by the two women he loved most in the world – his mother and Katharine.

11

Katharine and Angus

One of the most unenviable private aspects of the Queen's life is that, as head of the Royal Family, she alone can make decisions over the important romances of close relatives. Under the Royal Marriages Act of 1772, designed to prevent members of the family contracting unsuitable or embarrassing alliances, those in line of succession to the throne must secure the Queen's consent if they wish to marry before the age of twenty-five. At twenty-two and seventh in line, Edward, Duke of Kent, deeply in love as he was with Katharine Worsley, came into this category in 1958. Faced with his mother's adamant refusal to allow him to marry on the grounds that he was too young, he could have gone over her head and asked his cousin, the Queen, to give him her blessing. But, wisely, he made no such move. It was Katharine, two years his senior, who made sure that Eddie's head ruled his heart.

The differences within the Kent family, with Princess Alexandra taking the side of her older brother, came just as the Queen was recovering from her unhappy first experience of the implications of the Act, concerning her sister, Princess Margaret, and Group Captain Peter Townsend. What had begun as a complicated love affair had turned into a national issue which had left the Queen exhausted. She never wanted to find herself in such an agonizing position again.

Fifteen months later, still saddened by these events, the Queen interrupted her annual winter holiday at Sandringham on the cold but bright morning of 6 January 1957 to attend a birthday party for her cousin, Princess Alexandra, who had been twenty-one on Christmas Day 1956. More than two hundred people were invited on Twelfth Night to a buffet supper at Kensington Palace, and danced to the music of Sid Phillips and his Band to celebrate. Among the guests was the fair-haired Katharine Worsley. Only a few members of the family were aware of the conflict between Marina and her elder son. The Queen's fear that she might once again become embroiled in an emotional drama in the family was allayed by Princess Marina. While prepared to keep the Queen fully in the picture, she was nevertheless determined to handle the matter of her son's marriage herself, hoping that Eddie would accept the advice she believed his father would have given had he been alive. In the face of his protestations she remained unyielding, taking the same firm line that she had in the past whenever strongly motivated over family issues. With the destiny of the Kents uppermost in her mind, she made it clear to her son that he could not marry until he was older and until she was convinced that he was sure of his feelings. Eddie pleaded and cajoled, but to no avail. He threatened to take matters into his own hands. For the first time in his life Eddie Kent recognized that his normally easy-going and tolerant mother could be adamant. A younger, sympathetic but wiser Princess Alexandra, who realized that the Queen would support Marina, warned her brother, 'They'll argue for delay. They always do.' The person who exercised the greatest restraining influence on him was Katharine. She, anyway, was in no mood to be rushed into marriage. She had grave doubts about her ability to fulfil the role of a royal duchess and, despite Eddie's encouragement, insisted that he gave her more time to think. She handled Eddie's wild suggestion that they should elope 'and hang the consequences' with gentle amusement. Had Katharine been a bold adventuress there is little doubt that the Kent story would have had a very different ending. The Queen would never have forgiven such an offence.

In the hope that, once having met her, they would help to persuade Marina to change her mind, Eddie began to introduce Katharine to other members of the family. In June 1957 she was invited to lunch with Eddie and the Queen Mother at Royal Lodge, a charming Georgian and Regency pink-washed house almost four miles down the Long Walk from Windsor Castle. As Lady Elizabeth Bowes-Lyon, the Queen Mother had known what it was like to be courted by a royal duke and to be thrust suddenly into the Royal Family. She had waited for more than a year before accepting a proposal from George VI when he was Duke of York. She was charmed by her nephew's quiet, somewhat self-effacing girlfriend, and fully understood Katharine's initial uncertainty. On 10 July 1957 Eddie was encouraged when the Queen and Prince Philip, on an official tour of Yorkshire, made a special detour to visit Hovingham Hall and meet Katharine with her parents, Sir William and Lady

Worsley. It was a relaxed occasion and, although Eddie's name was not mentioned, it was obvious to the Worsleys that this was no ordinary visit.

From their early encounters Marina recognized a basic strength in Katharine Worsley, an essential quality in a future partner for her elder son who had always needed her strong hand to curb his wilfulness and enthusiasm. In February 1958, when Eddie was posted for six weeks to Aldershot, he took Katharine to Clarence House to meet his cousin, Princess Margaret. The two women got on well but Margaret kept her own romantic secret to herself. Only a few months earlier, at a private dinner party given by her lady in waiting, Lady Elizabeth Cavendish, at her home in Cheyne Walk overlooking the Thames at Chelsea, she had met society photographer Anthony Armstrong-Jones for the first time. Margaret was more than sympathetic to Eddie, but she was in no position to intercede on his behalf. Other members of the family found Katharine quite charming and believed that she had all the potential qualities required for a future Duchess of Kent, only needing to gain greater confidence. She had a calming influence on Eddie and his devotion to her was touchingly obvious. Nevertheless the Queen, Prince Philip and the Queen Mother agreed with Marina that Eddie posed a problem. As a royal duke he could not afford to make a mistake in marriage. They wondered, 'Does he really know his own mind?' It was decided that Eddie must be told to wait.

No one had counted upon Katharine's own attitude to the prospect of becoming a member of the Royal Family. The more she moved in royal circles with Eddie, the more alarmed she became at what marriage into the family would entail. Princess Alexandra was her confidante and friend, but as Katharine observed the public lifestyle of her future sister-in-law she became increasingly anxious. Katharine was a home-loving girl who had only occasionally assisted her mother in her capacity as wife of the Lord Lieutenant at Yorkshire functions. Eddie did his best to diffuse her anxiety, although he could not deny that sooner or later his Army career would be interrupted by royal duties. When Katharine said that she could never face a great wedding in Westminster Abbey, Eddie came up with a romantic solution. They could, if she wished, marry in the small church at Hovingham with as little fuss as possible. He put this idea to his mother, without avail. It only served further to convince Marina that her son was still too inexperienced and too impulsive to marry and settle down.

Everything came to a head in August 1958 when Eddie learned to his dismay that in the autumn he was being posted to Germany for two years. Once again he pleaded with Marina to allow him to marry so that Katharine could join him. His departure for Europe gave Marina her opportunity. She presented Eddie with an ultimatum. She said she would only reconsider her decision if Eddie and Katharine agreed not to see each other for a year. On 9 October 1958 Eddie celebrated his twenty-third birthday at Hovingham Hall with Katharine and her parents. Unhappy and distressed, the couple agreed to accept Marina's edict. Five days later Eddie flew from London Airport to Hanover with his regiment.

It was Katharine Worsley, with all her sound commonsense, who successfully averted a second emotional drama for the Queen. Eddie was all for defying his family, marrying Katharine and damning the consequences. Only the Yorkshire girl's wisdom made him come to terms with the real significance of Marina's move. She recognized that unless they proved that their love could stand the test of time and separation, they were lost. She had seen enough of the self-discipline exercised by the Royal Family to know that Eddie, as a senior duke, must not be found lacking. Of equal importance, and despite her own distress, Katharine was not prepared to join Eddie in any rash escapade that would inevitably become a scandal involving not only the Kents and the Worsleys, but also the Queen. How could they face a future together without the blessing of the Queen and Marina? Parting, said Katharine, was inevitable.

This was bold advice. Katharine could not be sure that the young officer she loved, gregarious and sought after because he was royal, might not become lonely and find someone else. To make life more bearable in his absence she said she planned to visit her brother John and his family in Toronto and friends in the United States. This only added to Eddie's unease. Would Katharine be swept off her feet by someone else when she was on the other side of the Atlantic, a man who did not present her with anxieties about life as a member of the Royal Family? In the event they remained faithful to one another. Eddie found escape in off-duty hours at racetracks in Holland and Germany, and on the few occasions when he was in England he was only ever seen in the company of one other girl – his sister and trusted ally, Princess Alexandra. For much of the time when she was in Canada Katharine was depressed, and for days on end her brother could not persuade her to leave the house. When she returned to Hovingham friends assumed – and she said nothing to the contrary – that she had been only a passing fancy for the Duke of Kent. By the summer of 1959, when even the Queen and the Queen Mother were inclined to the view that the couple had been separated for long enough, Marina insisted that the unwritten contract she had made with them must be observed until the time limit was up. In this she had the full support of Sir William and Lady Worsley.

With the rank of temporary captain and posted to the War Office in London, Eddie Kent, excited and overjoyed at the prospect of seeing Katharine for the first time in over a year, flew home from Germany in November 1959. Katharine arrived at Kensington Palace to discover that Eddie had arrived there before her. In his haste to greet her as she stepped into the hall he stumbled, fell down a steep flight of stairs and broke a bone in his foot. Far worse, they discovered that the year-long wait was not to be rewarded with permission to announce their engagement. During their separation Princess Margaret had fallen in love with Anthony Armstrong-Jones and she, as a senior member of the family, must have priority in the announcement of a betrothal. This was made on 26 February 1960. The couple were to be married in Westminster Abbey on 6 May 1960. The word from the Queen was that, regrettably, Eddie and Katharine must postpone their engagement and their marriage. She said there could not be two royal weddings in the same year.

Not until 8 March 1961, six years after their first meeting at Hovingham, did they become engaged. That same week Katharine had her first experience of court formality when she attended a state dinner in Buckingham Palace for the Commonwealth Prime Ministers. She was relaxed and at ease, for she had been well tutored. In the last year, while she and Eddie had been unofficially engaged, Marina and Princess Alexandra had dispelled her fears and built up her confidence so much that she quite simply gave every appearance of looking forward to being royal. Her steadying influence on her future husband had been impressive, and when Katharine said she would prefer to be married in York Minster and not Westminster Abbey, the Queen deferred to her wishes. The restrictions imposed upon the couple by Marina, with the support of the Queen and the Queen Mother, were hard, and it is unlikely that any of the present generation of the family would accept them. Yet in the case of the Duke of Kent the challenge of facing up to a parting from the woman he loved developed in him qualities that might otherwise have lain dormant. The years of waiting transformed a somewhat feckless, playboy youth into a man of dignity with a sense of purpose.

The wedding of Princess Margaret in May 1960, followed by the Kent engagement· in March 1961, eclipsed the fact that Princess Alexandra was fully occupied with public engagements. An arduous five-week tour of Australia in 1959 had been celebrated with a dinner and dance in her honour given by the Queen at Buckingham Palace. In September 1960 she represented the Queen at the independence celebrations in Nigeria, where she read the Queen's speech from the throne of Parliament House in Lagos. One success followed close upon the heels of another, and in November 1960 the Queen made her a Dame of the Grand Cross of the Royal Victorian Order, a rare order only given for 'personal service to the Sovereign'. During the aftermath of the Townsend affair, when Princess Margaret suffered bouts of depression, Alexandra had frequently stood in for her cousin at public engagements, often at very short notice. There were other ways, too, in which she had pleased the Queen, who appointed her cousin a Counsellor of State when she and Prince Philip paid a state visit to Italy in May 1961.

Alexandra never quite captured her mother's charisma, even though they bore a striking resemblance to one another. Nevertheless a natural spontaneity, thoughtfulness and meticulous attention to detail contributed to Alexandra being voted the most popular member of the Royal Family after the Queen. Her name was often linked with young men of aristocratic background, but when she celebrated her twenty-fifth birthday in 1961 there was no indication outside the family that she had anyone seriously in mind. She actively enjoyed her job, especially the ever-increasing amount of travelling which that winter had taken her to Hong Kong, Japan, Burma and Thailand. At an early age she had come to accept royal duties, happy to spend much of her time in the company of distinguished men and women so much older than herself. As much at ease with statesmen, presidents and diplomats abroad as she was with factory managers and civic dignitaries at home, she was essentially the first princess with whom the public could identify easily. When she made speeches it was in a rich, deep voice and she was always cheerful. That she thoroughly enjoyed her job came over very clearly. Her work schedule was heavy, and when she had some free time she danced and dined with a small coterie of friends, many of whom she had known all her life.

Marina, who had had none of the anxieties over Alexandra that she experienced with the emotional Eddie, was glad that her daughter showed no signs of rushing into marriage. She herself had married at the age of twenty-seven and felt that this was about the right time for a girl to consider settling down. She wanted Alexandra to enjoy her youth without the added responsibilities of a family. For Alexandra every official journey abroad was an exhilarating adventure, and with her youth and infectious enthusiasm she presented a new, refreshing image of British royalty that people had not seen before. She formed a close friendship with the King and Queen of Thailand which is still maintained today. Marina often pondered over the attitude a prospective son-in-law might adopt over Alexandra's job which, she knew, she would never relinquish. Anthony Armstrong-Jones, then in his second year of marriage, and ennobled as Lord Snowdon, had not found a satisfactory independent working lifestyle of his own and his boredom, on the rare occasions when he accompanied Princess Margaret on engagements, was all too obvious. Marina had never enthused over the Snowdon marriage, if only because she regarded Armstong-Jones as unlikely to respond to the discipline demanded from members of the family in their private as well as public lives. She held the conviction that this was something that could never be learned overnight by a commoner. Fundamentally, though, it was a matter of temperament, a quality she recognized in Katharine Worsley but thought had eluded the bohemian Armstrong-Jones.

The ideal husband for Alexandra would be a man with a knowledge of the Royal Family that would enable him to enter fully into the nature of her working life, which now seemed to be essential for her personal wellbeing and future development. Over the years there was only one man whom Alexandra had been devoted. He was eight years her senior, and she had known him eight years. Angus Ogilvy was the second son of the twelfth Earl of Airlie, who had been close to the Royal Family all his life and was the scion of one of the most patrician Scottish families. Their history was woven in the plaid of Highland history and could be traced back to an Earl of Angus in 1138. An old ballad, still sung in the hills, is called 'The Bonnie House of Airlie'. His father owned two estates, both with castles – one with 600,000 acres, Corachy Castle in Kirriemuir, where Angus was born, and another at Airlie –

and had been lord in waiting to George V and Lord Chamberlain to the Queen Mother. His grandmother, Mabell, Lady Airlie, had been one of Queen Mary's closest friends. He and his elder brother, David, the present Earl of Airlie and also Lord Chamberlain, had known the Queen and Princess Margaret since childhood, and his younger brother, James, became a close friend of Eddie Kent when they were at Eton together.

Compulsory post-war national service had made it impossible for Angus to go straight from Eton to university. Instead, during 1946–48 he first served in the ranks with the Scots Guards, his father's regiment. During a period in Austria as an Army ski instructor he took a bad fall, injured his back and had to have a plastic kneecap inserted. His service years, which included seven months in Malaya, left him yearning for some form of adventure, but in the meantime he settled for Trinity College, Oxford, where in 1950 he attained an honours degree in Modern Greats – economics, history and philosophy. It was his good fortune that his tutor in economics, the man who developed his acumen for City life, was the Labour intellectual, the late Tony Crosland. When Angus left Oxford, still undecided about what to do with the rest of his life, he astonished the Airlies by joining the Merchant Navy and signing up on an old freighter bound for the Baltic ports. His spell at sea was short-lived. Twelve days of constant seasickness in an appalling North Sea gale scuppered any notion that he could become a sailor. He signed off at Hamburg. There were other odd escapades when he was young. He once worked in the kitchens of the Savoy Hotel for a few days. Following this unsettled period he had begun to work in the City, and at this time first met Alexandra.

Shortly before Marina went on an official tour of the Far East in 1953 she invited Angus to lunch at Coppins to talk about Malaya, where he had felt so much at home as a national serviceman. Princess Alexandra, who had recently left Heathfield School, was unimpressed by the visitor, who teased her. Their next encounter was by chance, but could never have happened if Angus had not belonged to a family close to the Queen. The Airlies, with their six sons, were part of the trusted, closely knit circle of the Queen's personal friends, accustomed to attending the same family gatherings of weddings, christenings and funerals and joining in the same house parties.

Among the Queen's favourite hosts were Sir Harold and Lady Zia Wernher at Luton Hoo in Bedfordshire. Here, where she always spent her wedding anniversary, the Queen relaxed more than with any other friends, one of her greatest bonds with the Wernhers being their love and support of the British turf. Lady Wernher, christened Anastasia but known as Zia, had great public support as a racehorse owner and her green and yellow colours were famous. Her most popular horse was perhaps Meld, a triple classic winner in 1955 of the One Thousand Guineas, the Oaks and the St Leger. Like Marina, another great friend, she was of Russian ancestry. Her great-grandfather was the Tsar Nicholas I, and her father Grand Duke Michael of Russia. With her husband, the son of a diamond magnate and a millionaire industrialist in his own right, she had a cosmopolitan outlook that charmed the Queen. It was by no means unusual, therefore, that Alexandra and Ogilvy were included among the guests at a Luton Hoo house party given one August weekend in 1956. In the splendour of a home that contained priceless works of art and Fabergé objets, set in gardens laid out by Capability Brown, they met again. Angus, a somewhat with-drawn man of twenty-six, was amused and entertained by the young princess who was now so much more sure of herself and so elegant.

From that beginning they began to see more of each other. They coincidentally moved in the same circles, and when Alexandra was not working and Angus not on a business trip abroad they often found themselves invited to the same cocktail and dinner parties. His familiarity with the Royal Family automatically made him one of the few men with whom Alexandra was totally at ease. She became a frequent visitor to his modest flat at 17 Park West, a modern block near Marble Arch, and later to his larger, white-painted Georgian town house with a pillared entrance, one of fourteen in Culross Street, Mayfair. On the patio which led off the drawing room into the small garden she found that, with her chain-smoking companion, she could discuss and receive sound advice about her royal patronages. Regarded by many people as a dark horse, Angus was more than a bright business executive. He was a caring man, already actively involved in several charitable organizations including the Friends of the Poor and on the finance committee of the National Association of Youth Clubs. With his ever-increasing number of directorships in companies having such diverse interests as goldmines, supermarkets and cattle breeding, many people in the City saw him as a tycoon in the making, developing on similar lines to his successful older brother David, a merchant banker.

Both Angus and Alexandra enjoyed riding, tennis and the theatre, but their mutual passion was music. Alexandra is an outstanding pianist who could well have reached concert standard if she had had the inclination. One side of Angus's personality that appealed to Alexandra, however, was his complete understanding of the royal life and royal duties which meant so much to her. He also shared the same wide interests of her much travelled relatives, which gave zest to all their lives. Marina recognized these compatibilities as she observed the increasing closeness between her daughter and the second son of the Earl of Airlie.

Some people never fully understood Marina's hope that her children might one day find partners within one of the European royal houses. She herself had been an important agent for change within the family, in that she had revolutionized the upbringing of royal children by ensuring that her own three children grew up unfettered by protocol. She had kept their feet on the ground by making sure their young heads were never turned after visits to Buckingham Palace, with its liveried footmen, or by the grandeur of Sandringham and Balmoral. Her aim was never to separate them from their heritage, but to make her children realize that the social position and vast wealth of the sovereign's immediate family would never be shared by them, even though they were certainly privileged. That her children accepted this without any sense of resentment was another of Marina's great achievements.

She had no problem with sibling envy, unlike the less fortunate Queen Mother, who had difficulties with her second daughter, Princess Margaret, and later the Queen, who experienced similar problems with her second child, Princess Anne. As children and long into adulthood, both these princesses were affected by childish jealousy, Princess Margaret for her elder sister, the Queen, and Princess Anne for her elder brother, Prince Charles.

When her two elder children entered their late teens Marina's preoccupations with their possible future marriages was made clear to the Greek relatives with whom she was still so close. She recognized that this was a situation outside her control. The very independence she had given them made it unlikely that their future partners would be of her choosing. If they made a mistake in the selection of a wife or husband it would be a more critical issue than in her generation, since the Queen's success depended largely upon the support she received from junior branches of the family, who at that time were thin on the ground. The person who epitomized for Marina a modern royal mistake in marriage was her niece, Princess Margaret. She had fallen in love with Anthony Armstrong-Jones, successful in his own field as a photographer but unequipped by nature to be of real support to a member of the family. His world was too far apart to offer the understanding that Eddie, Alexandra and one day Michael would need.

For Katharine Worsley, as future Duchess of Kent, she envisaged problems, but at least not troubles of an unsurmountable nature. For the Hon. Angus Ogilvy she foresaw difficulties – but difficulties he would face head on, with the advantage of his early close contacts with royalty. In 1960, flanked by two children very much in love, she had every reason to be hopeful.

12

Two Weddings

Deaths and marriages always bring great changes to any family, but few people experience a more poignant sense of loss on the marriage of their children than a widowed royal mother in middle age. When Eddie married Marina was automatically deprived of her title as Duchess of Kent and decided to give up Coppins, which had been her home for twenty-six years.

After the wedding of Edward and Katharine Worsley on 8 June 1961, when her daughter-in-law became Duchess of Kent, Marina could, if she had wished, have been called the Dowager Duchess of Kent. However like all royal widows since the late eighteenth century she found this title grim, forbidding and at odds with her own image of herself. Instead she chose to be known simply as Princess Marina.

On the death of his father Coppins had been left in trust to Edward, who had inherited the property on his twenty-first birthday in October 1956. It had then remained the Kent family home, run by Marina until her son's engagement in March 1961. It is a curious aspect of twentieth-century royal marriages that no royal prince has ever chosen a bride of massive wealth, and Eddie was no exception. Katharine, who was to inherit £100,000 after the death of her father in 1973, had no private income. Generations before she married Eddie, the traditional dowry expected by princes of the blood royal from their brides had ended. George V married the almost penniless Princess Mary of Teck, George VI married Lady Elizabeth Bowes-Lyon, who had no private income, and Elizabeth II married Philip Mountbatten when he had a very small bank balance indeed. By the time Eddie proposed to Katharine he was in much the same position as any ordinary husband-to-be faced with the problem of supporting a wife without any expectation of extra monies. The young couple needed a home of their own but Eddie's only income was that of a captain in the Royal Scots Greys, and Marina told her son that there was no alternative but for her to move out of Coppins and live with Alexandra and Michael, when he was home from Eton, in the grace and favour apartments in Kensington Palace. Despite all attempts by the engaged couple to persuade Marina to share Coppins with them after their marriage, she insisted that they must enjoy married life without the encumbrance of a resident mother-in-law. To Alexander Koziell, grandson of her old friend, Baroness Agnes de Stoeckl, she observed, 'It was the only sensible thing to do.' She bade farewell to Coppins one afternoon in March 1961, taking with her only a few personal belongings. As she closed the door on her late husband's study she left it quite undisturbed, as it had been since his death. On the writing table was the last note he had ever written, now faded with time. It read, 'Please do not move anything on this desk.'

At the age of fifty-two and despite careful budgeting, Marina was still beset by the financial problems which had worried her throughout widowhood and which were never to be resolved in her lifetime. The costs of running Coppins, educating three children and maintaining (by royal standards) a relatively modest staff had often left her financially hard-pressed. In June 1960 she had been forced to sell off still more valuables, this time a rare collection of Fabergé and other items of sentimental value from childhood days, including a magnificent canteen of silver cutlery which had belonged to her parents and was used for family dinner parties. The sale at Sotheby's raised about £15,000 and Marina was confident that she and Alexandra, their working expenses covered by a special allowance from the Civil List, could now make ends meet without disposing of further heirlooms. For the young Duke of Kent the financial outlook was uncertain. At twenty-five he faced married life and the upkeep of Coppins and, apart from a few investments, was mainly dependent on his pay as an Army officer. He was hopeful that within a few years, when he began to carry out more royal duties, he too would receive some income from the Civil List like his mother and sister. While Marina harboured private doubts, Edward felt certain that somehow he would manage. It never occurred to him that one day, not so very far ahead, he would no longer be able to afford to keep up Coppins.

Yet in many ways their upbringing in a home far less wealthy than those of any of their relatives was to stand Edward and Alexandra in good stead when they fell in love. Eddie's passion for fast cars was short-lived. It began when he was nineteen and came to an abrupt end soon after he met Katharine Worsley. Her influence, even then, was powerful enough to curb what she regarded as a dangerous and extravagant pastime. When Alexandra discovered from Angus Ogilvy that his greatest anxiety was an income which he felt was insufficient for a royal princess, she was easily able to dispel his doubts. After spending so many years watching her mother's financial caution, she had not the slightest doubt that she could run her home on economical lines. Brother and sister had, by strange coincidence, met future partners who complemented them in a remarkable way. Eddie needed someone stronger and older than he, whilst Alexandra found a man who needed her confidence, and, later, her support through ill-health and financial adversity.

The first Kent in this generation to marry was Edward, who showed no immediate anxiety about the future on his wedding day. He may not have realized it at the time, but by choosing York Minster, built on the site of a church founded by Edwin, King of Northumbria, in 627, his bride saved the crown and the state a great deal of money. It was essentially a Yorkshire county wedding with a minimum of formality. It thus did not involve a costly procession to and from Buckingham Palace and Westminster Abbey. The only uniforms to be seen in the splendid setting of the Minster, with its glorious five sisters window in the north transept, were those of the Queen's Body Guard of the Honourable Corps of Gentlemen-at-Arms in their fine red tunics and plumed helmets of gleaming gold. Eddie, a tall, slim figure in the red tunic and full ceremonial dress of the Royal Scots Greys with the blue riband of the Grand Cross of the Victorian Order across his chest, impressed everyone. Standing at his side as they awaited the arrival of the bride was his brother Michael, in the dress uniform of a Sandhurst officer cadet. The Duke of Edinburgh was in the scarlet and black uniform of a field marshal. Softer hues were provided by the women in the Royal Family, the Queen in lilac, the Queen Mother in pale turquoise and Princess Margaret in ice blue. Marina outshone them all in gold silk. The vast Minster, however, was dominated by friends of the Worsleys, the men for the most part in well-used tight-fitting morning dress and carrying grey toppers, their wives in colourful summer hats and dresses. If the ceremony lacked the pageantry of Westminster Abbey it was more than outweighed by the simplicity of the service at the first royal wedding in York Minster for 633 years, when Edward III had married Philippa of Hainault in 1328.

A pale sun broke through grey skies outside, and then there was a dramatic fanfare of trumpets as Katharine entered the great west door on the arm of her father and walked towards the waiting Duke of Kent. She wore a gown of shimmering white silk, with gauze mounted within layers of organdie. There was a moment of near disaster when the fabric of the bride's long veil and train caught for a moment on the side of one of the pews, and for an instant it seemed as though her tiara, a gift from Marina which held the finely pleated veil in place, would crash to the floor. Quick action on the part of an observant usher saved the day. One of the great bonds between Marina and her daughter-in-law was their religious devotion, and the music for the service, the Toccata from Widor's Fifth Symphony, the Grand Choeur Dialogue by Eugène Gigour and Bach's Prelude and Fugue in E flat, was a joint decision. Yet Katharine surprised her mother-in-law in the choice of a favourite prayer attributed to St Francis of Assisi. Marina, who had never heard it before, found it so moving that she later learned it by heart. It was, indeed, remarkable, and is worth recalling since it meant so much to both the former and the new Duchess of Kent.

Lord, make us instruments of Thy Will; where there is hate may we bring love; where there is offence may we bring pardon; where there is discord may we bring peace; where there is error may we bring truth; where there is doubt may we bring faith; where there is despair may we bring hope; where there is darkness may we bring light.

Master, make us seek not so much to be consoled as to console, to be understood as to understand, to be loved as to love. For it is in giving that we receive; in self-forgetfulness that we find; in pardon that we are pardoned; in dying that we shall wake to the life eternal where Thou livest and reignest in the glory of the Blessed Trinity, one God, world without end.

Marina, with Alexandra at her side, was only a few feet away from the bridal couple as they exchanged their vows. Her eyes rested on her son's face. When he said in a firm and clear voice, 'With this ring I thee wed . . .' and placed a plain gold band on his bride's finger, tears welled in Marina's eyes. She opened a small coffee-coloured handbag and took out a white handkerchief. No one of Marina's age in the Royal Family was surprised that she was briefly overcome. Like the Queen Mother, the Duke and Duchess of Gloucester and Lord and Lady Mountbatten, she was startled at the bridegroom's powerful resemblance to his late father on his wedding day.

What made this the most informal of royal weddings for generations was Katharine's insistence that the reception should be held in the grounds of her family home, Hovingham Hall. There would be no speeches. This was a complete break in tradition – the customary highlights of royal weddings were the witty and amusing toasts at family wedding breakfasts in Buckingham Palace. Prince Philip, who had been at his mischievous best at the luncheon given at the Palace after the marriage of Princess Margaret and Anthony Armstrong-Jones in May 1960, was disappointed not to find himself in the same role again. Katharine made another break with the royal past: she did not allow her wedding presents to be displayed. The afternoon celebrations, with marquees on the green lawns of the Worsley home, became a relaxed family garden party where Yorkshire gentleman farmers, landowners, civic dignitaries and their wives mixed easily with royal guests. Queen Eugenie of Spain, a granddaughter of Queen Victoria, voted it 'one of the happiest of days'. That Lady Worsley had quite forgotten to curtsey to her only, and now royal, daughter, bothered no one, although in later years she always did so whenever she greeted the Duke and Duchess in public. By the time the bride and groom boarded a Heron aircraft of the Queen's Flight to spend the first part of their honeymoon at Birkhall, the Queen Mother's home on the Balmoral Estate, they were extremely hungry. They had been so flushed with happiness and excitement that, apart from sipping a glass of champagne, neither of them had tasted the splendid buffet of caviar, chicken and strawberries and cream. This had not passed unobserved by the Queen, who quietly arranged for a hamper of champagne, coffee and a large quantity of sandwiches to be sent to the RAF station at Linton before the couple took off for Dyce Airport in Aberdeenshire. As Eddie and Katharine continued their honeymoon in Majorca at the Villa Quiros, loaned to them by million-aire Rolls Royce chief Mr Whitney Straight, Marina may have wondered whether she would learn the date of the next wedding in the Kent family. If so, she did not have to wait for long.

The long romance between Alexandra and Angus Ogilvy was con-ducted so discreetly that when their engagement was announced on 29 November 1962, the anniversary of Marina's wedding twenty-eight years earlier, it came as a complete surprise to everyone outside their families and intimate circle of friends. Both Angus and Alexandra had been dismayed by the publicity that had surrounded Princess Margaret, first in her association with Peter Townsend and later at the time of her engagement, when Anthony Armstrong-Jones became a virtual prisoner in Buckingham Palace until his wedding day. They were determined not to find themselves in the same unhappy position. Princess Alexandra was then by far the most popular member of the Royal Family, and had her secret leaked out it could have had disastrous consequences. Angus, a sensitive and essentially retiring man, would not have enjoyed the pressure of the media. Together they deliberately planned false trails so that Alexandra was seen spending weekends at the family homes of aristocratic young men who were only too happy to act as decoys and guard the royal secret. Two of her best foils were the Marquess of Hamilton, heir of the Duke of Abercorn, and Lord O'Neil, the Irish peer who lived in Shane Castle, Co. Tyrone. She made sure she was seen dancing with her cousin, Crown Prince Constantine of Greece, three years her junior but whom many people felt Marina hoped she would one day marry. In Holland she was seen with Prince Karl of Hesse. Unlike Princess Margaret, Alexandra was not easily recognized in public and, wearing a headscarf and dark glasses, she was able to enjoy London with Angus without attracting much attention.

Although they had been devoted to one another for a long time, Angus was slow to propose because of what he felt might be the insurmountable problems that marriage to Alexandra would present to both of them. He was determined to continue with his professional career in the City and did not want to be involved in what he called 'the royal rounds'. The public life on which Alexandra thrived appalled him. At the same time he recognized that it would be wrong to ask Alexandra to consider carrying out fewer public duties just because she was a married woman. Work was her life blood and Angus could not envisage a satisfactory compromise. He was also very much aware that Marina regarded Anthony Armstrong-Jones as an unsuitable partner for Princess Margaret, not only because he was a commoner, but especially because after months of relentless pressure he insisted that for his own wellbeing he must be allowed to take up his work as a professional photographer again. In 1961 there was no reason for Angus to believe that a City businessman would be considered the right choice as a husband for Alexandra. Another factor which he felt to be against him was that he was not a man of means. He earned a very good salary and his personal investments were sound enough, but as the second son in the Airlie family he had no prospect of inheriting property or money. It was impossible for him to offer Alexandra the lifestyle that might have been expected from a prospective husband of a member of the

Royal Family – certainly the one who was the most popular princess in the country. But although Angus Ogilvy was a commoner in that he was not of royal blood, he had an aristocratic Scottish family lineage and close Airlie connections with Queen Mary and the Queen Mother. So he worried needlessly. It had been Princess Margaret and not the Queen who had been against Armstrong-Jones continuing with his career after marriage. Margaret felt strongly that it was her husband's duty to share in her public engagements, and in the early days of marriage her husband, still finding his feet in the Royal Family, acquiesced without revealing inner resentment. It was not until he got to know the Queen much better and became relaxed in her company that he actually raised the issue of his career with her. To Armstrong-Jones's surprise, the Queen not only applauded his idea of taking a job in his own professional field but urged him not to delay matters. How to bring Princess Margaret round to this way of thinking was to be their own affair.

In October 1962 the Queen Mother invited both Alexandra and Angus to a house party at Birkhall, her eighteenth-century white stone house lying slightly north of the River Muick about eight miles from Balmoral Castle. It was here, during a mild autumn weekend in the old-fashioned gardens filled with globe thistles and giant Himalayan lilies, that Angus asked Alexandra to marry him, and was accepted on the spot. There was no reason, they decided, why they could not both pursue their own careers just like any other married couple. Alexandra was actually glad that Angus had no desire to take any part in the official side of her life and this, had he known it earlier, was part of his initial attraction for her. That October weekend the couple went their separate ways on the Balmoral Estate to seek permission to marry. Angus went to Alt-na-Guitasach, one of the fine lodges in the grounds, where Marina was staying, and Alexandra to the castle to inform the Queen of her wish to marry. The news came as no surprise to members of the family, who had been quietly waiting for months to learn that Angus had proposed.

The Queen was so delighted by the match that for the first time in her reign she insisted on taking part in preparations for the wedding on 24 April 1963, which was in total contrast to the simple ceremony of the Duke and Duchess of Kent in June 1961. She was intrigued to discover that Alexandra had taken the unusual step, for royalty, of providing several London stores, including Harrods, with a list of desired wedding presents for the benefit of friends. Items on the list included a Zeiss Contaflex camera, table silver, decanters, glasses, kitchen and bed linen, an ironing board, a sewing machine and garden furniture. The Queen was determined that it should be a splendid occasion, and on the wedding eve gave a state ball for two thousand people at Windsor Castle, quite the most brilliant occasion staged at the fabulous royal residence since early in the reign of Queen Victoria. No expense was spared, and over a period of two months the great chandeliers in the State Apartments, which contain as many as eight thousand pieces of crystal, were taken down and each crystal prism washed and polished. New lighting was installed to spotlight priceless pictures and ornate carved ceilings. Accompanied by the Yeoman of the Pantry, the Queen went into the strong rooms of the castle, which houses hundreds of priceless pieces of gold and silver, and personally selected gold plate and table decorations for a private family dinner party before the ball. The State Apartments, which include the Rubens Room, once the King's Withdrawing Room, the King's Closet and the Queen's Closet, were opened and filled with spring flowers. Highly skilled craftsmen from the Windsor workshops, seamstresses, upholsterers, cabinet-makers, goldsmiths and metalsmiths, made sure that everything was in perfect order. The wedding ball was held in the magnificent Waterloo Chamber, one of the largest rooms in Europe, and looking down on the scene were great portraits by Sir Thomas Lawrence of sovereigns, statesmen and generals who had contributed in some way to the downfall of Napoleon; the vast room was decorated with a mass of hydrangeas, bold and beautiful in strong blues and pinks, and yellow, red and pink gladioli from Malta. With guests dancing to the music of Joe Loss and his Orchestra, and pipers of the Scots Guards for the Scottish reels, the ball lasted until four o'clock in the morning.

The wedding day dawned with sunshine streaking through an overcast sky as Alexandra left Kensington Palace for Westminster Abbey in a gown that was a triumph of simplicity, stateliness and sentiment. The Princess shunned the tight-waisted traditional style and instead chose a slender shaped shift with no seams, a high monastic round neck and long tight sleeves. Worked into the gown by the young London designer, John Cavanagh, was a piece of Valenciennes lace from the wedding gown of her Greek grandmother, Princess Nicholas, and some of the original lace from the train worn by Marina on her own wedding day.

The marriage of a descendant of the fourteenth-century Fair Maid of Kent and the Scottish family of Ogilvy lasted just over an hour. The Queen was looking slightly solemn as she saw her smiling young cousin and Angus come towards her, curtsey and bow respectively, and lead the way out of the Abbey, but she beamed with happiness as the couple stepped into the famous Glass Coach, used for royal weddings since 1923. For the first time for a hundred years the Queen gave Alexandra a reception in the magnificent state rooms of St James's Palace – two rooms built by James II in the early seventeenth century – and the Armoury and Tapestry Rooms, dating from the reign of Henry III.

Three days after Alexandra and Angus flew away on honeymoon to Spain, Marina left London on a private holiday with her sister. Young Michael was at Sandhurst. When she returned to Kensington Palace, Princess Marina, for whom family life had always meant a great deal, was quite alone.

13

The Kents and Freemasonry

Marina always hoped that her elder son would follow his father's footsteps. Shortly before he was posted to Hong Kong in November 1962 as second in command of C Squadron of the Royal Scots Greys, the Duke of Kent took a firm line over an issue that divided the men in the Royal Family. He was invited to join the freemasons, and agreed to do so. This required determination on his part since there was a powerful group of men close to the Queen who were strongly opposed to freemasonry. Headed by Lord Mountbatten, they took the view that the craft, which in Britain was formally set up in 1717 when Anthony Sayer, Gentleman, was appointed the first Grand Master of England, was an outmoded secret society which no longer served a useful purpose. They regarded freemasonry as a reactionary movement in opposition to their own creeds.

Considerable pressure was brought to bear upon the twenty-seven-year-old Duke to reconsider his decision but, despite the openly expressed antipathy of relatives much older than himself, including Mountbatten and Prince Philip, he refused to change his mind. One of the arguments he put forward was that his father had been a freemason and he thus wished to become one too.

Royal links with British freemasonry have always been cloaked in mystery, as are all masonic activities, but they have existed for centuries. England originally had four Grand Lodges and the oldest known was founded at the Apple Tree Tavern in Charles Street, Covent Garden in 1717. Members of this lodge trace their records back to a meeting of masons called in York in 926 by Athelstan, grandson of Alfred the Great, and the first man to be crowned King of England. Although freemasonry has long existed it evolved in Britain from the masons who built their religious edifices across Europe from the tenth to the sixteenth century. The distaff side of British monarchy has played an important part in the craft since the eighteenth century. The Kents have always held high masonic office and Edward, Duke of Kent, the father of Queen Victoria, was initiated as a mason in 1790. He later became Grand Master of the Ancient Grand Lodge in 1813. That year, with his brother the Duke of Sussex, he helped found the one United Grand Lodge of England in an Act of Union which still stands today.

Present-day royal involvement can be traced back to Frederick, Prince of Wales, the son of George II, who was initiated in 1737. Since then there have been twenty-three royal masons including Queen Victoria's father, and, of course, the present Duke of Kent's father who, as Prince George, was initiated in 1928 at the age of twenty-six.

Since the nineteenth century there has always been tacit royal support for freemasonry, even from men who declined to join. Prince Albert, for instance, was not a mason, but Queen Victoria became Patroness of the Masonic Girls' School in 1882. Their son, Edward VII, was initiated in Sweden in 1868 and with his wife, as Prince and Princess of Wales, opened a new wing of the school in 1891. George V rejected the craft but with Queen Mary he opened the Senior School for Girls at Rickmansworth in Hertfordshire. Both Edward VIII, as Prince of Wales, and George VI, as Duke of York, were initiated in 1919. The Queen Mother opened a new wing of the Royal Masonic Hospital in 1958 and new homes on behalf of the Royal Masonic Benevolent Institution at Oadby in Leicestershire in 1966.

The present Duke of Kent received no support from Prince Philip when he chose to follow in his father's footsteps. Philip had paid lip service to masonry in 1947 when he became engaged to the Queen, then Princess Elizabeth. His future father-in-law, George VI, had extracted a promise from him to join.

As Stephen Knight observed in *The Brotherhood*,

George died before Philip was able to fulfil the promise, but despite his own reservations (he regarded the whole thing as a silly joke), and his uncle's (Mountbatten) hostility, he felt bound to honour his promise to the King.

But having been initiated into Freemasonry as an Entered Apprentice, Philip felt honour was satisfied and he was free to act as he chose – which was to forget the whole business as quickly as possible, and while nominally a member of the Brotherhood, the Duke has taken no active part for thirty years and has refused all invitations to climb the masonic ladder and achieve grand rank.

When the Duke of Kent returned to Britain from Hong Kong in November 1963 with his wife and ten-month-old son and heir, George,

Earl of St Andrews, he came under close scrutiny from high-ranking freemasons. A successor was being sought for the Earl of Scarborough, the Grand Master of England and most senior mason in Britain. Was the Duke of Kent potential Grand Master material? The fact that, in view of Philip's disinterest, Eddie Kent was the only adult male member of the Royal Family available at the time was not in itself a deciding factor. Other qualifications were required, one of the most important of which was dedication to the craft. Lord Scarborough, Lord Chamberlain to the Queen from 1952 to 1963, was a tough act for Eddie to follow. A banker, he had a senior position in the Royal Household, was Lord Lieutenant of York and the West Riding, and above all he was a man of strong personality. As stage censor he banned the showing of such plays as *Cat on a Hot Tin Roof* by Tennessee Williams, and *A View from the Bridge* by Arthur Miller, though it was Scarborough who, in 1958, ended the ban on plays dealing with homosexuality provided they were 'sincere and serious'.

For three years Eddie worked hard at freemasonry; all members, especially those in high office, require a remarkable memory, for the mastery of secret rituals is demanding. In 1966 he succeeded Scarborough as Grand Master, subsequently marked by what Stephen Knight described as 'the greatest Masonic spectacular of all time – the 250th anniversary celebrations at the Royal Albert Hall in June 1967 when Masons from all over the world attended in full regalia and Arab Mason walked with Israeli Mason only ten days after the Six Days War'. There had been hopes that Prince Charles would follow the Duke of Kent into the brotherhood after his twenty-first birthday in 1969. However, perhaps influenced by Philip and Mountbatten, he said he did not want to join 'any secret society'. Prince Michael of Kent soon followed his elder brother. He was initiated in 1974 and became Provincial Grand Master of the Middlesex Lodge.

The Duchess of Kent and Princess Alexandra have attended masonic ladies' nights, held once a year, and are thus among the few women in Britain to know the identity of some of the most senior masons. In 1967 Princess Alexandra opened new homes for the Royal Masonic Benevolent Institution at Cramlington in Northumberland, and in 1982 the Duchess of Kent was present at the naming and dedication ceremony of the lifeboat *Duchess of Kent*, presented by the masons to the Royal National Lifeboat Institution.

There has been great speculation about members of the Royal Family who have become masons. After the death of Frederick, Prince of Wales, in 1751, he was followed by these royal figures (I in parentheses indicates the date of the initiation).

1766 Edward August, Duke of York (I)

1766 William Henry, Duke of Gloucester (I)

1767 Henry Frederick, Duke of Cumberland (I)

1786 William Henry, Duke of Clarence, later King William IV (I)

1787 George, Prince of Wales, later King George IV (I)

1787 Frederick, Duke of York (I)

1790 Edward, Duke of Kent, father of Queen Victoria (I)

1796 Ernest Augustus, Duke of Cumberland, King of Hanover (I)

1798 Augustus Frederick, Duke of Sussex (I)

1813 After the Prince of Wales became Prince Regent he resigned as Grand Master, a post he had held since 1790, and his brother the Duke of Sussex was elected Grand Master in his place

1813 Duke of Kent installed as Grand Master of Ancient Grand Lodge

1813 Duke of Sussex and Duke of Kent signed Articles of Union

1814 Duke of Sussex installed as Grand Master of the United Grand Lodge of England

1868 Prince Albert Edward, Prince of Wales, later King Edward VII, initiated in Sweden

1874 Prince Arthur, Duke of Connaught and Strathearn (I)

1874 Prince Leopold, Duke of Albany (I)

1885 Prince Albert Victor, Duke of Clarence and Avondale (I)

1911 Prince Arthur of Connaught (I)

1919 Prince Edward, Prince of Wales, later Edward VIII (I)

1919 Prince Albert, Duke of York, later George VI (I)

1928 Prince George, Duke of Kent (I)

1952 Duke of Edinburgh (I)

1963 Duke of Kent (I)

1966 Duke of Kent installed as Grand Master

1974 Prince Michael of Kent (I)

14

In Sickness and in Health

During the early summer of 1968 and in the twenty-sixth year of her widowhood, Princess Marina was looking forward to a holiday at the Italian home of her sister Olga in Florence. At sixty-one, but looking ten years younger, she had constantly taken on extra duties between 1960 and 1966 as four of her younger relatives became pregnant and temporarily relinquished their royal duties. The royal baby boom began when the Queen gave birth to Prince Andrew in February 1960 and then Prince Edward in March 1964, followed by Princess Margaret who gave birth to David, Viscount Linley in November 1961 and then Lady Sarah Armstrong-Jones in May 1964. The Duchess of Kent became the mother of George, Earl of St Andrews in June 1962 and Lady Helen Windsor in April 1964. Princess Alexandra had James Ogilvy in February 1964 and Marina Ogilvy in July 1966.

Although she was increasingly troubled by a weakness in her left leg which sometimes caused her to stumble, Marina gave no outward indication of anxiety. She took all her patronages seriously; when, as Chancellor of the left-wing University of Kent, she wanted to get to know some of the students better, she gave a garden party for sixty of them at Kensington Palace. It proved to be such an entertaining afternoon that the visitors left thirty minutes after the strictly appointed time. Marina, always astonished by her popularity, observed, 'Somehow I always thought you would have preferred an academic.' She had been on her feet for three hours. Like many of her parties, private or official, this one lacked grandeur and had a delightful impromptu atmosphere. When it was over the then President of the Student Union, Ruth Bundey, observed, 'She's wonderful. She understands us.'

During the rest of a taxing month, giving no hint about the weakness in her leg, Marina was at the Queen's birthday parade, presented awards to the Royal Geographical Society, toured Alexandra Rose Day depots in London, attended the Lawn Tennis Championship at Wimbledon as President of the All-England Lawn Tennis Association, and spent a day touring Rochester in Kent with the Friends of Rochester Cathedral. Whenever the opportunity presented itself she would pause to take the weight off her left leg, but not long enough for people to notice. On 19 July, for the first time in her royal working life, which had begun in the autumn of 1934, she cancelled a visit to the Frimley and Camberley Cadet Corps because of 'a slight knee injury'. Princess Alexandra carried out the engagement instead.

Marina dreaded the prospect of old age. Not long before, she had said, during a speech reported in the *Daily Telegraph*, 'It's bad enough to lose one's sight or hearing at any time in life. But it is worse when we are old. The loss of one's faculties nearly always means a loss of independence, and we all hate to be dependent on others.' Some months later she put it more fatalistically. 'We all grow old and we must face it. And most of us, I think, feel some anxiety as to what may be in store for us then. For whatever our misfortunes have been, the disabilities and infirmities of old age are universal.' They were not to be so for Marina. On 18 July 1968, after a bad tumble, she was admitted to the National Hospital in London for treatment to her leg and three days later returned home to Kensington Palace, advised by her doctors to cancel her holiday in Italy and take a complete rest. Convinced that she was suffering from some sort of rheumatism, she knelt in her bedroom on the morning of Sunday 25 August, saying prayers for her late husband on the anniversary of his air crash in Scotland in 1942. Shortly before lunchtime the next day she said, 'I feel tired. I think I will go to sleep.' Marina never recovered consciousness and died from an inoperable brain tumour on 27 August, not knowing the true nature of her illness.

The evening before her funeral on 30 August, according to her wishes, the body of the late Duke of Kent was taken from the vaults of St George's Chapel so that they could be buried side by side at Frogmore, the private royal burial grounds in Windsor Great Park. The service in the Chapel was essentially private, despite the hundred and fifty mourners headed by the Queen and including members of the British Royal Family and reigning and exiled monarchs from all over Europe. Held on a fresh day with a hint of autumn in the air, it was conducted by the then Archbishop of Canterbury, Dr Michael Ramsey, and by his side the Archimandrite Gregory Theodorus, Chancellor of the Greek diocese of Thyatira.

The service lasted for thirty minutes and included Psalm 23, 'The Lord Is My Shepherd', two hymns, 'He Who Would Valiant Be' and 'Lord of Our Life and God of Our Salvation'. There was also an anthem, the Collect hymn from the burial service of the Greek Orthodox Church of which Marina was a lifelong member. Two wreaths lay on the coffin which had been brought from Kensington Palace. A large one of red, pink and yellow roses was from the Duke and Duchess of Kent, Princess Alexandra and Angus Ogilvy, and Prince Michael, while a smaller one in blue and white, the Greek colours, was from her sister Olga.

Sitting behind the Queen near the altar in the second row of the Garter Stalls, pale and tense, was Marina's brother-in-law, the Duke of Windsor, who had flown to London from Paris where he then lived. On 21 March 1965, when the Duke was staying with his wife at Claridges Hotel in London, recuperating from three eye operations, Marina had made a dramatic gesture: she telephoned the ex-King, whom she had not seen since the abdication crisis in November 1936. Marina said that she would like to visit the Duke, who was actually to outlive her by seven years. When she walked into the second-floor suite of the exiled Windsors, the former Mrs Wallis Simpson curtseyed before her royal sister-in-law. And then they embraced. With tears in her eyes, Marina bent down and kissed her seated ailing brother-in-law. The trio, who had been close friends from Marina's wedding in November 1934 until the bitter days leading up to the abdication, never lost touch again. Marina promised the Windsors that her children would call and see them whenever they were in Paris, and Edward and Katharine, Alexandra and Angus, and Michael all did so on separate occasions. Through Marina's children, the Duke of Windsor renewed and strengthened his links with his family and was always stunned by his nephew Edward's likeness to George, the brother he had loved so dearly.

After death duties were paid Marina finally left only £17,398, one of the smallest sums ever left by a member of the Royal Family. She left £76,186 gross, but liabilities reduced it to £54,121 net. Then massive death duties of £36,723 (67 per cent of the net figure) had to be paid. These were so high because, although Marina had made considerable settlements on former employees, these gifts had been made within the previous seven years and so were liable to tax.

Of all the tributes paid to her one of the most moving was by the author Kenneth Rose, who knew the family well. He wrote in the

Sunday Telegraph, 'So the years passed, leaving scarcely a shadow on her beauty. The most adoring of mothers, she watched over her children with a fidelity that was not wholly maternal. She taught them that their lives belong as much to their country as to themselves.'

Sadly, the loss of their mother at a relatively early age was not the only burden that two of the Kents, Edward and Alexandra, had to bear. Both shared the same remarkably robust constitution of most members of the Royal Family and, like the Queen and the Queen Mother, had the sort of stamina that sustained them on trips abroad, during which they never displayed fatigue despite engagements which lasted from early morning until late at night. Although Marina had always been a heavy smoker, addicted to Turkish cigarettes, none of her children had copied the habit. They had been brought up among relatives who regarded physical fitness as vital. As very young children, when they were evacuated to Badminton House with Queen Mary, there had always been emphasis on outdoor activity. They were regularly roped in to join Queen Mary's Ivy Squad in her private battle against ivy when everyone, including grandchildren, equerries, ladies in waiting and four dispatch riders, was obliged to attack the creeper wherever it appeared in the grounds, on stonework, brickwork or trees. Their grandmother exacted the same concentrated effort from them which she threw into the work herself.

Later brother and sister became serious walkers when they spent part of their summer holidays at Balmoral. A day out on the Deeside estate meant several hours tramping over moorland, struggling through bracken with only a short pause for a picnic lunch before retracing their footsteps back to the castle for tea. An autumn or winter afternoon stroll with the Queen Mother could last until early evening. When dusk was falling she would appear out of the gloom in a worn mac and floppy rain hat with Edward and Alexandra on either side of her, quite unperturbed that anxiety might be mounting among members of her staff. For all the Kent children Christmas holidays meant long hours out of doors when, on the coldest of days, they went skating on the lake or rode or walked for miles with other members of the family and, after dinner, joined in energetic Scottish reels and other dances until the early hours of the morning.

It would have been surprising if either Edward or Alexandra had found partners with the same degree of energy. Although Marina could always relax with a book or listen to music, her children were far more attuned to the Queen and Prince Philip's pattern, which allowed no time for putting their feet up during the day. It is doubtful whether either of them ever saw a member of the family taking an afternoon nap. Both Katharine Worsley and Angus Ogilvy were relatively active people before they married, but their early days in the Royal Family taxed their physical fitness greatly. For Ogilvy, keeping up with his in-laws was not always easy. His back trouble, a legacy of the skiing accident he had had during national service, was exacerbated when, while swimming on his honeymoon in Spain, a small boat crashed into him. He made light of the pain, but as time went by he was unable to sit down for any length of time and often never managed to sleep for more than two hours at a stretch. Although he is a stable, well-balanced and self-disciplined man, blessed with a good sense of humour, his own false pride caused stress which did not ease his back. He turned down the Queen's offer of an earldom, an offer that had been accepted three years before by the only other commoner to marry a princess, Anthony Armstrong-Jones. Ogilvy said, 'I don't see why I should get a peerage just because I've married a Princess.' His wife gave him full support and, although no overt criticism was made by the Queen, his independent line did not find favour with his in-laws, in particular the Queen Mother. In 1963 the Queen held the view that it was the right of Alexandra's children, should she have any, to grow up with a title, and there was no reason to believe that she would ever think otherwise. Ogilvy's attitude, however, was to be of tremendous help to Princess Anne in 1970 when she cited his case after her engagement to Captain Mark Phillips. Neither Anne nor Mark wanted a title for their future children, and it was largely because Ogilvy had taken an independent line nine years earlier that the Queen reluctantly acquiesced.

Soon after he refused a title, Ogilvy adopted an independent attitude to another question. He declined the Queen's offer of a grace and favour residence in Kensington Palace which would have meant the couple could have lived rent free, in style, and with ample provision for Alexandra's hard-pressed official secretariat which at that time included three ladies in waiting. Instead Angus, with an income in the region of £60,000 a year, sold his house in Culross Street, Mayfair, and took out a mortgage of about £200,000 to buy the seventeenth-century Thatched House Lodge set in the heart of Richmond Park, seven miles south-west of Hyde Park Corner. In his determination not to be a kept man, Ogilvy believed that the purchase of a home for himself and Alexandra could only meet with approval. The Queen, however, was disappointed by his decision, since she did not regard her grace and favour offer as a royal perk, but a necessity for someone who travelled so much and worked as hard as Princess Alexandra. The Queen guards her prestigious grace and favour properties jealously and only busy members of the family, senior members of the Royal Household and, on occasion, retired Household officials of long standing stand any chance of ever living in one. An older and wiser Angus Ogilvy would probably have buried his pride, but in the early days of marriage, when he and Alexandra turned up for engagements in his rather battered but much-loved Jaguar, he was glad to have maintained some independence. The Ogilvys may have felt they could not accept the situation of Anthony Armstrong-Jones, who had had no choice but to come to terms with the inevitability of his wife's royal home. Armstrong-Jones was much less well off than Ogilvy and could never had afforded to provide Princess Margaret with the sort of home to which she had always been accustomed and would never have been prepared to relinquish.

The couple successfully pursued their own careers, with Angus occasionally joining his wife on foreign tours. However in 1969, six years after his marriage, Ogilvy had the misfortune to be linked with a City scandal that was to shatter not only his business career but his health as well.

Two years before his marriage Ogilvy had been invited by the financier Harley Drayton to join his group of companies which included a small mining concern with Rhodesian interests called Lonrho. Because Ogilvy had a good working knowledge of Africa he was asked to fly to Rhodesia to find someone with drive whom Drayton needed to develop the Lonrho enterprise. Ogilvy's choice was a man known as Tiny Rowland – because of his great height. Early in 1969, when there were rumours circulating in the City about sanction busting in Ian Smith's unilaterally independent Rhodesia, Ogilvy was secretly urged by Sir Burke Trend, secretary of the cabinet, to 'consider his position carefully'. In other words, he was being asked to resign from the Lonrho board. Ogilvy was reluctant to sacrifice personal independence and resign and received assurances from Lonrho's then chairman, Alan Ball, that there was no substance for the City gossip. Three years later Department of Trade inspectors accused Ogilvy of being 'negligent in his duties to an extent that merits severe criticism'.

Ogilvy issued a denial of all the charges, instancing '58 errors of fact' and more of omission in the report. Because the inspectors' charges were protected by privilege they could not be challenged in a court of law. For anyone marrying a relative of the Queen there can be no suggestion of impropriety in public at any level. Thus Ogilvy at once resigned from the sixteen directorships he held. It was eighteen months before the Director of Public Prosecutions cleared Ogilvy's name completely and ruled that no legal action should be taken. Had Ogilvy been a private individual and not married into the Royal Family, there would have been no reason whatsoever for him to have given up any of his City directorships. However, fearful that he might embarrass his wife or her family, he said that it was the only course open to him and 'the honourable thing to do'. His income was estimated to have been slashed from £90,000 to less than £9,000 a year and he admitted, 'From now on we'll be cutting our coat to suit our cloth. Thatched House Lodge may have to go. We'll see.' As it was, he had to sell 200 acres of land near Crieff in Perthshire, where he and Alexandra had one day hoped to build a modest holiday cottage. Ogilvy was left with few financial reserves. Ever since his marriage he had found himself in a not dissimilar situation to Marina. Over the years Princess Alexandra had received a rather inadequate allowance from the Civil List and her royal work had been continually subsidized by her husband. The subject of money has always been a royal blind spot, and the fact that no one close to the Queen ever pointed out the Ogilvys' invidious financial plight remains today quite incomprehensible to many people. Since it was not in their nature for either Alexandra or her husband to face the Queen with their difficulties, no move was made to provide the Princess with an allowance that fully covered her working expenses until ten years after her marriage.

Ogilvy had suffered bouts of ill health from the time he went into St Mary's Hospital, Paddington with gastro-intestinal problems in January 1965. His most troublesome year was 1973, when he was in and out of hospital with back trouble, had an attack of colitis and flew home from Montreal in a Jumbo jet, going straight into Westminster Hospital with a chest complaint. He had a painful experience during a visit to a museum in Sao Paulo, Brazil, when his plastic kneecap slipped out of position. The strain of waiting for his name to be cleared after the Lonrho affair played further havoc with his health and he was soon smoking more than sixty cigarettes a day and suffering severe back trouble, which exercise did little to alleviate. He sought help from many sources but even homeopathic treatment did little to ease his constant pain. Nevertheless Ogilvy remained cheerful, and to people who sympathized with him he invariably replied, 'When I look around me, especially in the charities I am involved in, I see people who are much worse off than myself.' One aftermath of the City disaster was a bout of pneumonia, the second in nine years. He was admitted to the King Edward VII Hospital for Officers in Beaumont Street, London, and advised to take a long rest.

Like other members of her family, Alexandra had been trained never to reveal her emotions in public, and by neither a look nor a glance did she indicate her deep concern about her husband's health. As the more physically robust partner in one of the most successful and down-to-earth of royal marriages, she provided Angus with all the support and light-hearted relief he needed to maintain his spirits. Unlike most of her older relatives, who could seldom bring themselves to discuss any form of illness, she recognized that with time on his hands Angus would be more prone to depression. One of the most effective ways in which she bolstered a flagging ego was by persuading him to join her on more royal tours. This not only eased their mutual sense of dismay on parting, but gave an added dimension to her visits on foreign trade missions. Ogilvy, who had an astute business brain, was a natural for this sort of tour. It was undoubtedly a loss for the Royal Family that he had hitherto opted out. His easy manner and shrewd understanding of industrial and commercial potential put him on a par with Prince Philip as a successful roving ambassador for Britain. The corner was turned for Ogilvy, in his temporarily blighted career, when he was invited to join Sotheby's, the fine art auctioneers, as a financial adviser; Sir Philip Hay, treasurer to his brother-in-law, the Duke of Kent, was already a director of the company.

As Angus regained his old enthusiasms, although never free from a debilitating back, his brother-in-law the Duke of Kent faced a health problem in his own family, one that was to be of long duration and which demanded enormous understanding on his part. It began when his wife Katharine, who had always longed for a large family, found herself pregnant for the fourth time in July 1976. Forty-four is not an ideal age for child-bearing but, even if a little anxious, she was deeply happy at the prospect of reopening the Kent nursery. She loved babies and motherhood, and active participation in nursery life meant more to her than to any other woman in the Royal Family. The timing of the baby could not have been better from her point of view. George, Earl of St Andrews and heir to the dukedom, was fourteen, Lady Helen Windsor was twelve, and Lord Nicholas Windsor was a sturdy six-year-old.

Earlier in the year her husband had given up his career as a professional soldier. Eddie's decision to leave the Army can be traced back to 1971, when as a major in the Royal Scots Greys he was unceremoniously recalled from Ulster after a tour of duty lasting only three weeks. It was felt in Whitehall that, as a cousin of the Queen, no matter how dedicated a soldier he was, he could not risk being made a potential target for the IRA. There were fears not only that he could be killed but also that he might be kidnapped. Despite Eddie's strong protests he was recalled to the mainland. He felt that he was being restricted at a time when his role in the Army had begun to matter. Encouraged by Lord Mountbatten, who had become something of a father figure to him, he bided his time before explaining his dilemma to the Queen – not only did he want a job, but he needed one that paid a salary. Until then royal princes had only taken honorary appointments, and Eddie had his doubts about his cousin's reaction. Mountbatten had none. He had already paved the way for Kent's request and, as he had so often done for other members of the family, he saw to it that the Queen was fully briefed before the encounter. As a result, she was both sympathetic and understanding and, in a dramatic concession to modern times, allowed a member of her family to join the board of a public company in a job that combined his qualities of leadership and organizational ability developed by the Army, plus his flair for languages. Like his younger brother, Michael, this was a gift he had inherited from George particularly, and from Marina. As a Sandhurst cadet he won the Modern Languages prize and passed a stiff examination to become a French interpreter. A two-year tour of Germany during 1963–65 with the British Army of the Rhine brought his fluency in German to a high standard. When the position of vice-chairmanship of the British Overseas Trade Board came up in January 1976 it offered him an opening as a professional ambassador for British exports and he seized it. It was also something of a coup for the BOTC. By virtue of his official tours abroad, Eddie was suited to international commercial affairs.

Ironically he was to find himself in much the same financial plight as his late mother and his sister. Like other junior members of the family he found his allowance from the Civil List insufficient to cover all his official expenses, so he subsidized them out of his own pocket. Like Marina and Alexandra he could never bring himself to ask the Queen to consider increasing his allowance, aware as he was that, had he done so, he might well have been told to cut his coat according to his cloth. Yet neither he nor his wife was extravagant. As with other minor royals, high-powered men and women who worked for them did so for salaries that were a pittance compared with what they could have earned outside royal service. The Kents even recycled paper in order to cut down costs. Unable to cope with the overheads of Coppins, and only after much heart-searching, Eddie finally sold the family home in 1974 for an estimated £160,000.

His financial burdens were eased when the Queen, urged by Lord Mountbatten, gave the Kents York House in St James's Palace where George, the previous Duke of Kent, had been given a suite of rooms in 1930 by his elder brother David, Prince of Wales. The house was fronted by Clarence House, home of the Queen Mother, and stood only a few yards from Marlborough House, the last home of Queen Mary. It was there that Katharine learned that she was expecting her fourth baby some time around her forty-fifth birthday on 22 February 1976. This would have made her the oldest member of the Royal Family to give birth since Queen Charlotte, wife of George III, had her fourteenth child, Princess Amelia, in August 1783 at the age of forty-five and three months. She was also seven years older than Queen Elizabeth II when she had Prince Edward, her fourth child, in 1966. Because the early months of pregnancy are regarded as the most hazardous, Katharine was advised to lighten her duties until the end of September. She had always been a devout practising Christian and her strongly held personal views on abortion were voiced to the British Congress of Obstetrics and Gynaecology on 6 July 1977 when she backed abortion controls and said, 'If there is abuse, it could easily become the accepted standard. Human life is sacred and uniquely valuable. It is a gift of God and, as such, must never be taken for granted.'

On 4 October the Duchess of Kent complained that she did not feel well, so her husband cut short an important diplomatic mission to Iran, saying that he must be with his wife at York House. By then they were not the only royal couple expecting a baby. Princess Anne and the Duchess of Gloucester were also pregnant. It was a tense and pale Duke of Kent who got behind the wheel of the family car and drove his wife to the Edward VII Hospital for Officers in Beaumont Street. The following day the royal medical team, headed by Dr Richard Bayliss, the Queen's physician, and Mr George Pinker, the Queen's surgeon-gynaecologist, revealed that there were complications in what was then the fifth month of Katharine's pregnancy.

On the night of 5 October, after a thirty-six-hour struggle, the royal doctors lost their fight to save the Kent baby. Within a very short time Katharine's close friend, Dr Donald Coggan, the Archbishop of Canterbury, arrived at the hospital and spent nearly half an hour with a deeply distressed husband and wife. More than anyone, Dr Coggan knew the extent of Katharine's joy at her pregnancy and recognized that her sense of loss might well not be easily overcome. It was a taut, grim-faced Duke of Kent who left the hospital many hours after the Archbishop, murmuring, 'I'm afraid she's lost the baby. . . .'

At first Katharine was subdued, but there seemed no reason for alarm. She left hospital on 9 October for York· House in time to celebrate her husband's forty-second birthday. She appeared to be restored to her old self on 27 October when she stepped out for the Silver Jubilee Fashion Spectacular at the New London Theatre, and was bright and elegant in her uniform as Commander-in-Chief when she visited the Women's Royal Army College in Camberley, Surrey on 27 November. She seemed radiant when she put on a donkey jacket, safety helmet and wellington boots to descend 1,000 feet into Murton Colliery in County Durham to meet miners underground on 23 February 1978. Yet all was far from well. The first clue came when she cut short an official visit to a production of Wagner's *Das Rheingold* by students of the Royal Northern College of Music in Manchester. She cancelled plans to accompany her husband to Venezuela when he opened a British industrial exhibition on 9 March and, later, a tour of New Zealand was quietly cancelled by Eddie after he had received medical advice that his wife was not only not up to the trip but also needed his support. On 23 April Katharine was again in hospital, this time for a gall bladder operation, and the degree of anxiety in the family was such that, instead of returning to York House, she went to stay with the much concerned Queen at Windsor Castle. During the following months Katharine continued to struggle with mounting depression, sometimes appearing to be quite well but later finding herself uncertain and forced to cancel engagements at short notice. In October 1978 there seemed good reason for optimism when she entered and passed a competitive voice test and joined the famous Bach Choir, founded in 1876, as a soprano. For Eddie, like so many husbands faced with a partner in a low state, the months dragged slowly as Katharine varied in mood. The death of her mother, Lady Worsley, in January 1979 was the final straw in Katharine's battle against depression. Two months later she was admitted to hospital and gallant relatives such as her sister-in-law, Mrs Penelope Worsley, married to Katharine's brother John, said, 'She's been working terribly hard lately and she is exhausted.' She was in hospital for six weeks, during which time only her husband, children and very close relatives were allowed to visit her. Doctors decided that no harm would come to her if she left hospital to rehearse with the Bach Choir for a performance of David Fanshawe's *African Sanctus* in the Royal Albert Hall, provided she returned to the hospital immediately afterwards.

For the best part of eight years Eddie Kent had to contend with his wife's fluctuating depression. She was by then in what is sometimes known as 'the middle years', when many women suffer a variety of emotional turmoils, mainly characterized by anxiety for the future, regrets for the past, and sometimes even more severe depressive symptoms. The Duchess of Kent was fortunate in having a devoted and understanding husband, and the support of a loyal as well as a Royal Family. Her travail had been made the harder because her physical health during those years was beset with problems, ending with the removal of an ovarian cyst in 1983. Perhaps, more important, she had suffered the bitter loss of the baby she so much wanted and, shortly afterwards, the death of her greatly loved mother. That she eventually recovered her full health and resumed her royal duties was a tribute not only to her own fundamental stability but to those who had walked so faithfully beside her through the dark years.

15

HRH Princess Michael of Kent

It was traumatic for thirty-two-year-old Prince William of Gloucester to give up a career in the Diplomatic Service in order to take over royal responsibilities from his ailing father, the Duke of Gloucester. A small weekend shooting party in February 1972 at the family home, Barnwell Manor, a few miles south-west of Peterborough in Northamptonshire, promised some light relief. The person in whom William wanted to confide was his cousin and close friend, Prince Michael of Kent, a major in the Royal Hussars and two years his junior. He, more than anyone else, understood William's reluctance to exchange personal freedom for public life. The two cousins had much in common. Neither of them had involved himself in royal duties and had rarely appeared on the balcony of Buckingham Palace except during childhood and early teenage years. They were both highly eligible bachelors who had played the field without, apparently, ever having had marriage seriously in mind. Prince William, who had been with the British High Commission in Nigeria and then served as second secretary in the commercial section of the British Embassy in Tokyo, had no choice but to return to England and assume the duties his father could no longer perform. Prince Michael, however, a professional soldier in the mechanized cavalry, had no such royal obligations. The Kents' official duties were successfully carried out by his elder brother Eddie, Duke of Kent, and his sister Princess Alexandra, leaving Michael free to pursue his Army career and his private life. Michael did his best to boost the flagging spirits of his cousin, who explained his problems in trying to run the 2,500-acre Barnwell Estate on a businesslike basis. His aim was to make the dairy and beef farms show a profit for the first time. His problems were short-lived, for he plunged to his death in an air crash near Wolverhampton on 28 August that year while taking part in the Goodyear Air Race. At the time, however, all that Michael could do was commiserate with his cousin, relieved by the knowledge that he would never find himself in the same predicament.

Born only seven weeks before the death of his father in the Scottish hills in August 1942, Michael had always been somewhat of a loner. He had inherited a deep sense of family loyalty from Princess Marina, who had a natural tendency to spoil her youngest son, bearing as he did an even more striking resemblance to his father than did his elder brother. As a little boy he experienced all the rough and tumble of a family of three children, but even Eddie and Alexandra spoiled their cheerful younger brother. Michael nevertheless developed a strong streak of independence and with it a passion for dangerous sports. He competed in international bobsleigh races and had several narrow escapes, took part in powerboat races and once almost broke his neck. His greatest enthusiasm, however, was for motor racing, and he drove in scores of gruelling rallies, winning many trophies, even though he was often up against far more experienced drivers than himself. He had his mother's gift for languages, was fluent in French and German, and became the first member of the family to master Russian. After the marriages of Eddie in 1961 and Alexandra in 1963, Marina, accustomed to being surrounded by her children and their friends, found her grace and favour home in Kensington Palace a sad and silent place. Preoccupied as her two elder children were with their new lives, it was Michael who became her closest confidant in her last years. On leave from Sandhurst and later from the 11th Hussars, he became her regular escort to the theatres and concerts they both loved. Mother and son would often spend quiet evenings listening to classical music.

Quite unlike the extrovert Alexandra and more academic than Eddie, Michael was known as the shy member of the Royal Family. This was because, like his cousin William, the company he sought out and enjoyed comprised either members of the Royal Family or his own small coterie of friends, many of whom he had known since childhood. Like so many of his relatives, however, he was not a reserved man; what he did fear was that people enjoyed his company not for his own sake but because he was a member of the Royal Family. He was haunted by the same spectre that faced William, who once said, 'The path of love is not easy for a modern Prince – or Princess. You never know whether a girl loves you for yourself or because she would like to be a future Duchess.' When either William or Michael ever appeared to be getting seriously involved with a member of the opposite sex it was always a sign that the relationship would soon break up. Neither cousin could ever put out of his mind the abdication of their Uncle David, who had given up his throne for the love of an American divorcee. Although the Act of Abdication had been signed in 1936, three years before the outbreak of war and before either of them was born, it was still the subject of deep bitterness in the family. Divorce remained anathema to senior relatives, especially the Queen Mother and, to a slightly lesser degree, the Queen. When the Queen's cousin, the Earl of Harewood, was sued for adultery in January 1967 by his wife, the former concert pianist Marion Stein, it marked the beginning of great coolness towards him by the Royal Family. The Earl, who was eighteenth in succession to the throne, had been living with his former secretary, Patricia Tuckwell, a divorced Australian, and had a son, Mark, by her in 1964. The divorce did not formally concern the Queen, but under the Royal Marriages Act her consent was required when George Harewood wanted to remarry – as he did in July 1967 when his decree became absolute. For years he was cold-shouldered by his relatives.

When William and Michael were spending the weekend with friends at Barnwell in 1972 they both knew that the marriage of their cousin, Princess Margaret, with Lord Snowdon was precarious. This only served to increase William and Michael's caution in their choice of girlfriends. Both remained wary and, like the Prince of Wales in the 1920s and 1930s, they tended to seek out the company of divorcees. It was as though at some level they felt less threatened by women who had been married before, women they could never contemplate marrying because of the Queen's attitude to divorce.

Among the guests at the Barnwell winter house party was a merchant banker called Tom Troubridge, an old friend of William's from Eton, and his wife, Marie-Christine, a striking six-footer with corn-coloured hair and blue-green eyes whose charm and wit enlivened any gathering. The Troubridges were a scintillating couple but there was no reason to suppose that that particular weekend would linger in anyone's mind. Both the royal cousins were intrigued by Marie-Christine, and Michael, introduced to her then for the first time, noticed that she spoke English with a slight accent not unlike that of his mother. Mrs Troubridge had a wide range of interests and was as knowledgeable about modern art as was Prince Michael. He confessed later, 'I was very struck by this tall Austrian lady. I was very impressed. I remember we had a long talk about the history of art sitting in a hut eating sausages.' Afterwards

Marie-Christine was to recall that first meeting like this, 'I just thought he was the funniest man I had ever met. We just kept laughing and talking together. But I didn't think he really "noticed" me at all. He was with such a pretty girl.' Yet this brief encounter was destined to end with the introduction into the Royal Family of a woman whose energy and sheer force of personality were to have a profound influence on them all.

The Troubridges disappeared from the London social scene in the summer of 1972 when Tom Troubridge was posted by his bank to Bahrain, a move which facilitated a trial separation which would cause the least comment. Marie-Christine visited him when he had been there six months and remained three weeks, just long enough to settle him into his house. She then returned to London, and to her thriving interior design company which she could not leave for long in view of the firm contracts she had undertaken.

Prince Michael had often been entertained by the Troubridges, although their friendship was not close. A while after her return he met Marie-Christine at a Red Cross luncheon, and thereafter began to 'run into' her in Richmond Park, knowing she rode there most mornings. For him, the cosmopolitan Marie-Christine possessed some of the powerful characteristics which had attracted his Uncle David, when he was Prince of Wales, to Mrs Simpson. She was witty, clever and highly organized in her personal life. Empathy, combined with a genuine interest in all that was going on about her, attracted men into her orbit, yet she did not deliberately play on her femininity. In style and personality Marie-Christine, like Mrs Simpson in the 1930s, had an unerring instinct for the best, which she combined with a real love of domesticity and dislike of ostentation. With her self-confidence she was able to take anyone in her stride, royal or otherwise. From the start Prince Michael found himself as much at ease in her company as his bachelor uncle had been with Mrs Simpson many years before. But that was where any similarity between the two women ended. Marie-Christine was an acknowledged beauty. She had an impressive lineage and had inherited all the resilience and staying power of generations of middle-European aristocracy.

Although they did not know it when they first met, Michael and Marie-Christine had a common ancestor in the seventeenth-century Landgrave of Hesse-Cassel – a tenuous royal link but nevertheless a significant one. Her parents came from families which had served in the courts of Europe for generations, some holding political office of consequence. Her Czech-born father from Silesia, Baron Gunther von Reibnitz, had married the Hungarian Countess Marianna Szapary, granddaughter of the last Austro-Hungarian ambassador to the pre-revolutionary court of St Petersburg, and great-granddaughter of the Prime Minister of Austria-Hungary in 1880. Marie-Christine also had distant family links with Prince Philip through marriages within the maternal – Szapary – side of her family.

Only months after Marie-Christine's birth on 15 January 1945 in Karlsbad, Czechoslovakia, her parents, along with many of their aristocratic friends, recognized that there would be no future for them in a Communist country. With the few valuables they could carry by hand they sought refuge in Austria, and with their tiny daughter and three-year-old son, Frederick, settled in Vienna where they had relatives and friends from affluent pre-war days. The Reibnitz family had a hard time, caught up in the turmoil of post-war Europe. Thousands of refugees from Czechoslovakia, Poland and Hungary were seeking a new sense of identity, security and purpose in Austria and other countries west of the Iron Curtain. After three years of struggling to make ends meet, the family broke up. In 1950 Marie-Christine's parents divorced. Her father remarried and sought a new life as a licensed wild-game hunter and running a citrus farm in Mozambique. Her mother, with great courage, little money and few contacts, sailed with her two small children to Australia. Her intention was to stay there until life returned to normal in Europe. But as it transpired, after settling for one small job after another in Sydney, she found happiness in a second marriage to another exiled European of Polish descent, Count Thadeus Rogala-Koczorowska. He had started his new life as a senior clerk in the surveyor's office in Sydney Town Hall. She owned, and ran herself, for a time a very successful beauty salon. The children grew up in a small bungalow on the outskirts of Sydney in a happy and united family where only French was spoken at home. A step-brother, Matthias, was born in 1956. Marie-Christine's mother was determined to give her daughter a sound education, and by exercising economies she was able to send her to a Catholic school in Rose Bay which had a fine scholastic record. In Marie-Christine the nuns had an apt pupil who worked hard, and because she grew so tall she was nicknamed the Amazon. Throughout her schooldays her great longing had been to see the father she could not remember, and in 1961, when her schooldays had ended and she was uncertain about a future career, at his invitation she travelled to Mozambique.

It was traumatic for her. As Marie-Christine was to explain later in a radio interview,

I was a little bit too young for university and I thought, well, it's time to go and meet the father I do not know. This proved to be a terrible shock in itself since he was much older than I had imagined and he could have been my grandfather. However, this was my introduction to Africa which became a great love in my life. I loved going on safari but I couldn't bear to see animals shot.

Travels took Marie-Christine back to Austria where she linked up with relatives, including many cousins whom she had never seen before. Life in Vienna, where most girls seemed content at the prospect of finding a suitable husband and settling down, had no appeal for Marie-Christine. Two years later, with introductions from her mother who had made friends in England from her pre-war skiing days (she had represented Hungary in the 1936 Olympics), Marie-Christine went to London to study interior design. In 1967, at the age of twenty-two, she arrived in the capital with no financial backing but with a driving ambition to succeed and set herself up in a business of her own. She said,

First of all I was an apprentice interior decorator and learned everything I could about architecture. I even did some carpentry and learned how to mix paints and so on before I spent some time studying at the Victoria and Albert Museum. Then I had a brief spell in an advertising agency because I wanted to know how to run my own business and needed to know how to run an office – enough to tell others [how] to work for me.

Six months later she launched Szapar Designs, named after her mother's Hungarian family. Commissions came in thick and fast. As she admitted, 'I did very well and made lots of money. It was very successful.'

Marie-Christine first met her future husband Tom Troubridge in London. The banker had various links with the Royal Family apart from his friendship with Prince William. His brother was flag officer on board the royal yacht *Britannia*, and in the course of his job came to be known by them all as a dedicated and highly entertaining naval officer. Tom was captivated by Marie-Christine and they were married in Chelsea Old Church on 15 September 1971. They were an ambitious and extrovert couple. Some guests at the wedding were convinced that the couple had exchanged heated words in the vestry shortly before the ceremony was over. Their marriage proved to be short-lived – the main problem was that Marie-Christine wanted children and her husband did not. After she returned to London, leaving Tom in Bahrain, Marie-Christine was depressed at the prospect of never having a family of her own. Later in the year it became obvious to the Troubridges that their marriage was virtually over. In the summer of 1977, when they had not lived together for more than three years, the marriage was dissolved. In April 1978 the Vatican agreed to an annulment on the grounds that Tom had refused to give his wife children.

By then Prince Michael, thirty-six and attached to Military Intelligence at the War Office, and Marie-Christine, three years younger, were deeply in love and wanted to marry. There were, however, major obstacles that first had to be overcome. Marie-Christine was a devout Catholic, and under the Act of Settlement of 1701 no member of the Royal Family in line of succession – and Michael was sixteenth – could marry a Roman Catholic. Secondly, under the Royal Marriages Act of 1772 no member of the Royal Family could marry without the sovereign's consent. In a state of agitation the couple turned for advice to Lord Mountbatten, the shrewd elder statesman who was often the first person whom members of the family consulted when they were in any sort of doubt or difficulty. In the first-floor sitting room of Mountbatten's London home in Kinnerton Street, Belgravia, with its pale blue walls and centrepiece of a low, glass-topped table which charted Lady Mountbatten's world tours between 1921 and 1939, Prince Michael expressed his nervousness about making a direct approach to the Queen. Mountbatten's counsel was that the couple should keep their love for one another secret until the right occasion presented itself, when he could tactfully raise the matter with the Queen at one of their regular tête-à-tête Tuesday dinners at Buckingham Palace. Although he did not want to raise false hopes, he felt that, provided the Queen did not feel she was being rushed into making a decision, he could see no reason why she should not give her blessing to the match. Within two weeks the Queen gladly gave her permission for the marriage. However, since Marie-Christine was a Catholic, Prince Michael automatically forfeited his rights to the throne.

What no one had envisaged, however, was Pope Paul VI's refusal to grant the couple the dispensation for a mixed marriage to be solemnized in church. This was attributed to the fact that Prince Michael had publicly stated that any children of the marriage would be brought up as Anglicans. The Pope's edict was all the more extraordinary since the Vatican had announced in 1970 that Catholics no longer had to promise, when marrying out of their faith, that children would necessarily be brought up as Catholics. Marie-Christine put it succinctly when she said, 'The real problem was that Michael could not have Catholic children.' The outcome was that the disappointed couple, who had hoped to be married in Vienna's Schottenkirche, had to be content with the civil ceremony, which was to take place in the neo-Gothic Vienna Town Hall on 30 June 1978.

The Queen, privately incensed by the papal ruling, was determined that a strong family contingency should attend the wedding. It was headed by Lord Mountbatten and included Princess Anne, the Duke and Duchess of Kent, their fourteen-year-old daughter Lady Helen Windsor, and Princess Alexandra and Angus Ogilvy. She also insisted the the wedding luncheon should be given at the British Embassy in Vienna and hosted by the British ambassador, Mr Hugh Morgan. On the wedding day, without making any specific reference to his second cousin's marriage, Prince Charles launched a bitter attack on church leaders. Speaking at the opening of the Salvation Army's International Congress at Wembley, he said that Christians were still arguing about doctrinal matters 'which can only bring needless distress to a number of people'. He praised the Salvationists for having a Christianity 'unfettered by academic or theological concern for dogma or doctrine'. Whereas the Queen was forced to remain discreetly silent on the matter, Prince Charles had left no one in any doubt about his views.

Recalling the wedding, Marie-Christine observed,

We were always going to have a civil wedding followed by a church wedding because that is the law in Austria and most European countries. We missed out on the religious marriage but we had a wedding ball in Vienna. Michael and I opened the ball with the 'Gold and Silver Waltz' by Lehar. My husband said, 'Waltz?' and I said 'Waltz.' He murmured 'One, two, three, one, two, three . . .' and I said, 'No, darling. Spin at quarter time.' And that was the last time I ever said, 'Follow me, I shall lead.' He never quite got over the dizzying speed of the waltz but it started our adventure in life together.

The couple agree to spend their wedding night apart so that Marie-Christine could attend a private mass the following morning to set a personal religious seal on the marriage. A few days before they returned to London, after honeymooning in India and Iran, they had a moving experience in Paris. Marie-Christine, intrigued by the love story of the Windsors, had always longed to meet the Duchess. Prince Michael had come to know the Duke and Duchess well a number of years before when he spent some time in Paris studying Russian. He, naturally, would not have liked to have visited the city again without paying his respects to the Duchess; and, equally naturally, she would have wanted to meet his wife. The Duchess sent a message to the newly-weds, inviting them to visit her. And so they went one afternoon to the lovely house in the Bois de Boulogne which had been her and the late Duke's home for many years, to take tea. They never saw her again.

As it transpired they were the last members of the royal family to visit the Duchess of Windsor. The very few people close to the ailing and elderly woman believed that a friendly call from one of her husband's relatives would have provided a much needed mental boost. On the occasions when senior members of the royal family paid private visits to Paris, the medical team caring for the Duchess in her lonely home, waited hopefully for telephone calls that never came. As the years went by and the Duchess of Windsor became more and more enfeebled, it became apparent that she was never destined to see another member of the House of Windsor again.

Distressed for her cousin and his wife at being denied a church wedding, the Queen registered her own approval of the marriage by giving them a welcome-home reception in the seldom used magnificent State Apartments of St James's Palace. She also gave the Kents a grace and favour home in Kensington Palace, one of the most enchanting royal residences in London. It has a maze of cobbled passageways and the courtyards are still lit by gas lamps. For Marie-Christine, now Her Royal Highness Princess Michael of Kent, the high-ceilinged rooms were an exciting challenge which demanded and received all her expertise as an interior decorator. No. 10 Kensington Palace, their official address, was once described by Princess Margaret, who lived there during the early days of her marriage to Lord Snowdon, as 'a doll's house'. For Marie-Christine, however, the four-storey house (to which she added a roof garden in 1980) was a joy and soon she had transformed the beautifully proportioned ground-floor drawing room, dining room and panelled hall and the suite of fine first-floor bedrooms. It soon became obvious to her royal in-laws that Marie-Christine was also in the process of transforming the life of her young husband. For Marie-Christine the most important part of her new life in the Royal

Family was work, and she took on official duties, at Lord Mountbatten's suggestion, to familiarise the public with their unknown prince.

She appeared on the British public scene at a time when the Royal Family had great need of a woman with poise, elegance, style and a sense of fun. At thirty, Prince Charles had not committed himself to marriage, so there was still no future Princess of Wales in sight. Princess Anne had married Captain Mark Phillips in November 1973 and already had one child, Peter. She worked hard but had built up an image of irritability, partly because she was unable to come to terms with the constant intrusion that was part and parcel of her role. Her tendency to pout or frown when in repose did nothing to help matters. After her divorce from Lord Snowdon on 26 May 1978 which became absolute on 11 July that year, Princess Margaret had initiated a friendship with Roddy Llewellyn, sixteen years her junior, which was the subject of constant criticism. Llewellyn, a landscape gardener and son of Lt-Col. Sir Harry Llewellyn, only encouraged further attacks when he returned from Princess Margaret's holiday villa on Mustique in the West Indies, saying, 'I don't care what they say about us. I shall go on seeing Princess Margaret when and where I like. Let them all criticise. I don't mind.' Less and less was heard of the Duchess of Kent, who was far from well, and the domesticated Danish-born Duchess of Gloucester, dedicated as she was to her job, was too quiet and retiring to make any real impact.

It was hardly surprising, therefore, that Prince and Princess Michael of Kent, obviously deeply in love and often seen hand in hand, soon captured the public imagination. Invitations flooded in from charities and other organizations, and Marie-Christine accepted them with a willingness that delighted her husband but left some of his relatives uneasy. The new Princess stepped out in style, wearing stunning clothes that outshone those of the other women in the family. She made it clear from the start that she loved being a royal princess. With an open and spontaneous manner, later to be seen in the Princess of Wales, she chatted freely to people, once admitting that she was often nervous before making a public appearance. 'I always say a little prayer, "Please don't let me make a gaffe," ' she said.

Her marriage gave Princess Michael a natural outlet for her abundant energies. She gave the impression that she loved 'being royal' and longed for the day when, like her in-laws, she too would be invited to plant commemorative trees, open hospital wings and perhaps even be made colonel-in-chief of a regiment. Dynamic and full of energy and ideas, she was overjoyed as more and more engagements piled on her willing shoulders. She did not want so much to be involved in pomp and pageantry as in everyday routine work which she regarded as duty for both herself and her husband because of their privileged position. If Princess Michael had been able to curb her enthusiasms and been prepared to stay quietly in the background for the first year or two of her marriage, she would have had fewer image problems. People sometimes found her pushy. Instead, while the Queen observed Michael's changed lifestyle with affection and some degree of amusement, Marie-Christine aroused envy among some royal relatives because she cut too much of a dash. By comparison at that time, Princess Margaret seemed old for her years and Princess Anne had little charisma. When women in the Royal Family walked into a crowded room they did so at a slow, well-regulated pace, smiling to the left, smiling to the right, pausing now and then to talk to an often prearranged group. For the most part conversation was stilted until people like the Queen Mother or Princess Alexandra, with their vast experience, put everyone at ease. Marie-Christine adopted a different manner. With her height and striking good looks she could make a grand entrance anywhere, effortlessly. Her habit was to ask direct questions and give honest replies, with the result that she had become well known as a stimulating and highly articulate princess. She was deeply hurt to discover that someone in the family had nicknamed her Princess Pushy, but not deterred.

When a gauche and naïve Viscount Linley made a snide remark about Princess Michael in November 1983 it boomeranged on him. Asked by a magazine what he would give his worst enemy for Christmas, he replied, 'Dinner with Princess Michael.' He was severely reprimanded by the Queen and his father, Lord Snowdon, and soon discovered how popular his second cousin-by-marriage was with the British public. Within forty-eight hours of Linley's comment appearing in the newspapers, Princess Michael was inundated with mail telling her to forget all about his remark.

She is devoted to cats and when one of her pets disappeared she received more than two thousand letters of sympathy. Seven moggies remain at the Kents' pleasant but unostentatious country house, Nether Lypiatt Manor near Stroud in Gloucestershire, but three favoured oriental cats travel backwards and forwards to London with her.

Spurred on by the support and encouragement of both her sisters-in-law, Princess Alexandra and the Duchess of Kent, Marie-Christine worked harder than ever. She ran her home on efficient and economic lines, the only member of the Royal Family to manage without a butler or a cook. She provided classic Austrian and continental dishes of *cordon bleu* standard for small dinner parties at which the guests were stimulating men and woman from the arts and politics including Leon Brittan, a future Home Secretary, the critic Bernard Levin, the then Foreign Secretary, Lord Carrington, Sir Roy Strong, head of the Victoria and Albert Museum, and the journalist Richard Kershaw. Only for larger cocktail parties did she employ outside caterers.

As was customary within the Royal family, the couple had been informed prior to their marriage of their own style and title and that of their children. So, when Princess Michael became pregnant in the summer of 1978, she knew that her baby would have an automatic right to a title. Whereas Princess Anne had caused the Queen considerable unhappiness by insisting that her children should be plain Master Phillips and Miss Phillips, Marie-Christine was happy to think that she and her husband's children should have a title. This would not be, as some might think, a rank bestowed by the Queen, but an example of earlier Royal foresight. As a result of a proclamation made by George V in 1917, when he made provision for titles to be borne by future members of the family, her son was entitled to the courtesy title of Lord. This was because George V, not wishing the change from prince to commoner to be too sudden, decreed that the younger sons in the third generation should rank as the younger sons of dukes.

Thus Lord Frederick Michael George David Louis Windsor was delivered on 6 April 1979 by the Queen's surgeon-gynaecologist, Mr George Pinker, in the Lindo Wing of St Mary's Hospital, Paddington, to be followed on 23 April 1981 by his sister, Lady Gabriella (after her maternal grandmother) Marina (after her paternal grandmother) Alexandra Ophelia Windsor. For Prince and Princess Michael their happiness was almost complete. In December 1980 Prince Michael left the Army. He was not eligible for promotion without commanding his regiment, which meant Northern Ireland. As he was considered a security risk, he was not permitted to serve there. So, he exchanged a military career for full-time employment in the City. In 1981 he accepted a directorship with Standard Telephones and Cables, the

British branch of the American multi-national STC, and in 1982 became a director of Aitken Hume Bank.

When they were first getting to know one another, Prince and Princess Michael found privacy riding together in Richmond Park. Princess Alexandra, the first member of the family to learn of the developing friendship, offered them the use of her stables in the grounds of Thatched House Lodge, her home in the Park, for saddling their horses. Princess Michael had ridden all her life and kept a horse at a private polo stable in Richmond for five years. In 1982, when they were spending more of their time at Nether Lypiatt Manor, their country home in Gloucestershire, Princess Michael began taking riding lessons at the Talland School of Equitation. Her family neighbours in the country were the Prince and Princess of Wales at Highgrove in the village of Tetbury and Princess Anne and Captain Mark Phillips at Gatcombe Park.

Princess Michael's instructor, Pamela Sivewright, impressed by her pupil's decision to take up eventing in 1983, two years before her fortieth birthday, observed, 'It is very commendable. She's not going to be the greatest rider in the world – there's no question of her doing a Badminton – but I think she will soon be winning ribbons.'

Princess Michael was undeterred by accidents. She damaged a shin-bone when her horse ran into an iron railing and for six weeks she was unable to wear boots. Another time she cut her face but turned up for an official engagement later the same evening. Towards the end of a faultless ride at one county event she had a setback. The show commentator observed, 'She made a complete botch of the fence. She lost the reins, she lost the stirrups. But she didn't lose her head. She stayed in the saddle, recovered herself and completed the course.'

Marie-Christine's determination to succeed in her new hobby encouraged her husband to take up carriage driving, a favourite sport of Prince Philip in middle age. Then in April 1984 when he was forty-one Prince Michael joined Prince Philip, Prince Charles and Prince Andrew when he qualified for his pilot's licence. Two months later he passed the Institute of Advanced Motorists' tough motor-cycle test on his four-year-old V-registered Honda CX 500 – twenty-two years after he passed the Institute's test as a motorist.

Six years after her marriage Princess Michael reflected upon her years as a member of the Royal Family and expressed the opinion that her early years would have been easier if Princess Marina had still been alive. In an interview with *Majesty* magazine, she said,

Everyone thinks that before you marry into the family you know what you are doing and what you are getting into. You know, I have heard comments that I *must* have known because the royal family is so *visible*. There is no way that you know what it's going to be like.

When my husband and I were courting, I saw the family, I had a jolly good look and I thought long and hard. I would have been much happier and I think I would have had a much easier transition into the family if I had had a mother-in-law to help me. The Duchess of Gloucester, for example, had the benefit of her mother-in-law, an older, benign guiding hand, as did my sister-in-law, the Duchess of Kent.

My husband hadn't a household of his own before our marriage, because he wasn't always around. He was a much loved, much younger member of the family who, as agreed a long time before, was doing his own thing.

And I think that if I had a mother-in-law, I would not have made some of the mistakes I made out of ignorance. I have had it said to me, 'Why didn't you ask for help?' But who *do* you ask? That said, I think lack of communication is one of the great problems in life today . . . we so often misunderstand one another. Admittedly, we didn't realise that we would be so public. My husband never had been, so we didn't think that anybody would find us all that interesting. We thought we'd be able to slip in under the woodwork.

Princess Michael was obviously sincere in what she said. What she perhaps did not realise was that she had unwittingly revealed the sense of loneliness that most men and women experience when they marry into the royal family and discover there is no set of rules to guide them. Nor do they receive any constructive words of criticism to help them – still less, occasional praise.

Ultimate happiness came for the couple in July 1983 when Princess Michael won her five-year fight to have her marriage recognized by the Roman Catholic Church. Pope John Paul II reversed the decision made by Pope Paul VI in June 1978 and gave his approval of the marriage and a service of validation – the term used for a service of approval. On 29 July 1983 Prince Michael, forty-three, and Princess Michael, thirty-eight, entered the tiny wood-lined private chapel in Archbishop House at Westminster Cathedral for the blessing of their marriage. Their vows were repeated before Monsignor Ralph Brown, Vicar-General of the Westminster Archdiocese, and witnessed by the Duke of Kent and Princess Alexandra. Princess Michael had flowers in her hair and wore the same cream silk Hardy Amies suit that she had worn on her wedding day in 1978. As well as establishing the marriage in the eyes of the Roman Catholic Church, the ceremony also meant that the Princess could once again receive Holy Communion. The couple brought their children up as Anglicans, and as regular churchgoers continued to attend a Church of England service one week and a Roman Catholic service the next.

Three years after her marriage Princess Michael returned to Australia on a five-day visit to Sydney, this time with her royal husband. They gave a party on a boat for all her old friends and a private lunch for her mother, her stepfather, her brother, Freddie von Reibnitz, now employed by the Australian government in Canberra, and her half-brother Mario. She was able to take the opportunity for a private visit to her mother in her charming bungalow, a journey which must have evoked many memories in the Princess, who had left Sydney to seek her fortune in Europe eleven years earlier and finally married the cousin of the Queen of England.

In the spring of 1985 Princess Michael experienced a ten day personal ordeal and emerged from it having aroused nothing but admiration for the courage and dignity she displayed. It concerned the war-time activities of her father, Baron Gunther von Reibnitz, who died in Mozambique in 1983.

The drama broke on the morning of 16 April when the tabloid *Daily Mirror* revealed in front page banner headlines that the Baron had been a member of Hitler's SS. In an article headed, 'This Bloody Disgrace', the *Mirror* commented 'He joined it in 1933, and later obtained a position on the recommendation of Herman Goering . . . he was not just an ordinary party member. The SS was Hitler's elite. It ran concentration camps . . .' This 'world exclusive' ended with the words, 'The Royal Family is Britain's prize possession. Even 40 years on, the taint of Nazism undermines it. The only course open now is to be full, frank and honest. And so far honesty has been missing'.

Yet Princess Michael had not personally been involved in any conspiracy of silence. Only when she had been advised several hours before of the impending publication did she telephone her mother in Australia. Then she learned for the first time that her father had been associated with the SS. However, ten agonising days of rumour and allegations were to follow before official papers from a de-Nazification court classified her father as only a 'minor Nazi official'.

In the meantime Princess Michael held her head high and on the night of the disclosure, wearing a flowing blue silk gown and her hair swept up under a diamond tiara, attended a State banquet given by the Queen at Windsor Castle for Dr Hastings Banda, President of Malawi. She remained calm and poised. It was clear she had the support of the royal family who surrounded her on that splendid occasion.

The following day widespread support came from members of all political parties for the view expressed by Prime Minister Mrs Margaret Thatcher to her colleagues: 'You can't choose your parents'.

Mr Norman St John Stevas, a leading Roman Catholic and Tory MP said he had seen documents which showed that von Reibnitz was only an honorary member of the SS 'Not every SS member carried out atrocities as some half-baked journalists tend to assume,' he said.

Mr Harold Brooks Baker, publishing director of Burke's Peerage went on television to say that genealogists had known of the connection for some time. 'It is nonsense to raise this now,' he said. 'Why should the sins of the father be visited upon the daughter?'

Messages of sympathy poured into Princess Michael's home in Kensington Palace. From Mr Ron Bishop, secretary of the Royal British Legion at Chalford, Stroud, near her Gloucestershire country home: 'My members and I are appalled that this has been dragged up now. It was not her fault that her father was a Nazi officer and we would be the last to condemn her for it.'

From Mr Barry Green, Warden of the Cheltenham and District Hebrew Congregation: 'It doesn't really matter whether she knew about her father's past or not.'

It was left to Princess Michael's mother to explain to the world why she had kept her late husband's links with the Nazis from her daughter. They had divorced in Bavaria in 1946.

Speaking from her home in Sydney she said, 'I hadn't been on very good terms with my first husband. I said to myself, "Why should I say anything?" I regret it very much in hindsight now. I should have told her (Princess Michael). You see, I didn't think it mattered so much. It wouldn't have served much purpose. Now, of course, I'm terribly sorry.'

But until clearance documents about her father's war-time career could be gathered together – and at one point it was suggested that he had been a member of Hitler's 'stud farm team chosen to sire master race children' – Princess Michael felt it necessary to take action.

On 20 April, four days after the *Daily Mirror* launched their story which became sensationalized on TV and radio networks and in newspapers all over the world, she decided to end speculation about her knowledge of her father's association with the SS. She appeared in one of the most dramatic television interviews ever given by a member of the royal family. On Britain's TV AM, a breakfast-time programme, wearing a white dress, her long blonde hair hanging loosely over her shoulders, she replied spontaneously to a series of questions put to her by interviewer Nick Owen.

Princess Michael: 'I immediately telephoned my mother when I was told this report was coming out in the *Mirror* and I said more or less to the effect, "Guess what they are trying to pin on me now?" and she said "But I am afraid that it is true." And so I said, "Well, how is that possible?" And she told me.'

Owen: 'And what was your reaction?'

Princess Michael: 'Well, it was a total shock, to everything I have been taught to believe, you know. But my shoulders are broad and I shall have to carry it.'

Owen: 'What has your husband said to the news that has broken?'

Princess Michael: 'Well, he is extremely supportive of me and as devastated as I am.'

Owen: 'Do you feel in some way that you will be uncomfortable now performing your public duties? Because presumably the public perception of you will have changed to some extent?'

Princess Michael: 'I don't know what I shall feel. I just think that when dreadful things come to you out of the blue you have to live with them. I mean, it is like suddenly discovering you are adopted, you know. Here I am, forty years old, and I suddenly discover something that is really quite unpleasant and I shall have to live with it. What the public's perception of me will be, I don't know. I wasn't alive when all this happened so I hope that they will judge me on my own performance and what I am and what I stand for.'

Owen: 'What has it been like for you, the last thirty-six hours or so?'

Princess Michael: 'I think I have been in a sort of state of

shell-shock but it is something I will have to come to terms with – and
I know I shall.'

Three days later a copy of an appeal tribunal held in Upper Bavaria
on 14 May 1948 was issued by Kensington Palace to the Press
Association. The tribunal found that Baron von Reibnitz joined the
Nazi party in 1931 'in the belief that National Socialism would bring
about economic recovery'.

It also revealed:

* He continued to be politically inactive and accepted no party
office;
* He obtained his SS rank as an honorary title through his post as
chief ranger responsible for hunting in his area of Germany;
* He never served with the SS in such rank, had no authority to
give orders and merely had the right to wear uniform;
* He came into conflict with the party authorities as early as 1934
and by 1944 it had intensified to such a degree that he was dismissed
from the SS;
* He made no secret about his disappointment over political
developments and found himself 'in difficulties' with his Gauleiter;
* In his post as chief ranger he permitted Jews to participate in
hunting and concerned himself with the well-being of foreign
workers, going beyond 'normal limits' in helping those subjected to
racial persecution;
* His devout outlook – he became a firm Roman Catholic –
incurred the displeasure of the Nazi party.

The judgement concluded: 'He was to be regarded as falling within
the category of nominal party member since he took only a nominal part
in National Socialism and lent it only insignificant support.'

Colonel Michael Farmer, Princess Michael's Press Secretary,
accurately summed up the situation when he said: 'This effectively put
him in the lowest grade possible without taking up arms against Hitler.'

Princess Michael's mother added a tribute to the late Baron. She
explained that she personally had incurred the wrath of the Nazi
regime. She had refused to rise to 'Heil Hitler' when she went to Tachau
to run a timber business she had inherited from her grandfather. She
had been caught listening to the BBC and the Germans, who had

over-run Czechoslovakia, saw her as totally non-supportive of the Führer. As a result her passport was stamped 'undesirable'. Baron von Reibnitz was in a position to help. Under regular treatment for a heart condition, he did not return to his regiment but married her in December 1941 when she was 28 and returned to his pre-war job as chief ranger for Silesia. When she was summoned to Berlin to appear before the Gestapo, the Baron went with her. 'They released me in his care,' she said. 'He had to say something like, "I'll see to it that she behaves." He showed enormous courage.'

The stress of the whole affair caused Princess Michael to break down in tears at the Doctor of the Year lunch held on 25 April at the Savoy Hotel. 'It has not been an easy ten days . . .' she told 450 doctors in a quiet voice. It soon became clear that the Princess was extremely upset and she began to choke with emotion. 'I would just like to take this opportunity . . .' she persisted, 'to thank the thousands of people who have written to me.' Princess Michael was by now in tears and had to stop speaking as she was given a standing ovation. As she left she was given a bouquet of white flowers and received another enthusiastic ovation from the doctors.

During this unhappy business *The Times* published a remarkable lead letter 'From Lord Onslow and others'. It was headed 'Press Treatment of Princess Michael' and signed by thirty members of the House of Lords. It read: 'Sir, All of us are regular attenders of the House of Lords, of all parties, and we would like to say how outrageous we feel the treatment of the Princess Michael of Kent has been by the *Daily Mirror*.

'No-one is responsible for the actions of their parents, unlike editors who are totally responsible for the actions of their papers.'

16

The Common Touch

The first indication that George, Earl of St Andrews and heir to the dukedom of Kent, differed from other children in the Royal Family came in May 1975 when he was twelve and competed with seventy-six other candidates for fifteen Eton scholarships. It was regarded as a particularly gruelling examination and although Mr James Edwards, headmaster of Heatherdown, his prep. school at Ascot, thought the Queen's young second cousin would do well, he kept this cautious optimism for himself. A month before his thirteenth birthday on 26 June it was announced by the Eton authorities that George had not only come overall top in French but was also well above average in his general papers. He came eighth in the success list and thus the first member of the family ever to win a scholarship, and the first to become a King's Scholar at Eton since the scholarships were founded by Henry VI in the fifteenth century. George's success earned a half holiday for his fellow pupils at Heatherdown and Mr Edwards said, 'It is normal for us to celebrate the success of our boys in this way. We are all delighted, of course. The Earl of St Andrews is a clever boy.' George had every reason to be proud. With other King's Scholars he was to live in the oldest part of Eton, known as College, which has produced a steady succession of stimulating personalities and men of eminence.

There had been other bright children in the Royal Family before George, but none had been given the opportunity to develop freely without parental intervention, which often had disastrous consequences. George's paternal grandfather was also a clever boy. He became the victim of frustration and stress because of a father who was determined that, although Georgie hated the sea, he should nevertheless make his career in the Royal Navy. George's father, Eddie Kent, was sent to Eton on the advice of his uncle, George VI.

Despite their diversity of personal interests, members of the Royal

Family have never been renowned for their intellectual pursuits, and patronage of the arts was for years little more than a dutiful and graceful gesture. When Queen Mary married the future George V on 6 July 1893 she found herself living in what seemed to her a cultural desert, unable as she was to find relatives who shared her joy in literature and in the treasures and heirlooms which filled the royal residences. Three decades were to pass before a royal couple emerged with a true interest in the arts, music and literature. They were George's grandparents, George and Marina, who after their marriage in 1934 found their stimulus in creative men and women of the theatre, composers and established writers.

The most important influence within the family after World War II came from Prince Philip, not an intellectual, but a man of mental energy who added a new impetus to royal participation in the cultural scene. This was later to enthuse his eldest son, Prince Charles and, to a lesser degree, Prince Andrew. All three painted better-than-average watercolours. Philip's greatest influence, however, was on the Queen. As heir presumptive to the throne she had been tutored by her father, during her teenage years, in the history of the constitution and in statesmanship. However, her ultimate emergence as a highly intelligent woman with expertise in many fields was due in no small way to the stimulation and constant encouragement she received from her husband.

Unlike his grandfather, who found rapport only with his mother, Queen Mary, George St Andrews grew up among relatives with a changed outlook, men and women who held wide-ranging interests, by the very nature of their jobs, which brought them into direct contact with commercial, industrial and scientific developments and also produced a new style of royal patronage. George entered the Royal Family at a time when support for the arts was no longer a token matter but one which demanded clear proof of personal involvement. His second cousin Prince Charles, a man with only an average school record and a B.A. honours degree from Cambridge, also cared deeply about these ideas.

During his adolescence, at family gatherings, weekends at Windsor Castle, and more especially during the part of his summer holidays spent at Balmoral, George, the eldest member of the new generation of Kents, found himself in the company of people who were beginning to care about some of the pursuits of educated commoners. The traditional royal preoccupations with hunting, shooting, fishing and large house parties were gradually giving way to wider interests, and for a highly intelligent boy like George tremendous stimulus was to be found within the ranks of his own family. For the first time children like George were surrounded by relations who were well read and who delighted in history, architecture, photography, painting and a wide range of other hobbies. This, combined with the greater personal freedom granted by their parents, meant that the present generation of Kents, along with other royal children, was growing up in a Royal Family that was yielding to the common touch.

George was the first direct male descendant of George V not to bear the titles of Prince and HRH. His paternal great-grandfather had foreseen a proliferation of princes and princesses, so that in his proclamation of July 1917 he decreed that the style HRH and the title of Prince should be granted, in the male line, for two generations only of the sovereign's descendants. Thus after his grandfather, His Royal Highness the first Duke of Kent, and his father, His Royal Highness the second Duke of Kent, George took his father's secondary title, that of Earl of St Andrews. One outcome of George V's action was that his descendants in the third generation came to regard their royal status in a new and less important light. From the time they were able to understand the significance of their birthright they each revealed a marked reluctance to participate in any form of public life. Significantly, they registered no envy of past royal privileges and only wanted to pursue their own independent careers. George had seen enough of his parents' disciplined lifestyle to observe with real feeling when he was nineteen, 'Fortunately I am never going to carry out engagements like my parents. I have managed to remain anonymous so far in life and I want to stay that way.' Such a statement could never had been made by either his grandfather, a naval officer for eight years, or his father, who held a commission in the Royal Scots Greys for thirteen years. Neither of these men ever questioned his responsibilities as an active member of the Royal Family. George's grandfather had a strong streak of independence, as witnessed by his years as a factory inspector, but his hopes of ever doing an ordinary job never came to fruition. His father, George V, always puzzled by his youngest son's desire to work at factory floor level, saw to that. Given the heavy schedules of royal duties he had to carry out during the 1930s it was impossible for him to maintain any sort of continuity in his Home Office job. That four decades later his grandson, Lord St Andrews, was able freely to express his total disinterest in public life without causing the slightest ripple of indignation from any quarter illustrates the dramatically changing attitude of the Kent family and British royalty as a whole in the 1980s.

However in 1984 George St Andrews, twenty-two, his sister Lady Helen Windsor, twenty, and his younger brother Lord Nicholas Windsor, fourteen, could not have taken part in the quiet revolution which had begun in the 1970s without the full approval of the Queen. Her attitude to the future of the House of Windsor is based very much on the views of her grandfather when he restricted the business of being royal to those members of the family closest in line of succession. In the event the desire for all her young relatives, with the exception of her own four children, Prince Charles, Princess Anne, Prince Andrew and Prince Edward, to live their own private lives has proved a bonus for the Queen in her wish to limit working members of the family to a relatively small and manageable number. What we are witnessing, then, is a Royal Family that is paring itself down of its own volition and without any external political or ideological pressures.

At no point in his early life was Lord St Andrews given to understand that he was in any way different from other children. His only public activities took place in 1966, when he was three years old. In January of that year he was a pageboy on two occasions, first at the wedding of Miss Fiona Bowes-Lyon, a great-niece of the Queen Mother, to Mr Joseph Goodheart; in the middle of the ceremony he burst into tears. Later in the month he showed greater self-control at the marriage of Miss Claire Pelly and Lord Herbert. He rounded off the year when his mother took him with a group of friends to *Sooty's Christmas Show* in the West End. When volunteers from the audience were invited to sing a song in an improvised talent contest George was first up on the stage, and for his splendidly gutsy rendering of 'Away in a Manger' he received the first prize – a Sooty glove puppet. When the late Harry Corbett, who masterminded Sooty, asked the boy what his father did for a living, George replied, 'He changes in and out of uniform.'

As his father was a serving officer in the Royal Scots Greys, George travelled a great deal as a baby. Loath to leave him at home, the Duke and Duchess of Kent took him with them when they represented the Queen at the Ugandan Independence celebrations in 1962, and this was followed by a year with the regiment in Hong Kong. The Kents lived in unfashionable and cramped officers' quarters and made do with a second-floor three-bedroomed flat that had seen better days. The Duchess was delighted to be relieved of official duties, apart from occasional Army social occasions, during the baby's first year, and when she wheeled him in his pram, sometimes accompanied by a Chinese ayah, there was nothing to indicate that the trim figure in a simple cotton dress, bare legs and fair hair almost to her shoulders was a member of the Royal Family. At hand to help her was Miss Mary McPherson who, like so many royal nannies, was Scottish and had links with the family in that she had once been a nursemaid to the Factor of Balmoral. It was only after long discussion that the Duke and Duchess agreed to leave George behind with Miss McPherson when they flew to London to attend the wedding of Princess Alexandra and Angus Ogilvy in April 1963. The Duchess, determined not to be parted from her young son any longer than was absolutely necessary, returned to Hong Kong within forty-eight hours of the great service in Westminster Abbey.

In 1963 the Duke, accompanied by his wife and son, spent two years with his regiment in Germany, stationed in the small town of Fallingbostel. In the spring of 1964 the Duchess flew home to England for the birth of her daughter, Lady Helen Marina Lucy Windsor, at Coppins on 24 April. The early days of the two babies when the family returned to England in the autumn of 1965 differed little from those which had been enjoyed at Coppins by their father, his sister Princess Alexandra, and his younger brother Prince Michael. Some of their pre-war toys were discovered in a dusty attic and brought out for use again and an old swing, made by George, Duke of Kent before World War II, was once again a source of great fun. The domestic lifestyle of Eddie Kent and his wife Katharine, however, was in total contrast to that of the previous Duke and Duchess, whose regular dinner parties were famous and who seldom had a weekend free of house guests. Eddie and Katharine did not cultivate celebrities and their social life was on the whole limited to close friends and relations. Because of Eddie's postings abroad the children inevitably saw more of their mother, who gave birth to her third and last child, Lord Nicholas Windsor, at King's College Hospital, Denmark Hill, on 26 July 1970. Katharine was a born mother, and when she began to take on important duties, which included becoming Controller Commandant of the Women's Royal Army Corps and the youngest-ever Chancellor of Leeds University, she still always tried to be home every night.

Of all the young Kents, George was by far the most sensitive and reserved. Fortunately he was surrounded not only by his extrovert sister, Helen, but also by five other young cousins born between 1961 and 1967, all destined to experience an upbringing with little emphasis on their royal status, with the one exception of the Queen's youngest son, Prince Edward, born on 15 November 1967.

Both the Duke and Duchess of Kent, and Princess Alexandra and Angus Ogilvy, played down the royal connections of their children, but at the same time found this difficult, unable as they were to reject their own roles. Princess Margaret once tartly commented, 'My children are not royal. It just happens their aunt is the Queen.' Princess Alexandra insisted on putting her children before royal duties and she refused to carry out any official engagements during their school holidays. She felt that her son and daughter, James and Marina, were subject to the same outside influences as other children and regarded it as imperative to devote her time to them when they were at home. Angus Ogilvy said,

I think the time is coming very shortly when if we don't see more of our children, we're going to pay the price at the other end, when they're older. But it's very difficult. You decide to spend an evening with the children, but then someone rings up and says, 'Will you please come to a film premiere? If you come it will help us raise another £1,500 and this could help three hundred spastics.' Well, who are more important, three hundred spastics or your own children?

Both sets of parents found themselves embarrassed by another aspect of bringing up their children. Every summer, like other members of the family, they were all invited to join the Queen during her annual summer holiday at Balmoral during part of August or September, and Windsor Castle was a must for everyone from 23 December until New Year's Day. Again, Ogilvy summed up the situation. He said,

It is very difficult for the children when they go back to school at the end of a holiday. They are inevitably asked where they went and they can only reply truthfully, 'Balmoral' or 'Windsor Castle'. You can imagine what happens then. They are bombarded with questions such as 'What is the Queen really like?', 'Do you eat with the Queen?', 'Is Princess Alexandra as nice as she seems?' We are trying to bring up two children with their feet firmly on the ground. When they grow up they will each have to earn their own livings. Being related to the Queen will not help them and nor will the fact that they spend holidays in magnificent royal castles assist them to get on in life. My wife and I have done our best to make our children recognize that the royal way of life they experience now and then is something to enjoy and appreciate but that will never be a permanent part of their future lives.

The new Kent generation grew up in elegant homes and the standard of living to which they became accustomed was very much the same as that of most children from aristocratic backgrounds. The Ogilvy family remained at Thatched House Lodge in Richmond Park, and shortly after 1973, when the Duke of Kent had to sell Coppins and was given grace and favour apartments in St James's Palace, he acquired Anmer Hall, a six-bedroomed Georgian house standing in ten acres in the village of Anmer, part of the Sandringham Estate.

In July 1979 George St Andrews suffered a setback when he failed two of his three A-level examinations. He was devoted to his mother, whose mounting illness during the previous year had placed a strain on the entire family. George's anxiety and worry were reflected in his school work, and when he resat the examinations some months later he passed with top grades in history, English and French. Eton masters had no hesitation in reporting to the Duke and Duchess of Kent that their son, the first academic in the family, was destined for a brilliant career. With his Eton days behind him, George wanted to spend some time on a worthwhile project and to see something of the world. At his mother's suggestion and at his own expense he spent four months working in India for the Boys' Town Trust and the Save the Children Fund. He travelled incognito and, known simply as George Andrews, spent most of his time helping in town organizations in Calcutta, Madras and Kashmir and some of the remote villages in the baking interior. He returned home appalled by the poverty he had seen at first hand, and determined to return to India at the first possible opportunity in the same voluntary capacity. He achieved his great ambition to follow Prince Charles to Cambridge and in 1981 was accepted by Downing College where he is reading history. In June 1984 George failed his History Tripos (Part One). However, it is well known that academic promise is not always fulfilled in the shape of examination success. Fair-haired and blue-eyed and bearing a strong resemblance to his paternal grandfather, he has remained very much a loner at college, striking up few close friendships and preferring to spend the long vacations with his family at Anmer Hall. Always labelled the egghead in the Royal Family, his future is yet undecided but if he fulfils the hopes of his tutors the strong possibility remains that he will become a don and perhaps the first royal to be a Fellow of his college.

Not as academically minded as George, Lady Helen Windsor inherited the combined artistic qualities of both her paternal grandparents and her parents. She went to four schools, Eton End, like George, St Paul's Junior School for Girls in London, St Mary's Convent School at Wantage in Oxfordshire, and finally she spent a year at Gordonstoun where she took her A-levels. Her results were not good enough to guarantee her a university place but she was not unduly disappointed. Her somewhat vague ambition was to establish herself in the art business and, as a stepping stone, she took a job on the reception desk of Mayfair's prestigious Mayor Gallery. Until then she had always kept well out of the limelight, like her brothers, and it was not until her father, with whom she was very close, took her official fourteenth birthday photograph, published in the national newspapers, that she was seen not so much as a pretty schoolgirl but as a potentially stunning beauty. This was more than confirmed four years later on her eighteenth birthday, when Lord Snowdon's lens revealed a mature girl with an attractive pouting mouth, a slightly turned-up nose and the sparkling eyes of her mother. In both sets of pictures she appeared demure, but in private life she had very much a mind of her own. In temperament she was gregarious, unlike her elder brother, and was often seen dining and dancing in the best nightspots in London. Like so many adolescents adjusting to adult life she yearned to possess her own front-door key, and when she told her parents that she would like to have greater independence and leave York House they raised no objections. Neither the Duke nor the Duchess had ever been possessive about their children and regarded Helen's request in much the same way that Earl Spencer had regarded his daughter Lady Diana's wish to share a London flat with close girlfriends. Early in 1983 Helen moved to a small flat in Kensington shared with an old schoolfriend, shopped in supermarkets, bought clothes off-the-peg and determined to be financially independent as soon as possible. In some ways she resembled the Princess of Wales in that she had a soft voice and never used phrases or pronunciations traditionally associated with royalty, such as 'orf', 'one', or 'hyce' for house.

Her sense of fashion, however, was bolder than that of the Princess of Wales and highly individualistic. At the Badminton Horse Trials, where the women in the Royal Family, with the exception of a competing Princess Anne, were always seen in sensible flat shoes, tweed skirts, twinsets and headscarves, Helen appeared in striking striped jeans and a denim jacket and was observed drinking beer from a can and smoking. From the age of eighteen she was seen with a variety of boyfriends, of which her favourite for a long time seemed to be John Benson, a stockbroker's son, who ran a private disco between terms at Edinburgh University. When the Duke and Duchess of Kent stayed in a rented villa on a package holiday to the Greek island of Corfu, John went along with Helen. Some people raised their eyebrows when they heard that a topless Helen had been seen swimming in the blue waters of the Ionian Sea, but there was no adverse comment from her parents. Once, when she was asked whether she had marriage in mind, Helen's brusque reply was, 'Do you know how old I am? I'm just nineteen. Give me a chance!' Both her mother and Princess Alexandra share Princess Marina's view that twenty-seven or twenty-eight is about the right age for a girl to marry. Lady Helen Windsor still has the world at her feet and she is leaving all her options open until she completes a period in France where she is studying the history of French art, a subject that absorbed Princess Marina when she was exiled in Paris in the 1920s until her marriage in 1934.

The Duke and Duchess of Kent made a complete break with family tradition when they rejected Eton for their youngest son, Lord Nicholas Windsor, who started public school as a day boy at Westminster in the heart of London in the winter of 1983. At the time the Duchess was recovering from an operation for the removal of an ovarian cyst and both parents felt that Nicholas would be a great comfort to her, coming home every evening to York House rather than spending eight months of the year at boarding school. Westminster, only a ten-minute walk across St James's Park for Nicholas, was founded in 1560 by Elizabeth I on the site of a Benedictine Abbey. It was therefore Nicholas to whom the Duchess turned for company as she began to recuperate, and together they flew to Canada to spend two weeks with her brother, John Worsley, a cattle breeder in Alberta. Nicholas has inherited the Kents' love of music, and at the age of ten was the first member of the Royal Family to perform in a Covent Garden opera when he had a walk-on part in Mozart's *The Magic Flute*. At thirteen he entered the Hunstanton tennis tournament in Norfolk, listed as N. Windsor, the first member of the Royal Family to play tournament tennis since George VI as Duke of York was at Wimbledon in the men's doubles in 1926. Nicholas was beaten, but he did have the misfortune to come up against one of the seeds in the first round.

James Ogilvy, with his open face and likeable personality, is an old Etonian who shows all the signs of inheriting his father's financial flair. Sturdy and gutsy, he is the young royal who most resembles his second cousin, Prince Charles, and in the family he is often dubbed Action Man Two. In the spring of 1983, quietly and without fuss, he was accepted for a short-service commission as a second lieutenant in the Scots Guards and then went up to St Andrew's University in the autumn. He filled the intervening time with various odd jobs, including one in a south London factory screwing on bottle tops. Once at St Andrew's he tried to get a glossy magazine off the ground which he called *Freeway*. Despite much hard work the venture did not succeed. His father observed, and not without a touch of pride, 'At least James's magazine washed its face. But he is certainly not going to be a newspaper proprietor.'

His sister Marina is far more forthright and has been known to use the fiery language favoured by Princess Anne when something or somebody upsets her. At seventeen, and still at St Mary's Convent School at Wantage, she is an extremely good pianist, like Princess Alexandra, and reached Grade 8 in the Royal College of Music examinations. What she lacks on the academic side is more than made up for in the arts. She had the lead part in two school plays, *Salad Days* and *Kiss Me Kate*, and built up a reputation as a good swimmer. When Marina left school in the summer of 1984 she rejected the idea of a university life for one of adventure. Her first experience of spartan living was at Captain John Ridgeway's tough adventure school in Scotland. Her ambition is to go to Central America in the spring of 1985 where she will carry out social work under the direction of Colonel John Blashford Snell.

For the two children of Prince and Princess Michael of Kent, years of schooling still lie ahead. Six-year-old Lord Frederick Windsor, now at a London nursery school, is destined to go to Harrow and will be required to sit an entrance examination in 1991 like all other hopefuls. At five his sister, Lady Gabriella Windsor, is the youngest member of the Kent family and, despite her mother's enthusiastic involvement in public life, will be so far down the line of succession when she grows up that, like her brother and five much older cousins, her future will be in her own hands. No matter whether Queen Elizabeth II or King Charles

III is on the throne when she reaches maturity, her lifestyle will bear no comparison with that of her mother, who found her natural outlet in royal duties, possibly the last member of the Kents who will ever do so.

The story of the Kent family tells of the changing face of royalty in this country today. The pomp and splendour of the royal houses of Europe vanished under the impact of social and ideological forces, rumbling in the late nineteenth century, and bursting into storm before and during World War I. The French Revolution, more than a century earlier, had started the avalanche and was a savage indictment of the selfish and mindless subjugation of the masses by hereditary power and privilege. The few monarchies which survive, or have been restored, are carefully tuned to the political ethos of their countries. Why then has the British Royal Family retained for so long its place in the hearts of the great majority of the people? How is it that a monarch who has no constitutional powers, except the right to be consulted, to encourage and to warn, can command such allegiance, in spite of a minority of dissenters who deplore the concept of divine right and the money required to support it? There can be no doubt that the pageantry and glamour of state occasions provide joyous excitement and enthusiasm in the streets, and high-rating television viewing in homes. The thread of history is spun into these displays and most subjects feel a sense of personal heritage. Yet these events are not enough to explain the public interest in members of the Royal Family, so that scarcely a day goes by without the national newspapers reporting accounts of their activities, or speculating on their private lives. In the same almost unique way this particular family has captured the imagination not only of the British people but of the whole world. As individuals they have become invaluable ambassadors and as a group they have contributed to the image and even the economy of the nation, if only by the tourist attraction of their homes and themselves.

By some magic, perhaps inherent in themselves and in the British character they have acquired over the years, these people have managed to adapt to what is required of them in this age. Whatever their personal views, they are scrupulously apolitical, just as the Queen speaks of 'My Government' whatever party may be in power. We often see them in their grandeur but sometimes in their human roles. The Queen is unashamedly excited at race meetings and when travelling to Balmoral with a train of corgis at her heels. Prince Philip and the Prince of Wales speak openly and sometimes forcefully – not always with restraint – on matters which engage their interest, compassion or concern.

Those more distant from the throne, such as the Kents, are slowly divesting themselves of the trappings of royalty, moving towards the lifestyle that they want. They walk at times with kings and queens, but they are acquiring a flair for the common touch.

THE SUMMERHOUSE

Val Mulkerns

'A remarkable book, full of insight and feeling . . .'
Evening Press

It crouched forlornly in the kitchen – a crumbling
fretwork summerhouse, a symbol of failure and
decay, perfectly appropriate to the family that
drifted round its disintegrating form, sniping bitchily
at each other.

Eleanor, beautiful, frustrated, feeding on her
contempt for her spineless husband Con; Margaret,
mother of Martin, slowly sinking back into the
clinging folds of her family from which she had all
too briefly escaped; their mother, senile and
overbearing; Hanny, spinster daughter, finding her
only satisfaction in eroding her sisters' confidence
and self image; and Ruth, Martin's wife, a crisp if
timid observer of the lethal family minuet . . .

Told in the voices of five separate but intertwined
characters, THE SUMMERHOUSE evokes the lives of
an Irish family whose tragedies and occasional joys
will haunt every reader.

'evocative' *The Irish Press*

FUTURA PUBLICATIONS
FICTION
0 7088 2623 7

PRENEZ GARDE

Terence de Vere White

PRENEZ GARDE
'If Sinn Fein had its way there would be no more
visits to Mrs Heber, no more tennis for Miss Morris,
no Bank for Uncle Lindy, no job in Court for my
father, no King, no Queen, no Prince of Wales, no
visits to Dublin to buy Christmas presents and have
tea at Mitchells in Grafton Street. Everything would
be given up to men in black hats and trench coats
with badges in their button-holes and cigarettes
behind their ears.'

Nine-year-old Brian was living in a time of fearful
political disturbance – though he was not supposed
to be aware of it. The solicitous parental warning
'prenez garde de l'enfant' could not exclude the
atmosphere of Ireland in the troubled 1920s. Seen
through Brian's eyes, PRENEZ GARDE tells of
horrible happenings (did the Black and Tans really
skin babies alive?); soul-destroying remorse (Brian
believes he might have committed two murders . . .
not to mention adultery!); and romantic dreams (if
only the lovely Miss Morris would wait for Brain to
be 21) . . .

'Beautifully cool and wistful. A rare and intensely
personal kind of re-creation'
Guardian

'Very enjoyable. Deliciously funny'
Scotsman

'A charming and witty novel'
Punch

FUTURA PUBLICATIONS
FICTION
0 7088 2944 9